JAPAN

A Sunset Travel Book

LANE BOOKS • MENLO PARK, CALIFORNIA

FOREWORD

In this book we bring together in guide form many details on where to go, what to see, what to do—and blend with these facts some of the experiences of reporters of the Japan scene. Because of Japan's complexity and diversity, we can provide only a brief summary of the Japan travel panorama. But we hope it gives you enough of a glimpse that you'll be moved to meet the Japanese on their own ground, partake of their unusual foods, absorb their rich culture, capture in your memory some of their scenery and pageantry and obtain some feeling for the dynamics of their economic and industrial growth that has led to Japan's pre-eminence among the nations of Asia.

Additional information on Japan may be obtained from the offices of the Japan National Tourist Organization. Their main office is at 2-13 Yurakucho, Tokyo, Japan. Their overseas offices are located at 1737 Post Street, San Francisco, California 94115; 727 W. 7th Street, Los Angeles, California 90017; 45 Rockefeller Plaza, New York, N.Y. 10020; 109 Kaiulani Avenue, Honolulu, Hawaii 96815; 165 University Avenue, Toronto 1, Canada; 333 N. Michigan Avenue, Chicago, Illinois 60601; 1420 Commerce Street, Dallas, Texas 75201.

Special acknowledgments should be made for help in writing this book to the following persons and organizations: Japan Air Lines for the many photographs they provided; the Japan National Tourist Organization for photographs; Cecelia Arima in Tokyo for research and careful checking; Martha Guthrie of Tokyo and New Haven, Connecticut; Brigitte Weeks of Hampshire, England; Mary Benton Smith and Mimi Bell for their research on the project; the Pacific Area Travel Association and the editors of their official publication *Pacific Travel News* in San Francisco for the use of their photo and information files; and Kiyoko Ishimoto, San Francisco, for her contributions of information and checking of the manuscript.

Supervising Editor: Frederic M. Rea, Publisher, Pacific Travel News

Research and Text: Frances Coleberd

Coordinating Editor: Sherry Gellner

FRONT COVER PHOTOGRAPH, by Jack Cannon, shows *geisha* girls looking out over gardens of *ryokan* in Kyoto.

Executive Editor, Sunset Books: David E. Clark

First Printing February 1973

CONTENTS

SPECIAL FEATURES

COUNTRY AND CITYSCAPES: row upon row of tea plants (above), and ribbons of concrete in Tokyo's freeway system (far right). The splendid Kumamoto Castle, in a park-like setting, its approach lined with cherry trees.

Japan...Thriving, Zestful Half Moon of Islands

Japan has a different meaning for almost every day and for every pair of eyes that see it. You may go seeking a remote, mysterious, Zen-filled land of tradition and calm. You'll find tradition and serene retreats, but you'll also find the 20th century in full reign. It's a 20th century, we might add, with a certain ineffable touch that makes it Japan's own unique version of the 20th century.

Japan means school kids—navy-clad youngsters solemnly filing out of buses at yet another Shinto shrine on their annual school tour, the boys with Buster Brown haircuts and girls with braids. They'll unabashedly stare at you, the tourist, and happily try out their *harros* (translated hello).

In the decade of the 1970's, it is the 20th century that predominates over the past. For Japan is a thriving, building, industrial nation, the most powerful in the Orient. From one end of the island nation to another, from Nagasaki to Sapporo, the country is alive with the activity, the vitality and the change that is so necessary to support the 100 million plus who live in a mountainous land a little smaller than California.

It is perhaps the various aspects of change, coupled with still-rooted traditions, that lend to the traveler's Japan its paradoxical fascination and make the meaning of Japan such a personal matter.

For instance:

You will certainly want to see Mt. Fuji, never-changing symbol of the country. But you probably won't see it from Hiroshige's vantage-points. Most likely, weather and cloud cover permitting, you'll view it from the window of a Tokyo to Osaka plane, from the swaying gondola of an aerial ropeway near Lake Hakone, or from the train window of the New Tokkaido Line's super express.

You can retrace the steps of years of history (Japan's *written* history covers more than 2,000 years). However, your trip to storied Nikko will most likely not be along

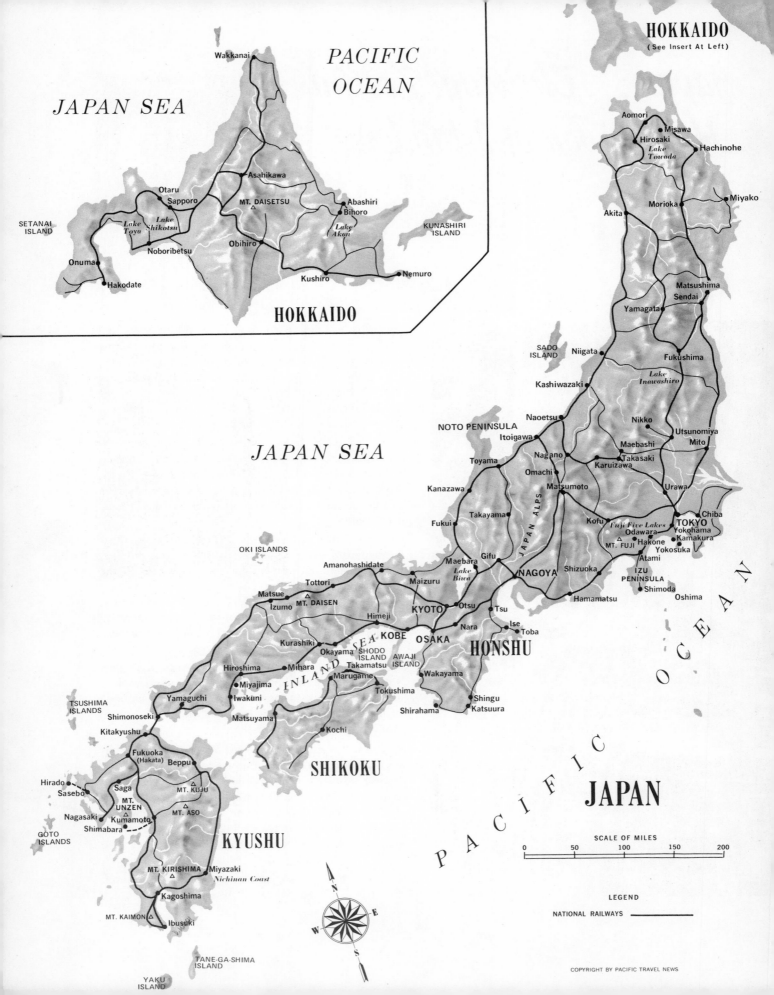

PACIFIC OCEAN

JAPAN SEA

HOKKAIDO
(See Insert At Left)

HOKKAIDO

JAPAN SEA

PACIFIC OCEAN

HONSHU

SHIKOKU

KYUSHU

JAPAN

Wakkanai

Otaru
Sapporo
Asahikawa
MT. DAISETSU
Abashiri
Bihoro
Lake Akan
KUNASHIRI ISLAND

SETANAI ISLAND
Lake Toya
Lake Shikotsu
Noboribetsu
Obihiro

Onuma
Hakodate
Kushiro
Nemuro

Aomori
Misawa
Hirosaki
Hachinohe
Lake Towada
Morioka
Miyako
Akita

Niigata
Matsushima
Sendai
Yamagata
Fukushima
SADO ISLAND
Lake Inawashiro
Kashiwazaki
Nikko
Utsunomiya
Mito
Naoetsu
Itoigawa
NOTO PENINSULA
Toyama
Nagano
Maebashi
Takasaki
Karuizawa
Kanazawa
Omachi
Matsumoto
Urawa
Takayama
JAPAN ALPS
Kofu
Fuji Five Lakes
Chiba
TOKYO
Fukui
Odawara
Yokohama
Hakone
Kamakura
MT. FUJI
Yokosuka
Maebara
Gifu
Atami
Lake Biwa
Shizuoka
IZU PENINSULA
Amanohashidate
Maizuru
NAGOYA
Shimoda
Tottori
KYOTO
Otsu
Hamamatsu
Oshima
Matsue
MT. DAISEN
Izumo
Himeji
Tsu
OKI ISLANDS
Kurashiki
KOBE
Nara
Ise
Toba
Okayama
OSAKA
Hiroshima
Mihara
SHODO ISLAND
Takamatsu
AWAJI ISLAND
Miyajima
Marugame
Wakayama
Iwakuni
INLAND SEA
Tokushima
Shingu
Yamaguchi
Matsuyama
Shirahama
Katsuura
Shimonoseki
Kochi
TSUSHIMA ISLANDS
Kitakyushu
Fukuoka (Hakata)
Beppu
Hirado
Saga
MT. KUJU
Sasebo
MT. UNZEN
MT. ASO
Nagasaki
Kumamoto
Shimabara
KYUSHU
MT. KIRISHIMA
Miyazaki
GOTO ISLANDS
Nichinan Coast
Kagoshima
MT. KAIMON
Ibusuki

TANE-GA-SHIMA ISLAND

YAKU ISLAND

N W E S

SCALE OF MILES
0   50   100   150   200

LEGEND

NATIONAL RAILWAYS ━━━━━━

FACES OF JAPAN: *a bride in ceremonial and traditional headdress; the chief of an Ainu Village; a nursery school child; a girl taking notes on flower arranging; a* noh *actor; a Japanese merchant.*

the narrow highway lined by tall Cryptomeria, but by electric train. The train speeds through the hand-tended rice fields of the Kanto Plains, past tiled or thatched-roof farmhouses that have remained almost unchanged for eras. *Almost,* because there are television antennas on many of the roofs and shiny new tractors in the farm yards.

You'll be able to witness the pageantry of yesterday. But you will probably watch from the grounds of Kyoto's old Imperial Palace as self-conscious college students hired for the day amble past costumed as courtiers of old—while overhead a light airplane will circle and via loudspeaker its pilot will urge the spectators (mostly Japanese) to save now in order to marry stylishly or die in clover.

You can shop for the tradition of craftsmanship, and you'll find it both in the items of yesterday and the

20th century. You can buy the latest in zoom-lens cameras, tiny portable TV-sets, or stereo equipment. But, if you seek the unique, you can wander to a shop in the quiet back streets of Kyoto where a man, who's classed as a "national living treasure," turns out by hand magnificent miniature replicas of ancient armor that cost several times the current duty-free allowance.

You will certainly want to sample the traditional service and Japanese way-of-life you've heard so much about, and you'll be able to sample it in the *ryokans,* the Japanese inns. In the *ryokan* you can sleep in a room completely alien to your Western bedroom—but sleeping on the floor will be made less forbidding by foam rubber mattresses. Service in the *ryokan* will be unbelievably gracious. Even if you don't venture beyond the centrally-heated confines of the posh, Western-style luxury hotels, you will find the same fine tradition of service—

FOUR FACETS OF JAPAN: *the restrained* noh *actors on stage; a side street bedecked with signs and lanterns; a larger-than-life kite being lofted at a festival; a baseball game in progress.*

except that you can summon it via a marvelously complicated bedside pushbutton console.

If you scorn "Continental" fare, you can have your choice—if you take your appetite beyond the Western hotel's inevitable sukiyaki and tempura room—of some of the world's most gracious and elegant restaurants, where dining in a private room is the custom and where the check can easily reach summits as high as those in the West's brightest expense account establishments. The everyday cafes are not to be scorned either, whether you want a snack of *sushi* (popular Japanese dish of rice and fish made into small cakes), raw fish, succulent eel and rice, or coffee and pound cake. And when the exotic becomes tiresome, you can easily retreat to your beefsteak; for Japan's beer-fed, hand-massaged steers produce some of the best beef in the world.

If you seek drama in the old tradition, you will find it in the powerful *kabuki*, the slow-paced *noh*, the puppet drama called *Bunraku*, the frothy Geisha plays staged each spring in Kyoto. Today's *kabuki* players, however, are inclined to do Eugene O'Neill between runs, and you're likely to be more enthralled—or bowled over—by the all-girl extravaganzas, or by the culmination of modern showmanship at one of Tokyo's huge supper clubs which offer Las Vegas-like spectaculars complete with revolving stage and dancing waters twice nightly to 2,000 patrons per performance.

If you are interested in sports of old you will find it in *sumo*, the fantastic display of wrestling and ritual performed by the fattest of men. The sport packs arenas and is threatened by the orgy of over-popularity via constant color TV exposure. On the other hand, the Japanese also exhibit their passion for sports with a madness for baseball, skiing and golf.

In these pages, we hope to lead you to some of the best of Japan's seemingly inexhaustible supply of attractions, to introduce you to the Japanese people, their customs and traditions.

But, first, some details you'll want to know:

Instant geography lesson

Japan's big islands stretch in an irregular half moon for 1,200 miles from Hokkaido in the north to Kyushu in the southwest. Honshu, the largest of these, is almost 800 miles long. Shikoku, the smallest of the big islands, is only about 60 miles wide by 100 miles long.

For every square mile of land, there are 9 miles of coastline. More than 80 per cent of this land is mountainous—with parts of it marked by high peaks and deep valleys. Along the coast dance more than 3,000 islands— and hundreds of these islets dot the quiet, misty water of the Inland Sea, the protected waterway that stretches for 250 miles and separates big Honshu from little Shikoku.

How long to stay?

Most tourists start in Tokyo. If they spend a week in Japan, they usually add Nikko, Kamakura and parts of Hakone-Fuji-Izu Peninsula to their visit. If they stay

---

YOU HAVE A SPECIAL INTEREST? ASK TIC FOR INFORMATION

Travel for most of us involves the exploration of some of our special interests—skin diving, kayaking, hiking, bird watching, stamp collecting, the drama, rock hounding, whatever. And in many countries it is difficult to find our counterparts or the place where we can pursue our interest. In Japan, though, you should have no such problem.

The Japan National Tourist Organization (JNTO) has a Tourist Information Center (TIC) at Yuraku-cho (it's within walking distance from the Imperial Hotel) that is the best source for tourists seeking special information. TIC has scrapbooks full of the most esoteric information on just about anything, and the personnel in the office are unbelievably helpful. They will make phone calls in Japanese, supply you with special little maps, provide you with instructions

that can be handed to a taxi driver, give you time schedules, make whatever special arrangements are required.

TIC also keeps a definitive list of festivals, covering events both inside and outside of Tokyo, a list which generally cannot be found anywhere else. You can also pick up handy booklets covering a wide variety of subjects. You can also try JNTO's Tele Tourist Service: just dial (03) 503-2911 for pre-taped tourist information including the events of the week.

A second TIC office is located in Kyoto on the left-hand side of Karasuma Street across from the main train station and just past the Marubutsu Department Store. Your hotel desk can give you instructions (or will write out instructions for a taxi driver) on how to reach either of these offices.

GETTING THERE is made easy with signs in Japanese and English at the immigration station (upper left) and a luggage carousel (above) like those at home. An ocean liner (left) docks at Harumi Harbor in Yokohama.

is in the 10-day to two-week category, Ise-Shima and the Kyoto-Nara area are musts. From that point, weeks can be added to become months. One sophisticated world traveler tells us: "If I went to Japan once a year and stayed for six months, I could go for one hundred years and never see the same thing twice. There's an array of national, cultural, religious, mythological and political displays to be found in no other part of the world."

Veteran American tour operator Joseph A. Grace (who heads Japan's largest tour company, Travel Center of Japan) suggests that first-time visitors would be wise to take a half-day or full-day sightseeing tour—particularly in Tokyo and Kyoto. It covers the standard points of interest, gives you a little feeling for the city and its people, and orients you as to the location of your hotel in relation to the whole city. Usually, you'll feel a little more confident about venturing forth on streets that are labeled only with Japanese characters or not labeled at all. And once you gain that confidence, you'll find Japan to be

one of the safest countries in the world for independent exploration.

How to get there

Japan is served by major air and shipping lines from all parts of the world. Tokyo is the air transportation center and Yokohama is the principal seaport.

The distance from San Francisco or Los Angeles to Tokyo on the Great Circle Route via Alaska is about 5,200 miles. The distance by way of Honolulu is 6,300 miles. From Honolulu to Tokyo it is 3,900 miles. There's a time difference of 17 hours between the West Coast of the U. S. and Japan—when it is 9 A.M. (PST) Monday in San Francisco, it is 2 A.M. the next day (Tuesday) in Tokyo.

By air. Seven major airlines operate regular flights from the West Coast to Tokyo: China Airlines, CP Air, Japan Air Lines, Korean Air Lines, Pan American

World Airways, Northwest Orient Airlines and Varig. Trans World Airlines flies from Los Angeles to Okinawa, from which there are connecting flights to Tokyo. From Tokyo, domestic carriers operate connecting flights to Japanese cities and tourist areas. Flight time from the West Coast (Los Angeles or San Francisco) to Tokyo is approximately 11 hours on the Great Circle Route via Anchorage and about 14½ hours via Vancouver or on the Central Pacific Route via Honolulu. On the return, the trip may be as short as 8 or 9 hours (depending on winds).

Several airlines offer service direct from New York and other eastern cities westward to Tokyo—with a variety of intermediate U. S. or Canadian stops. These lines are CP Air, Japan Air Lines, Northwest Orient and Pan American. Many of the trans-Atlantic airlines continue east-ward through Europe and the Middle East or through Russia to Tokyo.

By sea. The trip by ship from the West Coast to Japan takes about 14 days and can be made on ships of any of the following lines: Mitsui-O.S.K. Lines, Orient Overseas Line and P & O Lines (North America).

A number of other steamship companies provide passenger service on cargo lines (from 4 to 12 persons) between West Coast ports and Japan ports. These are: American Mail Line, Barber Lines, Knutsen Line (eastbound only) and States Steamship Company.

Passports and visas

Traveling to Japan has become a relatively simple matter. There is a minimum of red tape involved in entering

---

THE FORMIDABLE JAPANESE LANGUAGE... AND WHAT TO DO ABOUT IT

If you had to, you could get around in Japan with a three-word Japanese vocabulary: *dozo* (please, pronounced doh-zo), *arigato* (thank you, pronounced ah-ree-gah-tow) and *ohayo* (good morning, pronounced like Ohio). But a little more familiarity with the Japanese language brings its own rewards.

It's a language so difficult to learn that it's frustrating to a foreigner. With no basic similarity to our own language, there are no familiar roots to go by. Pronunciation is less complicated. All syllables are generally pronounced and with equal emphasis. *A* is pronounced as in America; *e* as in egg; *i* as in pin; *o* as oh, and *u* as in yule. Often the letter *u* is not pronounced—particularly in words ending in "u." For instance, *desu*, which means "is" or "are," is pronounced "dess."

Because of the great difficulty of the language and because you can't count on finding an English-speaking person whenever you need to ask a question, an English-Japanese phrase book will prove helpful. You'll find them available at most hotels, at travel agent offices or through the Japanese National Tourist Organization's Tourist Information Center.

You'll have no trouble, of course, with communications at leading hotels; they all have English-speaking staffs. But if you go exploring, a bilingual guide is just about a must. If you find yourself without phrasebook or guide and need help, ask a young person. They are more likely to understand English than older people since high schools require four years' study of English.

A few things to remember before you try speaking Japanese to a Japanese: it is the most polite of languages, and therefore full of honorifics, some of which are not always used by men but always must be used by women. For example, a man's *ohayo* is acceptable, but a woman must say *ohayo gozaimasu* (oh-high-yoh goh-zah-ee-mahss). The last word is an honorific, adding delicacy to the greeting. *Arigato* would be *arigato gozaimasu*. *Furo* (bath) is properly *o-furo* (the honorable bath), and tea is never just *cha* when spoken either by a man or a woman. It is *o-cha, o* being one of those often-used syllables indicating extra respect.

Another thing to remember is that if you ask a question in the negative ("Aren't you ready?"), the Japanese answer will be "Yes" when he means "No," "No" when he means "Yes."

Here are a few words for starters: yes, *hai* (pronounced high); no, *iie* (ee-yeh); good afternoon, *konnichiwa*; good evening, *konbanwa*; good night, *oyasumi nasai*; hotel, *hoteru*; telephone, *denwa*; railway station, *eki;* consulate, *ryojikan;* toilet, *tearaijo;* department store, *depaato*. Doctor is *isha*; dentist, *haisha*; drugstore, *kusuriya*; breakfast, *choshoku*; barber, *tokoya*; water, *mizu*; good-by, *sayonara*.

Dozo means please, but *kudasai* is another way of saying it as the end of a sentence. "Bring me a bottle of beer," for example, would be *biiru o ippon kudasai*.

Everybody is a *san* in Japan. It follows the name and means Mr., Mrs., Miss, or, for that matter, Ms.

Many Japanese can read printed English when they can neither speak nor understand the language. So if you print the English word and follow it with *kudasai*, that may be all you need to know.

and leaving the country. All you need is your passport and a tourist visa; for a short stay no visa is required.

No visas are required of steamship passengers on overland tours (of 15 days) between two ports, nor for visitors who stay in Japan less than 72 hours. Your plans can change, however, so it's a good idea to pick up a tourist visa regardless. They are valid for four years. Citizens of the United States and Canada are exempt from visa fees when they enter Japan as tourists.

If there is a Japanese embassy or consulate near you (addresses available from any of the Japan National Tourist Organization offices—see page 2), and you want to apply in person for your tourist visa, take your passport with you to be stamped. You will not need extra photographs, but you will have to make out three applications.

Let your travel agent do the leg work for you in applying for visas. He has all the necessary forms and other information.

Customs regulations

You can take just about whatever you want into Japan duty-free, subject to these limitations: no more than 400 cigarettes, 100 cigars, 500 grams of pipe tobacco, three bottles of alcoholic beverages.

Be sure to register your foreign-made cameras, binoculars and any particularly valuable jewelry, particularly pearls, with American customs at your departure point. Then hang onto the certificate. Japanese officials may not want to see it, but you will need it to show to American customs officials when you come home.

When you go through Japanese customs, you will be given a form called *Record of Purchase of Commodities Tax-Exempt for Export.* Guard it right along with your passport because it can save you up to 20 per cent on the bulk of your purchases in Japan. This entitles you to buy, at designated stores, many of Japan's best bargains without paying the Japanese commodity tax. On it you must list the price and date of each tax-free purchase to show to customs inspectors when you leave.

Inoculations

Japan requires a smallpox vaccination. So be sure that your International Certificate of Inoculation and Vaccination states that you have been successfully vaccinated within the last three years. If you plan to enter Japan from a country where there would be any likelihood of cholera or yellow fever, shots will be required for those diseases before entering Japan (or re-entering the United States). All of your inoculations should be recorded on the International Certificate; you may obtain one from any local health department office or from your travel

agent. Your doctor will fill in the information, but the smallpox certification is not officially valid unless it also carries the official stamp of the U.S. Public Health Service.

Hotel accommodations

Western-style hotels comparable to the best hotels in America and Europe are found throughout Japan in all the large cities and leading tourist resorts. The best ones all belong to the Japan Hotel Association, which requires high standards in both service and facilities.

Japanese-style inns, or *ryokan,* are great fun if you want a true sample of Japanese life (see page 36). There are well over 70,000 *ryokan* in Japan. Again, reliability is confirmed if the inn is a member of the Japan Ryokan Association.

The Japan National Tourist Organization office (see page 2) can send you two up-to-date accommodations guides: the *Japan Hotel Guide,* listing and describing its 251 member hotels, and the *Ryokan,* which covers 1,625 members of the Japan Ryokan Association.

Hotel space is difficult to get at the height of the tourist season—usually April and May, August through October. Reservations made well in advance are a must if you want choice hotels. This is especially true in Tokyo and Kyoto. The *ryokan*—the really good ones—are almost always

*NEW TOKAIDO LINE TRAINS run between
Tokyo and Osaka at speeds up to 125 miles per hour.
The Hinoyama Youth Hostel (above) is in Yamaguchi
Prefecture. Tokyo's Keio Plaza Hotel is the tallest
building in the Orient. This ryokan (lower right) is
typical of many in Japan.*

heavily booked and require reservations well in advance. Six months is not too early to make reservations for either hotels or the better *ryokan.*

Young people traveling on low budgets can stay at youth hostels or in *minshuku* (private homes that take in guests) at very little cost. Illustrated folders listing the best-equipped hostels and giving addresses, capacity and access to each one are available from the Japan National Tourist Organization (see page 2). Youth hostels cost Y540 to Y940 per night including breakfast and dinner.

For the "get to know the real Japan" traveler, a truly memorable addition to your trip can be staying in a *minshuku.* They vary from large, almost *ryokan*-like places to smaller private homes that take in one or two guests. They cost between Y1,800 and Y2,000 per night, including two Japanese meals, often eaten in a kind of communal room (which can be quite a learning experience). You can book space in a *minshuku* at any Japan Travel Bureau office.

Currency and banking

Japan's unit of currency is the yen. Notes include these denominations: Y10,000, Y5,000, Y1,000, Y500 and Y100, and there are Y100, Y50, Y10, Y5 and Y1 coins. The official exchange rates will vary somewhat because of value of the floating dollar; but for an approximation, you can figure the U.S. $1 to equal about Y300; Y100 is equal to about 33 cents. You'll find minor daily variations in the exchange rate.

You can bring yen into Japan, or you can convert your money at airport or seaport (go through an authorized foreign exchange bank or authorized money changer). When you convert, you will be issued a paper, *Record of Purchase of Foreign Means of Payment.* You may be asked for this when you re-convert to dollars upon departure. Traveler's checks are usually accepted in payment of purchases at all leading hotels and stores. Most major credit cards are accepted in the big hotels.

Banking hours are similar to those at home, usually 9 A.M. to 3 P.M. on weekdays with some banks open from 9 A.M. to noon on Saturdays.

Health and Medical

There are no health problems for travelers in Japan. The drinking water is excellent in Japanese cities. Milk served in hotel dining rooms and restaurants is pasteurized.

Should you need a doctor, ask your hotel manager or your tour director or representative. Many Japanese doctors speak English. Medical care and hospitals are of high standards. Most U. S. and European drugs are available in all big cities. The drug store in most big hotels in Tokyo will look very much like what you would find in a big hotel in the United States.

Food and drink

To tour Japan eating the same type food that you eat at home would be to miss one of the most interesting differences between East and West.

Most Americans have at least a speaking knowledge of *sukiyaki*—it consists of paper-thin slices of beef, bean curd (*tofu*), Japanese leeks, Chinese lettuce, mushrooms, *shirataki* (fine vermicelli-like threads of gelatinous starch), *dashi* (soup stock), sometimes onion and other vegetables, and it is flavored with soy sauce, sugar and *mirin* (a type of rice and wine used for cooking).

To do it justice, you should sit on a *tatami* (mat) at a low table and eat it with chopsticks. There will be a bowl of raw egg into which you may dip the *sukiyaki*, cooling it a bit as it comes from the hot frying pan. Half the fun of a *sukiyaki* dinner is that the dish is cooked on a charcoal brazier on a low table right in front of you, and served by waitresses in kimonos.

Another popular method of Japanese cooking is *tempura,* usually a fish of some sort that's dipped in an egg batter and deep fried. It may be made with fresh prawns or shrimp or any type of seafood. A variety of vegetables are also usually dipped in the same batter and fried with the fish. This is generally done before you as you sit and watch. Before you eat it, you dip the *tempura* into a sauce made of *dashi*, soy sauce, sugar, *mirin*, and grated radish and a bit of grated ginger.

Sushi (soo-shee), a less familiar dish, is made of rice and fish. The fish may be eel, tuna, *kohada* (a small fish with bluish skin), clams or prawns. The fish is raw—but don't let that keep you from trying this one. Westerners usually soon come to like it. The fish in dainty slices (*sashimi*) tops rice that has been flavored with vinegar and salt, sometimes also with sugar, and rolled into oval cakes. You can try *sushi* at one of the many *sushi* shops, where you will sit at an immaculately clean counter and see the *sushiya-san* prepare your order. Eat it with your fingers or with chopsticks, and order hot tea with it. You'll find you can also buy *sushi* "to go"—the oval slices are neatly fitted into a wooden box, wrapped with decorative paper and bound together with a rubber band.

You may be surprised to find superb beef available in many restaurants and at the leading hotels. Steaks are excellent—particularly if you go to a restaurant that features Kobe, Matsusaka or Omi beef. These are the finest beef cattle in Japan (some say, in the world) and are the result of selective and careful breeding that began about 1825. But the Japanese say breeding is only part of the story— they also pamper their beef. Kobe steers, you will be told,

DINING ENTRY (above) is to a famous soba *(Japanese noodles) restaurant in Tokyo. Dinner is served (upper right) at Nakamura-ro, a restaurant in Kyoto.* Sushi *shops (lower right) specialize in small cakes of rice and raw fish.*

are massaged with *sake* in a daily ritual designed to spread the fat evenly and are fed two bottles of beer a day—which aids their digestion and makes contented cattle and, therefore, tender steaks.

And there are other wonderful dishes and menus to try: *mizutaki* beef or chicken, Mongolian barbecue, *yakitori* (grilled chicken), *kushi-katsu* (usually poultry or pork on a skewer), *Okaribayaki* (hunting style—wild game—cooked on a steel plate). But part of the experience is the setting, part the ritual. Here's a brief description of a visit to a Japanese restaurant:

After a taxi ride through the hodge-podge streets of Tokyo, you'll enter some quiet side street and stop before an unpretentious dun-colored building identified by a modest sign in Japanese lettering. But what a contrast when you step through the gateway. You'll be greeted by a bowing employee (sometimes the pro-

prietor) and escorted through the garden to the front door. The garden may be no larger than a postage-stamp, but rock stepping stones will make the path, several clumps of bamboo will suggest a forest, a huge earthenware jar with water trickling into it and over its sides will suggest a pool and stream.

At the entryway, you'll stand on cobblestone pavement, remove your street shoes and step up onto the polished wood of the landing. You'll then slip into slippers—that certainly won't stay on your Western-size feet —and pad carefully down the mirror slick corridor to your private dining room. All will be quiet, except for muffled conversations or laughter from this room or that.

At the door to your room, the maid will slide back the door, you'll step out of your slippers, walk in and take a seat on a floor cushion. Your dining room will be the ultimate in sophisticated simplicity—with walls

CLIMATIC EXTREMES. When it's summer in Japan, it's hot enough to bring crowds to the beaches on Honshu, Shikoku and Kyushu. When it's winter, the snow flies and the temperature drops so low in northern Honshu and Hokkaido that almost everyone stays inside.

of beige plaster, unpainted and waxed woodwork, a flower arrangement and scroll in a special alcove, a red or black round lacquer table (with built-in burner in the center), and dark green cushions on the springy tan tatami flooring. There may be a special lower door to one side through which the maid enters.

Hot towels for hands and face will be served first, then the serious business of dining will begin. What you'll eat will depend on the restaurant you've selected, for Japanese restaurants are inclined to specialize in certain foods—there's one in Tokyo, for instance, where sardines are served in 150 different ways!

Let's say you've selected one specializing in chicken. The chicken is probably shipped in daily from Nagoya. The first courses—the appetizers, really—may be chicken *sashimi* garnished with chopped, dry seaweed, followed by chicken broth. While you try these, the waitress will ready the iron cooking pot in which the main course will be cooked. From a black lacquer box she'll bring out the dishes of ingredients—white meat of chicken in bite sizes, liver and heart, meat balls, leeks, soy bean curd, big fresh

mushrooms—and begin cooking them in a soy-based sauce that imparts a subtle barbecue flavor to the meat. She'll show you how to grasp the bite-size pieces with your chopsticks and dip the hot bites in a little bowl containing grated radish, mustard and pepper; and she may give you some instruction on chopstick etiquette.

When this course is finished, another pot—this one filled with broth—appears and similar ingredients are gently boiled and served with another type of tangy radish relish.

Throughout the meal you will be served warm *sake*, the slightly sweet rice wine that is such a favorite with the Japanese. It's served in thimble-size pottery cups from narrow-necked pottery pitchers. As a finale, when chicken, leeks, curd and mushrooms are dispensed with, broad noodles will be put into the broth. After you've chased enough slippery noodles around your bowl with your chopsticks, the *sake* cups and cooking pots will be whisked away. Tea—along with a few other tidbits, just in case you're still hungry—will appear. First there'll be some soy bean soup, then a little bowl of rice and a dish of pickles, and finally a special last course: tea and a selection of fruits.

You'll always find some places in the major cities and tourist centers where you can find American type food; and in places like Tokyo, Kobe and Osaka, you'll find a wide variety of restaurants serving food representative of many other nations.

Climate

Japan's climate is temperate, but it does have decided seasonal changes. The country is around 1,300 miles long, so there are considerable differences in temperatures between Hokkaido, the northern island, and Kyushu, the southernmost.

The climate of the main island of Honshu is frequently compared to the middlewestern states of America, although Honshu's temperature changes are not nearly so extreme. The best months for visiting are March, April and May (blossom time) and October and November (brilliant foliage and chrysanthemum time). These months are usually mild (though March doesn't always remember that it is supposed to be a spring month).

Summer brings rain. It may start earlier, but from mid-June into early July you can just about count on daily rain. Though July, August and early September are hot (high 80s, low 90s and humid), there is air conditioning in all the big hotels and restaurants.

Winters are generally bright and clear. Hokkaido and northern Honshu get a considerable snowfall, but the southern half of Honshu and the large island of Kyushu have a very mild winter. Tokyo usually gets a few light snowfalls in January and February.

What to wear

You will find that dark suits and cocktail dresses usually suffice for dressy occasions in Japan. Jackets, sweaters, and lightweight coats will be needed both in spring and autumn, and they will be useful in summer as well for the air-conditioned hotels and dining places. Otherwise, take cool cottons and silks for summer months; woolens, top coats and furs for winter.

Two important wardrobe items are a raincoat and a pair of comfortable walking shoes. And women should have some full skirts along for sitting on the floor at tea ceremonies and in Japanese inns and restaurants.

What else to pack

If you wear reading glasses, take along an extra pair, or your prescription, or both (optical equipment is one of the good buys in Japan).

That one allowable carton of cigarettes will be a boon to smokers who don't like to experiment with unfamiliar makes. Cigars and American cigarettes are available, but rather high-priced in Japan (about 60 cents a pack for cigarettes). A couple of handy extras to have along are flints for lighters and refills for ballpoint pens.

Your single, most useful accessory will be a pair of warm, knitted slippers to wear on those frequent occasions when you must remove your shoes. Slippers are sometimes but not always supplied for you to wear when you enter shrines and temples.

Barbers, baths and beauty shops

Japan's barber and beauty shops are excellent, particularly in the leading hotels. If you are staying in a small inn where there are no such facilities, ask someone to make an appointment for you with a shop in any of the big hotels. Or try an out-of-the-hotel shop. They are fun, and you can probably make your wants known even if verbal communications bog down. In the cities several big Japanese cosmetic firms have luxurious salons on the order of Elizabeth Arden salons in the United States.

You may be coiffed, manicured and pedicured all at the same time in a Japanese beauty shop. The results are likely to be elegant, and the price for all this service much less than you would pay at home.

Many of the neighborhood barbershops employ women barbers, and they do a good job. Women also come in occasionally to have their faces shaved, so don't be astonished if you find you have female company in the chair next to you.

Wherever you go in Japan, you'll find steam and mineral water baths where you can be most skillfully steamed, scrubbed and massaged by efficient young masseuses. Or you can order a massage in your hotel room. Many hotels employ their own masseurs. Don't be surprised if he is blind. It is a profession in which the blind become adept.

Laundry and dry cleaning

In major hotels quick and efficient service is available for both laundry and dry cleaning. Laundry or cleaning collected before 10 A.M. in most of the big hotels will be returned the same day by 5 or 5:30. Two-hour service is also available for an extra fee, and you can always get pressing and mending attended to promptly. The service at inns and in smaller, out-of-the-way hotels is somewhat slower, as a rule.

Electric appliances

Electric razors, traveling irons and similar American electric appliances may be used in Japan. The electric current is about 100 volts, alternating current. Japanese outlets take American plugs.

Guide service

Tourist guide-interpreters licensed by the government may be hired through any authorized travel agency or hotel, or through the Japan Guide Association. If you would like a guide-interpreter for your entire Japanese tour, your travel agent will arrange for one before you leave home. Guide-interpreters speak Japanese, English, French, Spanish, German, Italian, Portuguese, and Russian; and they are classified into three grades of A, B and C according to their skill and experience.

Rates are Y3,500 (a guide fee only) for a half day for one to four persons. Full days (eight hours) cost Y5,000. For parties of more than four persons, Y100 is charged for each additional person. You also pay your guide's transportation, his meals and accommodation.

Tipping customs

In Japan the 10 per cent service charge, where levied by hotels and restaurants, is final. That is all you need to tip. Don't dig further into your wallet.

In Western-style hotels in the larger cities you will find printed notices to the effect that a 10 per cent service charge is added to the bill, with a request not to tip additionally. In Japanese inns a service charge of from 15 to 20 per cent is usually included in your bill; and if it is not added, it is expected.

In both Western-style and Japanese restaurants, 10 per cent of the bill will usually be added to the bill.

Tipping is unnecessary for taxi drivers, sighteeing bus drivers and guides, but a ten per cent tip is customary for drivers of hired cars.

A fixed fee per piece of luggage is charged at the international airport and station by porters.

Photography

Japan is as photogenic a country as there is in the world, and the Japanese are great picture-takers themselves. There are lots of camera shops, and you can buy good Japanese black and white film almost anywhere. The Japanese color film is not as satisfactory as American, but you'll find ample stocks of American film in any of the large cities.

Since you can take any kind of camera you like into Japan, do have one for quick, candid shots. Japanese children make ideal photo targets. If you are photographing older people, you can at least get the idea across, with a *ii desuka?* (is it all right?) and a few gestures, that you are asking their permission. They are generally quite willing. *Do* be appreciative. *Don't* as you might in Latin American countries, offer a tip. It could be considered an insult. Only occasionally will you encounter a sign requesting that no pictures be taken; but when you do, there is some reason of vast importance behind it as far as the Japanese are concerned, so be careful to respect the regulations.

Shopping

Shopping is half the fun in Japan. Men like it for there are many excellent buys that appeal to them, like cameras and binoculars, transistor radios, stereo record players, tape recorders and portable television sets. Women love it. Topping the list of treasures that typify the country are Japan's cultured pearls. Other favorites include raw silks and brocades, *kimonos* and *obis* (the broad sashes that go around the *kimono*), happi coats and bright embroideries, cloisonné, pottery and lacquer ware, dolls (their elaborate coiffures and costumes reminiscent of Japan's many historical periods), wood block prints and damascene.

Since Japan makes more time-keeping instruments than any other country in the world, it's obviously a good place to shop for watches, stop watches, clocks, chronometers, digital time pieces and even the new 24-hour clocks. At the other end of the scale, you can also find (if you search with enough diligence) some fascinating antique time pieces—masterpieces of wood, metal or porcelain artistry made during the last century.

Japan's *o-miyage* (souvenirs) are typically her own: things like lanterns, fans and parasols, *noh* masks (worn by the actors in *noh* plays), an infinite variety of toys made of paper, wood and lacquer, bamboo ware, wooden clogs, straw slippers and *origami* (paper folding).

Whenever you go shopping, always take along your record of purchases form that you received when you came through Japanese customs. You must present it in order to receive the 10 to 20 (usually 16) per cent tax discount allowed tourists. Only specially designated stores are permitted to offer this discount which represents the Japanese commodity tax. Remember that this tax is included in the amount marked on the price tag of any item for sale in the shops.

All the shops that allow the tax deduction are members of the Japan Souvenir Association, which is also a guarantee that their merchandise is of good quality and truly representative of Japan. Folders listing them are available at hotels, travel bureaus and the shops concerned, and each store makes it clear that it is a tax-free tourist center with a large sign in English.

Tax-free items for tourists include pearls and articles decorated with pearls, objects made of, plated or covered with precious metal, tortoise-shell, articles made of precious stones, coral and ivory ware, cloisonné, dolls, lacquered smoking accessories, radio sets, tape recorders, rifles and shotguns, slide projectors, record players, portable TV sets, furs, furniture made of fibres, toys, cameras,

ARTS AND CRAFTS in Tokyo: five doll heads
mark time in front of a doll manufacturing shop.
A dressmaker fits a kimono for a customer. A
salesgirl adds up the prices on an abacus. An artist
is at work on a scroll painting.

THE *MEISHI*—IT'S INDISPENSABLE

Calling cards, termed *meishi* (or name cards) by the Japanese, are virtually essential in Japan. They are used by the Japanese routinely in social as well as business situations. Name cards prove invaluable when you are meeting people, exchanging addresses, dealing with hotel personnel and others to whom you wish to make your identity known, in the pursuit of either business or pleasure. The calling card custom is so ingrained in the Japanese people that they ordinarily bring their own cards (with bilingual identification taking up both sides) when they travel to the United States and elsewhere. Sometimes their cards also carry a simple line map of Japan indicating the location of their place of residence.

To assist you in acquiring a supply of bilingual calling cards, several airlines have name card services.

For a small charge they will print the Japanese translation of your name (and your company and title if these pertain) on the blank side of your own cards; or they will make up new cards with your English and Japanese identification. They also print cards carrying only your own name translated into Japanese.

Printing of foreign names in Japanese is done through transliteration: the phonetic pronunciation of the name is spelled out in Japanese characters. If you have a name that is uncommon or difficult to pronounce, JAL advises that it is important to include the phonetic spelling of your name (for example, Rochambeau would be Roh-sham-boh). If you are an officer or member of the board of directors of your firm, indicate this. In Japan, such status is very important, particularly if you are doing business there.

---

projectors, telescopes and binoculars. When you leave Japan, you must take all tax-free purchases with you—you cannot dispose of them in the country.

If you are buying antiques (never tax-free), ask the salesman to attach a statement that the item you have bought is not a *national treasure*. Some antiques and art objects are so considered, and a national treasure is not permitted to be taken out of Japan.

The hotel arcades are the easiest places to shop, for they offer a fine variety of goods, and there's never any language problem. Shopping in a department store is a novel experience. The big stores are something like a small city, with theater, art gallery, tea house, play center for children, and sometimes even a zoo. Clerks wear tags indicating that they speak English.

Business hours seem to go on forever in Japanese cities, with many shops open on a seven-day basis. Most department stores close on one day, most often Monday or Thursday, and sometimes on Wednesday. But Sunday is the week's busiest shopping day. They are generally open from 10 A.M. to 5 or 6 P.M.

You may be surprised at the prices—particularly if you are accustomed to paying less for Japanese products at home. The products they export are competitively priced for world markets; many of the products they sell domestically won't fall into the category of a bargain. And bargaining, although it is expected everywhere else in the Orient, is not the custom in Japan. Prices are fairly well standardized in most city stores, just as they are at home.

Also, don't feel neglected if a shopkeeper pays no attention to you. Aggressive salesmanship is considered discourteous. Browse as long as you like. He will give you patient and polite service when you are ready.

How to get your treasures home

The better shops do a fine job of wrapping and mailing packages for you. There is a shop in the Imperial Hotel arcade in Tokyo that does nothing else. When you are arranging to have anything shipped home, make sure that the clerk really understands your name and address. Give him a personal calling card, or *print* your name and address carefully; *our* written language confuses *them* about as much as their calligraphy confuses us.

If you ship articles home by boat, count on 5 to 10 weeks for delivery. If you are traveling by plane, it will be less expensive to ship parcels by air express than to pay excess baggage costs.

Duty on your purchases

You are allowed to bring $100 worth of articles into the United States duty free. But customs officials give you the advantage by figuring a fair wholesale price on your purchases. And when you bring in more than $100 worth of items, they will usually assess charges on those items that carry the lowest duty.

You may also send home any number of gifts without declaring them so long as each gift is valued at under $10 (wholesale price), and so long as you send no more than one gift a day to the same person. Be sure that each package is marked *"Unsolicited gift, value less than $10."*

CRAFTSMAN GLAZES POTTERY in Shigaraki (above). Visitors to temples, shrines, inns and private homes remove their shoes (upper right) before entering. At some places, slippers are offered, but it's a good idea to carry your own. Karasugi, a famous craftsman (lower right), works at the potter's wheel.

Watching your souvenirs made

It is fun to bring home a lustrous lacquer tea set, a Japanese woodblock print, or a perfect string of pearls. But each will mean much more if you have watched such articles being made. And this is one of the delightful experiences open to you in Japan: to see the *mingei* (crafts) of the country being created.

In Kyoto, for example, you may see the long, painstaking processes essential to manufacturing lacquer. In Tokyo you may watch the many steps involved in turning out a finished woodblock print. You may see silk being made in Kyoto and lanterns in Gifu. Potters work at their wheels while you watch. And perhaps most exciting of all is to witness, at Ise Shima National Park, the creating of cultured pearls. You can watch the diving girls in Ago Bay, the precision-operation of injecting a tiny bit of foreign matter into each oyster, and finally, the grading of the finished jewels.

Transportation in Japan

There are no transportation problems for travelers in Japan (except those resulting from language difficulties) what with the excellent plane and train service available throughout the country. And numerous bus companies operate comfortable sightseeing tours, always with English-speaking escorts, in and around all major tourist centers. Chauffeur or guide-driven cars are available for

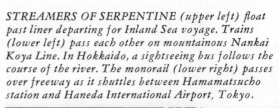

STREAMERS OF SERPENTINE (upper left) float past liner departing for Inland Sea voyage. Trains (lower left) pass each other on mountainous Nankai Koya Line. In Hokkaido, a sightseeing bus follows the course of the river. The monorail (lower right) passes over freeway as it shuttles between Hamamatsucho station and Haneda International Airport, Tokyo.

sightseeing, and U-drive cars may be hired. There are also some delightful water cruises for travelers in Japan, from steamship cruises on the Inland Sea to river rides in small boats.

Travel by train

Japan is a train-conscious country. Her railroad systems, serving the entire country, are efficient, punctual and pleasant. Travel by train is highly recommended to tourists.

The Japanese National Railways has a 13,000-mile network, while numerous private companies operate 4,500 miles of railways. Rates, the same on both the national and the private lines, are economical.

The national system has been converted to only one class, with particularly luxurious service available in the "A"-class coaches. The limited express trains, wherever available, have elegant service and are particularly recommended for tourist travel. The private trains, which also operate mono-class, also have some excellent deluxe trains.

The Japanese National Railways train that most tourists will use is the New Tokaido Line super express that runs between Tokyo and Osaka via Nagoya and Kyoto. This is the world's fastest train. Traveling more than 125 miles an hour, the 313-mile trip from Tokyo to Osaka takes three hours and 10 minutes. The total fare one way costs Y6,730 which includes the basic fare, and the extra charges for the super express and for a reserved seat in the "A"-class section.

Other than the New Tokaido super express, some 385 limited express trains and 1,209 expresses are run on Japan's principal trunk lines. The "A"-class coaches of all these deluxe trains are equipped with reclining seats, and all of the cars are air-conditioned in summer and heated in winter. Sleepers are available on all long distance services. "A"-class berth charges (over base price of ticket) range from Y3,800 for an upper to Y5,400 for a roomette. All of the berths are air-conditioned and vibration free.

Both Japanese- and Western-style meals are served in the dining cars, along with wine, beer, and liquor.

Super and limited expresses, known as *Hikari* and *Kodama* trains, accept telegrams for dispatch from trains, and telephone service is available to major Japan cities. All Japanese National Railways trains observe a "non-tip" system. New Tokaido Line and some limited express trains make announcements in English concerning scheduled stop-stations, and travel information. Porter service is available at main stations (where you *do* tip).

Travel by air

Internal airlines serve all major tourist centers in Japan. Japan Air Lines makes frequent daily flights from Tokyo to Osaka and Fukuoka to the west and to Sapporo to the north. JAL uses DC-8 and Boeing 727 jets on all of these flights. Passenger fares between Toyko and Osaka are Y7,900; between Tokyo and Sapporo, Y13,900.

All Nippon Airways, another nation-wide line, also operates regular domestic air services throughout Japan. Toa Domestic Airlines, another internal airline, provides service between Tokyo, Osaka, Sapporo, and other points.

Travel by bus

A few of the travel agents operate regular escorted bus tours in luxurious coaches, with English-speaking guides and hostesses. They range from half-day sightseeing trips to 12-day tours. Several tour operators are offering special 5 to 12-day bus trips out of Tokyo. The most popular bus tour pattern is one that follows the Old Imperial Highway (the Tokaido) between Tokyo and Kyoto. Accompanied by a veteran guide and hostess, these coach tours offer several departures weekly during spring, summer and fall, with less available in winter. Deluxe air-conditioned coaches with deep reclining seats are used.

Each major city has its selection of morning, afternoon and nighttime sightseeing tours. Your travel agent can arrange any of these trips for you.

Travel by car

Chauffeur-driven cars may be arranged for tourists through any travel agency in Japan. Both American and the small Japanese cars are available. Your best bet is to get a driver-guide who has some knowledge of English. In Tokyo rates average Y10,080 for up to three and one half hours. Out of Tokyo, rates vary depending on the time and distance—Y28,800 for a trip to Nikko, Y19,-800 for a trip to Kamakura.

Japan has many drive-yourself cars available from a host of rent-a-car agencies including some of the big international services like Avis and Hertz. But driving a car is not usually recommended for tourists. You have to drive on the left side of the road. Road and directional signs are usually in Japanese. Once you get off the super highways, you'll find country roads rutty and rough. And traffic in the cities, especially in Tokyo, can be a downright traumatic experience. Add to all this the fact that rent-a-car rates are very high in Japan.

Travel by boat

All-day cruises on the Inland Sea are operated daily by several steamship companies, the most recommendable of which is the Kansai Steamship Company. (See page 125 for the complete story.) Hydrofoils are now in service on short runs out of Gama-gori, Osaka, Kobe, Himeji, Hiroshima, Takamatsu, Sakate and Tonoshyo.

TRANQUILITY ENVELOPS the Jakkoin Nunnery in Ohara, Kyoto (above) while the manifestations of Western music are to be heard at Doshisha University's jazz festival in Kyoto and at a violin concert in which very young children participate.

The Japanese People ... Their Customs, Traditions, Art and Culture

We read from left to right on a horizontal line; the Japanese read from right to left along vertical lines. When we say "yes," we mean "yes"; but a Japanese may mean "no" when he says "yes." We paint our houses; the Japanese use not one drop of paint on theirs. Tea to us is a beverage like coffee; to the Japanese it can be the subject of a very formal ceremony. We bathe in privacy but dine with crowds. The Japanese bathe together quite casually, but they like privacy at their meals. In the United States, major decisions, ground breaking ceremonies, building dedications and other such important events are usually performed because it's time to start construction or it fits into our social or business schedule; in Japan major events are scheduled to fall on "an auspicious day."

Start from here, with the realization that in Japan you may often encounter points of view just the reverse of your own. A little study of the customs and traditions of the people, however, will help you bridge that gap between the ways of the East and the ways of the West.

Keep in mind how long the Japanese have been evolving their way of living. When the Pilgrims were landing at Plymouth Rock, the nation of Japan had known 12 centuries of development.

Isolated by governmental choice from the rest of the world, except for the few abortive decades when a handful of Portuguese and Dutch lived in a kind of social quarantine on an off-shore island near Nagasaki, Japan only met the civilization of the West in the middle of the last century. A treaty of friendship with the United States in 1854, one year after Commodore Perry's arrival off Yokohama, opened the first door to the outside world. Even then it was opened reluctantly.

Superstitions

The Japanese seem to us a strange mixture of sophistication and primitive superstition. You will find them in

Tokyo in enthusiastic attendance at a concert, say, of the London Symphony Orchestra, or avidly attending the theater. A highly literate people, you will find them jamming book stores and crowding into art exhibits.

On the other hand, you may witness a graveside ceremony for a broken doll; or see a doll being thrown into a river—the purpose, to avert misfortune. You could happen onto a memorial service for the spirits of cherry trees sacrificed to make wood block prints. You may see a comb thrown from the window of a passing bus, a comb no one will touch because it carries with it all the bad luck of the person who threw it away.

Among other unusual observances that are held largely out of superstition are the following: an annual festival for broken sewing needles; an annual service for the souls of eels, which are a favorite Japanese food. At the February Setsubun Festival, fathers throw pre-blessed beans into dark corners to chase out evil spirits. And mothers take their children to touch a certain stone at the Yuten-ji Temple in Tokyo in order to ward off a case of the measles. During the New Year's Festival, a rope of twisted straw is hung at the entrance to the home to indicate that the house is pure and has no evil spirits.

The Japanese have a special affinity for animals—using

A NATIONAL "TALENT BANK": UNIQUE TO JAPAN

Japan's corps of human national treasures, officially known as "Holders of Important Intangible Cultural Properties," might also be called a unique kind of talent bank. The idea behind this talent bank is one that helps preserve the ancient arts and crafts that had come perilously close to extinction by the end of World War II. General of the Army Douglas MacArthur was the proponent of the idea originally. When he realized the extent of wartime destruction in Japan, he persuaded the Japanese to forestall what would have been the death of ancient ways in the producing of certain types of arts and crafts.

So it is that 69 individuals are today designated as "living national treasures," carrying out the ancient and time-honored steps in the processes of producing something representative of some of Japan's finest arts and crafts. The arts practiced by these great craftsmen include pottery, the making of puppets, hand-dyed fabrics, hand-woven textiles, hand-forged swords, lacquer ware, metal arts, wood and bamboo crafts, doll-making and hand-made paper. Others—actors, musicians, dancers—preserve the ancient traditions of Japanese music and drama with particular emphasis on *noh*, *kabuki* and *Bunraku*.

All 69 artisans who comprise this talent bank are individuals who possess more than talent and skill. Each person must in addition be guided by a spirit that motivates him to the endless search for perfection in his chosen field.

The superiority of the artists' works has a tangible and lasting effect on a great deal of the hand-done work produced throughout Japan. The piece of lacquer ware you buy, for instance, may very likely be an object created in some small studio by an artisan whose spiritual mentor is one of the "Holders of Important Intangible Cultural Properties."

These artisans are protected from the public; their studios are not open to the casual visitor. If, however, you are also an artist or you have a special interest in one of the fields in which these craftsmen work, you can make arrangements through the Japan National Tourist Organization to visit their studios. The JNTO offices at the Tokyo airport and in Kyoto have a list of the artisans, their specialties and their locations.

SERIZAWA, *master of picture pattern dying on cloth.*

a dozen of them to name their years: the year of the rat, the bull, the tiger, the cock, and so forth. And wherever you go, you see symbolic statues of animals. The stone foxes you see so often at Inari-Jinja Shrines, for example, are symbols of worldly success. Great dogs guard Shinto shrines. Porcelain cats (*manekineko*), each with the left paw upraised, sit in shop windows—beckoning you inside, in a gesture the reverse of ours: the Japanese beckons with palm outward in a downward movement of the hand.

Jeans and bikini-clad youth not withstanding, Japanese young and old, still keep the fortune tellers very busy. Visit a mod center like Shinjuku (see page 61) any afternoon or evening, and you will see proof of this. A crowd of girls, plus a few men, will always be seen—asking the fortune tellers what the future holds for them.

Manners

If Japanese manners seem excessively polite, ours seem strange to them, too. A Japanese girl training to be a hostess on Japan Air Lines remarked that it was difficult to learn the "often so strange etiquette of the foreigners."

You may be told that when over 100 million people live in such a small area, it is necessary to be courteous to each other. There is no room for blowing off steam. But the habit of tranquility, which includes no show of emotion, is a Buddhist idea. A Japanese smiles even when he is telling you of personal grief. Courtesy also involves his personal honor. To lose his temper would be to lose face.

Strangers continue to be strangers in Japan, where formality rules. Japanese students may prove eager to speak with you, in order to practice their English, and they are likely to be helpful and friendly. But generally it is not the custom to strike up a conversation with a stranger, and Japanese who work together long remain on a bowing-acquaintance basis.

Everything the Japanese do they do with intensity. If you sample much of the night life in Tokyo, you may think that they have taken on Western customs with startling intensity. But this is but one facet in the meeting of two dissimilar civilizations. The Orientals may play the latest American jazz and stage tremendous *storippu* (strip-tease) shows for the entertainment of the tourist, but their traditions and beliefs have been deeply ingrained through generation upon generation.

Religion

Japan's two principal religions, Shinto and Buddhism, have become closely interrelated. Shinto enters much into everyday life; Buddhism into the spiritual life. Weddings are generally Shinto ceremonies; burials are Buddhist rites.

CHILDREN are in the spotlight on November 15 for Shishi-Go-San day (seven-five-three day) when parents take their children of corresponding ages to a shrine.

A THREE-YEAR-OLD is taught to scoop up water with a dipper so he can wash his hands and rinse out his mouth to purify himself before approaching the Shinto shrine.

THE GREAT BUDDHA *(left) at Todaiji Temple in Nara is famous for its chief object of worship, the 53-foot, 8th century bronze* Daibutsu. *One of the young shrine assistants (below) walks across the courtyard in the rain. A parade of parasols (lower right) marches down an empty road.*

Shintoism. Shinto has a great pantheon of gods that include ancestors, heroes, ancestral members of the Imperial Family, gods and goddesses of the sea, the mountains, the wind, but above all, of the sun. The Sun Goddess was presumed to have been the ancestress of Japan's first legendary Emperor, Jimmu, and only in 1946 did the present Emperor Hirohito disclaim for himself this line of divine descent.

Shinto shrines are everywhere in Japan. If you see a Japanese clap his hands before a shrine, it is to attract the attention of the special deity there enshrined. He may then drop a few coins into an offertory box, although food is the commonest offering. People collect the pieces of paper on which the seals of shrines have been printed, and hang them in their houses as protection against all manner of troubles.

A shrine you may often notice is one dedicated to *Jizo,* guardian of the souls of dead children. Some say this deity may have been adopted from Christianity's Jesus. Frequently a tiny bib or bit of clothing is hung about the stone statue of *Jizo* in hopes that the patron saint will assist the soul of a dead child.

Though numerous festivals pay special homage to certain deities at specified times during the year, there are no regular Shinto services of any kind. And Shrine festivals, even when they honor lost soldiers, are the gayest of events, something like carnivals. For the festival of Tokyo's Yasukuni Shrine, dedicated to the spirits of soldiers killed during this century, people come in bus loads. They buy souvenirs at the stalls leading to the shrine, watch dances and parades.

The *torii,* or high gate before each Shinto shrine, is another Japanese landmark. It dates from Japan's legendary pre-history, and to walk beneath it is a first step in purification.

Japan's most sacred Grand Shrine of Ise, consecrated to the Sun Goddess, is considered the top example of traditional Japanese architecture, from which Western modernists have borrowed so much. Built on pilings, it is a structure of elegant simplicity. It is reconstructed exactly the same way every 20 years. Here is where the mirror, one of the sacred symbol regalia of the Imperial Family, is kept. Another sacred symbol, a sword, which legend says was found by the brother of the Sun Goddess when he destroyed an eight-headed serpent, is kept at Atsuta Shrine in Nagoya.

Buddhism. Buddhism is an ascetic philosophy, a system of ethics in which the individual seeks to live in harmony with all nature and to find, as did the Buddha, eventual enlightenment. Austerity is a basic precept, particularly in the Zen cult.

Buddhism came to Japan from China via Korea in the sixth century. In due time it incorporated the Shinto gods

WORSHIPPERS at main hall of Tokyo's Asakusa Kannon Temple (Goddess of Mercy) smell burning incense.

as manifestations of Buddha. Like Shintoism it has no set day for any kind of service, but worshipers constantly visit the temples. Two of its most typical observances are the *O-Bon* Festival, which welcomes home departed souls, and the *Bon-Odori,* the all-soul's festival dance, which celebrates the liberation of dead souls into the Buddhist state of bliss. (See July listings under Festivals, page 153.)

Zen Buddhism also came to Japan from China, about the 12th century. Its stern discipline appealed to the *samurai,* those fierce fighters who were attached, by contract, to various warlords as their warriors. Its influence spread rapidly throughout Japan. The *cha-no-yu* (tea ceremony) which you will no doubt witness on aching knees, as you sit Japanese-style on the floor, was developed by Zen monks. It expresses the disciplined behavior and elaborate simplicity of Zen.

The graceful, lifted roof corners of Buddhist pagodas stand out against the Japanese skyline. The pagoda is often the focal point of a temple, which is not a single structure but a complex of buildings comprising a main hall, other dedicated halls or galleries and buildings that house the monks. Most temples, since they are always built of wood, have burned down again and again, and have been rebuilt in replica.

About two-thirds of the Japanese people are adherents of Buddhism though not all of them belong to one sect.

In addition to Zen Buddhism, there are a number of other sects—Nichiren, Ritsu, Shingon, Tendai to name a few—most of which have a number of branches and all of which have their special temples.

Art and architecture

Art is an inseparable part of all Japanese life, and the Japanese artist ranks high in his homeland. Art exhibits draw tremendous public response, and you see groups of school youngsters on outings, each with his drawing pad. To paint, to arrange flowers, to write poetry, to create beauty in everyday living is part of the Japanese character.

Buildings of outstanding architectural beauty and sculpture, carvings and paintings of unusual merit are recognized as such by the government and named as cultural properties of the nation or as National Treasures. Kyoto, with its some 2,000 shrines and temples, Nara, Nikko and other cultural centers abound in National Treasures. The murals at Nagoya Castle, for example, are so designated, and an ancient fan fashioned of strips of cypress and preserved in the Itsukushima Shrine at Miyajima is a National Treasure.

The theater

Japan's three unique traditional forms of theater are *kabuki*, *noh* and *Bunraku*. *Kabuki* is the one you are likely to find the most fascinating. It has fantastic plots, fabulous costuming, lots of action. Men take all the parts. Performances go on for hours. (See page 62 for a description of the *kabuki* theaters in Tokyo.)

A great deal goes on besides the acting and singing, what with the musicians seated on stage and the prop men who come out in their black hoods to hand performers a fan or flowers, to arrange their voluminous robes or, if a scene gets too violent, perhaps to rearrange an actor's wig.

Noh plays, stylized and highly symbolic, are of particular interest to students of serious drama. It is the classical drama of the early aristocrats, dating back to the 12th century. It is slow-paced, with musical background, on a bare stage with a huge pine tree painted on the backdrop. The main performers wear masks depicting the characters they portray, and they speak in strangely raucous, falsetto voices.

Noh plays are performed throughout the year. They take from three to six hours, depending on how many plays are presented in a performance. Most *noh* plays are given on weekends. Major *noh* stages are in Tokyo, but there are also four in Kyoto and two in Osaka.

Bunraku, or puppet plays, may not sound exciting, but Osaka's are considered one of the finest theatrical arts in Japan. The plays are really *kabuki* in miniature, specializing in heroic tales of *samurai*. The dolls are a little less than life-size, manipulated by puppeteers, in ceremonial robes, who are famous for their dexterity. Three operators sometimes manage one doll, a wonderfully mobile creature, even to its facial expressions. If you see hooded operators in the background, these are puppeteers of lesser skill who assist the experts.

Some of the finest performances of *Bunraku* are given at the Bunrakuza Theater in Osaka (see page 119); however you can also see the same company in performances at the National Theater in Tokyo. You can also see short puppet plays at the Gion Corner in Kyoto, and a less sophisticated *Bunraku* is flourishing on Shikoku Island where some of the puppets are made. Once fading in importance in the Japanese theatrical world, the puppet play has undergone a tremendous revival—much of it due to the performances at the National Theater and frequent productions on NKH-TV in Tokyo.

The all-girl revues in Tokyo and at Takarazuka are a light year away from *kabuki* and *noh*. They are spectacular vaudeville shows, with lots of girls, lots of color, and big orchestras capable of *M. fortissimo*.

The geisha dances of Kyoto, performed in autumn and spring, are charming. A *kabuki*-like play may be included with song and dance skits, and a feature in both seasons is the tea ceremony which is performed traditionally before the dance.

Japanese dress

Yofuku (Western dress) is the rule now in Japan rather than *wafuku* (Japanese dress). But at Japanese inns and hotsprings resorts you will see both men and women in *yukata*, the comfortable and loose fitting cotton *kimonos* that the inns provide to guests. For more about the *kimono*, see page 35.

Certain evening sightseeing tours in Kyoto let you have a glimpse of a *geisha* in her gorgeously colored *kimono*, with her elaborate coiffure. And when you visit a Shinto shrine, like the Heian Shrine in Kyoto, for example, you may even see a wedding party, the bride in *kimono* of stiff brocade, with heavy headdress. The groom and other men will be dignified in tails. The older women will be in their best *kimonos*, black with colorful embroidery and with gold and silver-thread brocade *obi*. Unmarried women will wear *kimonos* rivaling the rainbow.

The bride's traditional headdress has a wide boat shape which is supposed to cover the horns of jealousy, indicating that the husband need not fear the green-eyed demon in his wife no matter where he chooses to bestow his favors. For this reason, the headdress is looked upon with increasing disfavor by young, progressive Japanese women (many of whom will wear the ceremonial *kimono*).

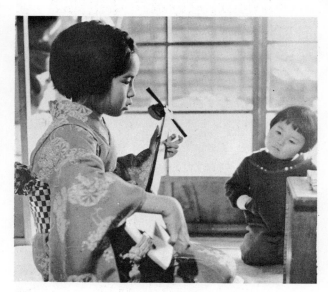

TRADITION FLOURISHES in theatrical performances such as kabuki *(above). Bride (upper right) accompanied by her mother, wears lovely embroidered* kimono *at Heian Shrine in Kyoto. Playing of the* samisen *(lower right) is learned in early childhood.*

Geta are the wooden clogs that the Japanese wear (the best made of light-weight paulownia wood); *zori* are loose sandals you'll be offered at temples. Women wear white *tabi* (ankle socks split for the sandal thong), while men's tabis are invariably dark blue.

Signs of the times: the young people of Japan are currently as wild about wearing blue jeans as American youth. Some of them are imported from the United States, but about 50 of Japan's clothing manufacturers are also turning out tens of thousands of them every month. You'll also see young people in hot pants, cotton denim shirts and many of the other international trappings of today's youth.

Japanese music

The Western ear needs some attuning to the eerie quality of Japanese music—part of which results from the fact that their music is based on a five-note scale.

The orchestra seated on stage at the performance of a *noh* play, for example, will play on a *fue,* or flute, and three types of drums: a *ko-tsuzumi* (shoulder drum), an *o-tsuzumi* (knee drum) and a *taiko* (flat drum). For the Japanese, the quality of the drumming by the leading drummer is all important to the atmosphere achieved by the play. As with *noh* actors, the drumming is often a hereditary art. The chanting of the chorus, called *Yokyoku,* at first may sound as strange as the instrumental music. Its purpose, like that of the ancient Greek chorus, is to fill in the action of the play with explanatory information.

The *samisen,* a three-stringed guitar-like affair covered with cat skin, is one of the most popular musical instruments in Japan. Playing it, along with learning such accomplishments as *ikebana* (flower arranging), is part of the training of Japanese girls. Geisha play the *samisen* in their professional entertaining; and if you should visit

SCHOOL CHILDREN *in Japan wear traditional uniforms—blue serge suits for boys (bottom right), middy blouses and navy blue skirts for girls (left). The tea ceremony (below left), normally held indoors, is a very formal occasion. Maiko (apprentice geishas) wear traditional costumes (below). You can arrange to visit a geisha house in Kyoto.*

a Japanese home, you would probably be offered a song to the accompaniment of the *samisen*.

The *koto* is more like a zither, and has 13 strings. The *biwa,* with four strings, is shaped a good deal like a mandolin. Lake Biwa, which you may visit in a side trip out of Kyoto (see page 112), is so named because its shape is like this instrument. A flute of bamboo is called a *shakuhachi*.

How to behave in Japan

The main thing in Japan is to try to match the over-whelming courtesy of the Japanese. Be particularly careful at temples and shrines. Although the Japanese people may seem almost off-hand at their religious centers, these places are sacrosanct. Show your respect by removing any head covering and your shoes, and by bowing as you enter a temple. And if you accept the hospitality of the Japanese in houses or inns, where they themselves remove their shoes, be prepared to do the same. To walk on *tatami* in shoes would be like walking in golf shoes on your most prized hardwood floors.

Dress in the cities as you would in American cities, and wear casual clothes in the country. Slacks on women, until recently considered a no-no in Japan, are perfectly acceptable even in the most remote districts (more Japanese women of all ages wear slacks than skirts). It is always all right to ask for directions, but that's about all. The Japanese usually like to be introduced. There are no taboos on picture taking except that you should be considerate of older persons who may adhere to a superstition that there must *not* be three persons in a picture.

Pay bills and tips as quietly as possible. The Japanese consider it offensive to hand over money; they like to enclose it in an envelope, and you may often have change handed you on a tray when you are shopping. You might want to remember that you won't be asked to give up your ticket until you get off a train, and you pay as you leave a streetcar.

Everybody bows to everybody in Japan. It is the expected polite greeting. And if somebody seems to hiss at you as he bows, be flattered. It is an extra show of respect.

In Japan, the number 4 is unlucky; it's like our 13. This superstition stems from the word for that numeral: *shi.* It not only means 4; it also means death.

Coming from a country where we take pleasure in kidding about our V.I.P.'s, it may come hard, but this taboo is important: *never* discuss the Emperor with members of the older generation.

Geisha

The *geisha* is a unique, well known, but frequently misunderstood feature of the Japan travel scene. There is no one quite like her in any other part of the world, and the Japanese themselves find it difficult to explain the role of the *geisha* to foreigners.

Geisha (pronounced *gay-sha,* with the plural either *geisha* or *geishas*) are trained entertainers who begin their apprenticeship as young girls. They occupy a highly respected place in Japanese society, and often spend their lives in the profession.

At *geisha* parties, given for a group of men (it's a favorite way for businessmen to entertain overseas visitors), the *geisha* is both hostess and entertainer. She is a fascinated listener, witty conversationalist, super waitress (she serves the food and keeps the *sake* cups full), tactful hostess (laughing at her guests' jokes), dancer and singer. Her music will be on *samisen* and drum, her dancing will use traditional steps and her costume will be the brilliant *kimono* of the *geisha* of three centuries ago.

Apprentice *geisha* have to pay for their strict instruction out of their later earnings, and, though these may be high eventually, the girls must continue to buy expensive *kimonos* for their evening appearances.

Charges for a *geisha's* services vary, depending on how much experience she has had and how popular she has become with patrons. But it is one of the important parts of the Japanese man's social life, especially as it relates to business associations. And so it has been for three centuries.

Once so much a part of Japanese business life, it was even said that the state of the economy could be judged by the financial health of the members of the Geisha Association. Still an important part of Japanese life, the center for *geisha* training today is Kyoto (see page 105). If you would like to attend a *geisha* party, you can do so through travel agents in Kyoto or Tokyo.

The tea ceremony

Japan's tea ceremony (*cha-no-yu*), carried on today as it has been for centuries, is one of the unique facets of Japanese life that you may witness as a tourist. The strict rules which regulate almost every movement of both host and guests in the tea rites have been relaxed for visitors not accustomed to finding relaxation in a two or three-hour, slow-motion session of squatting on the floor. But enough of the cult is performed that you begin to comprehend what the ritual means. It is designed to create a state of mental composure.

Like Buddhism itself, tea drinking came first from China. A priest who had studied in the south of China planted the first tea in Japan at the beginning of the 9th century. By the 16th century it had developed into a rigidly observed cult expressing the Zen Buddhist philosophy. The ceremonious though simple rites are intended to promote harmony, respect, purity, and tranquility.

You will walk down a garden path (the *roji*) designed to separate you from the hurly-burly outside and bring you to the serenity of the teahouse which, if it adhered to ancient rules, would be exactly four and a half *tatami* (mats) wide. There would also be just five guests at a proper tea ceremony, and they would enter through a low door (the *nijiriguchi*) on hands and knees to come in humbly.

Guests at a proper home ceremony would first bow or kneel before the *tokonoma* (alcove) and admire the scroll there. In the center of the otherwise-unadorned room, water is heated in an iron pot on a brazier, and the hot water is poured over powdered tea and beaten with a bamboo whisk. It is a thick brew, called *koi-cha*.

Remember that if you are served anything before the tea, you are expected to consume every morsel. Were you taking part in the entire ceremony, you would sit through two waiting periods, be served two courses before the actual tea service (all of which would be done by the host), and you would finish with a thin tea, or *usu-cha*.

Guests are expected to gaze at and admire each implement used: first the tea bowl, then the tea caddy and even the spoon, the object being to appreciate the artistry of the host's teaware and to concentrate on beauty.

You can always arrange to see the tea ceremony practiced in its abbreviated, for-the-tourist form. Two particularly pleasant places to see it are at the Happoen Garden in Tokyo (on various city bus tours) and at the Silver Pavilion (the Ginkakuji Temple) in Kyoto where one of the oldest tea houses in Japan is used.

Japanese wrestling—sumo

Watching Japan's ancient and highly different kind of wrestling, sumo, is fun if for nothing more than the elaborate pageantry which is such a large part of it. It provides all the bravado and bluff of an American wrestling match along with plenty of honest action and drama.

Centuries ago sumo was performed for the Emperor at the Imperial Court (when contestants fought it out to the death) and in shrine and temple compounds as a religious offering. Now the matches are held in huge arenas like the Kokugikan Stadium in Tokyo, attended by enthusiastic multitudes, and the matches are carried on television.

If you want a ring-side seat, you must squat shoeless on tatami mats in a four-person stall. If comfort is a requisite, you'll find chairs in the balcony, but take along your opera glasses.

The sumo wrestler is a man of mountainous bulk and profound dignity. (There are no limits on weight, and wrestlers are often well over 300 pounds.) The combatants are preceded into the 15-foot circular ring by a procession of leading wrestlers in brilliantly embroidered *keshomawashi* (aprons). In the ring, wearing loin cloths topped by wide belts of many layers of cloth, their hair, worn in medieval topknots, they look like overfed genies from Aladdin's lamp.

Each match is begun with a precise ritual. If it is an important one, big companies announce prizes and hire men to carry large silk flags, inscribed with trade names, around the ring.

Before the bout the wrestlers sip and spit out purifying water, and each throws a handful of salt into the ring. The referee, wearing archaic garb and carrying a fan, chants out information about the fight. Finally the grapplers crouch, glaring furiously at one another. Many new starts are made (with more salt thrown into the ring each time), building up tension for the eventual battle. Once under way, the match is likely to end in seconds, for it is all over when any part of the wrestler's body touches the floor, or when he is forced out of the ring. (The latter can cause ringside photographers to do some fancy dodging.) Matches continue in quick succession, and during intermission, a fantastic traditional ceremony of stomping and clapping called *dohyo-iri,* is performed in the ring by other wrestlers of higher rank.

One of the entertaining side lights to attending a sumo match is to watch the geishas who are nearly always on hand in their elaborate kimonos.

Judo

Judo is so popular in Japan that it is practiced by an estimated five million Japanese, and of those some 400,000 have achieved black-belt ratings, indicating a very high order of judo skill.

You may see this Japanese-originated sport being practiced at the gymnasium of the Kodokan Judo Institute, Japan's leading judo school, in the center of Tokyo. The gymnasium is one of the stops on various sightseeing bus tour itineraries. Exercises are held there from 3 to 7:30 every afternoon, and visitors, who watch from balconied seats, are always welcome.

Judo, or jujutsu, actually a unique system of self defense, is based on turning your opponent's strength to your own advantage. It utilizes 15 basic throwing positions and 10 basic grappling positions. The costumes of white trousers and heavy white cotton jackets, with various colored belts, each denoting the rank of the judoist, add a certain exotic flavor to the matches.

The all-Japan judo championship tournament is held every year on May 5, and the world championships are held every other year in November. The 1964 Tokyo Olympic Games were the first to include judo.

THE KIMONO . . . A STATIC BUT DELICATE BEAUTY

In this age of capricious fashion, the kimono is a gloriously graceful anachronism that has thus far survived the growing Westernization of Japan. Although the kimono seems unchanged and unchanging, it is in fact the product of a long and historical evolution, dating directly back to the Meiji period (1868-1912) and indirectly as far back as the Heian period (794-1185).

The kimono as such is original and purely Japanese in form, color and design—a characteristic handiwork of the Japanese people, closely linked with the climate and lifestyle of Japan. It is a long garment that reaches to the ankles. In the front, the left side is folded over the right side, and the whole thing is held snugly around the waist by an *obi*, or sash. It has no buttons or other means of fastening. The sleeves are wide as well as long. When the kimono is held up, the length of the sleeves usually measures about one third of the garment's length; in a woman's formal kimono, the length of the sleeve sometimes measures about two thirds of the length.

Called a *yukata*, the summer kimono is made of cotton. Unlined, usually blue printed on white or vice versa, it is a loose-fitting, wonderfully comfortable garment. In spring and fall, the kimono is lined (for extra warmth), and in winter it is padded and quilted.

The long evolution in clothing that led to the kimono probably started during the Heian period. This was the era in which Japan broke away from the prevalent Chinese-style clothing and adopted garments more suitable to the Japanese way of living. During this period, aristocracy was at its height; Japan was at peace, life was secure, the upper classes no longer had to do manual work. Clothing in general became looser and more decorative.

By the Muromachi period (1336-1568), the common people had achieved more power within a turbulent social structure, and a significant change appeared in dress: what was called the *kosode*—essentially the kimono—began to be worn more generally. During this period, the *obi* became more important.

Over the years, the kimono became more elaborate and more brilliant. The *obi* was widened, and it achieved a more ornamental quality. In the Edo period (1603-1867), the long-sleeved *furisode* (again a forerunner of today's kimono) came into being. It was in this period that almost every form of the present-day kimono, including those used for work, appeared on the scene.

Since the Edo period, there has been virtually no change in the kimono's basic style. But in the following period, the Meiji, the kimono as we know it today came into general usage. It was during the latter part of this era, too, that the traditional kimono gradually disappeared from the public life of many Japanese, although it continued to be worn in the home.

Today in the cities, while Western-style clothes predominate, you'll occasionally see a kimono-clad woman on the street. You see more of them, however, at family gatherings, wedding receptions and other social events in the early evenings at the major hotels. It's a more commonplace dress in the country.

All of the big department stores have kimono departments, and there are smaller shops in the main cities that specialize in the garment. You'll find inexpensive ones with the *obi* ready-wrapped and tied (perhaps made of synthetic materials). Others, made of silk and with handsomely embroidered *obis*, can cost several hundred dollars. The lightweight *yukata* makes an excellent traveling robe. And many an exquisitely colored and designed *obi* has graduated from its traditional function of encircling a lady's waist to a new role as a stunning wall hanging in elegant homes from Honolulu to Hong Kong.

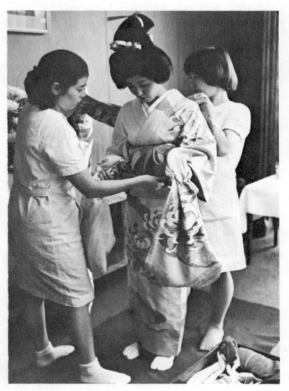

BRIDE, wearing traditional wedding kimono *needs assistance to properly wrap and tie the* obi.

RYOKANS are suffused with serenity. Sliding doors open onto a balcony where you may enjoy the perfection of a garden (above). Entering a ryokan, you leave your shoes behind (right). After much bowing and smiling, banto-sans (houseboys) carry your luggage (far right) and kimono-clad maids provide you with slippers.

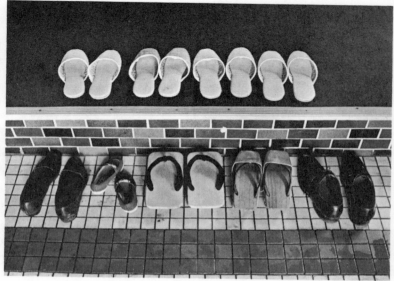

The Ryokan... an Experience in Japanese Living

A stay in a Japanese inn (*ryokan*) is an experience you should not deny yourself through fear of trying the unknown. You will find no other experience like it anywhere else in the world, and it is the nearest thing to living as the Japanese do in their own homes.

Just be certain that your reservations are for an inn that belongs to the Japan Ryokan Association. Member inns maintain a high standard. They are immaculate, the decor is charmingly Oriental, the atmosphere elegantly simple, and the service is excellent, with emphasis on making you comfortable and contented. Your travel agent can arrange for you to be booked at one of them.

Japanese inns do, however, have certain limitations. They can be cold in winter, for central heating is the exception. If you are young and warm-blooded, it may be a lark to wrap up in a quilt and huddle around a *kotatsu* (live coals placed in a pit beneath a low table). If you find yourself in an old *ryokan* during some of the cold months, you might find this to be the only way to stay warm. You put your feet on a board in the pit and wrap a quilt around the lower half of your body to conserve the warmth. (Some come equipped with a *genki kotatsu*, the same low table but with an infrared element on the underside which warms your legs under the table.) The obvious disadvantage of this kind of heating is that everyone must huddle around the table—or freeze. But it's about the only kind of heating found in the old *ryokan* outside Tokyo—and it's certainly cozy! But the warmth of the service, which outweighs most other drawbacks, may not make up for cold floors if your blood doesn't run as fast as it once did.

Inns that have catered to many foreigners usually have also solved the much-talked-about communal bathing problem. Rooms with private Japanese-style baths are available at many *ryokan*, while others have small baths and dressing rooms that may be used privately.

The fun of staying at an inn, however, is the experiment in living as the Japanese do, and once you have sampled life in a Japanese inn, with its overwhelming personal service, an Americanized hotel may seem something of a comedown. Even one night in typical Japanese style may be the highlight of your trip.

The language barrier? There's very little, for the *ryokan* that have encountered a number of foreign tourists usually have someone to cope with simple requests. And *dozo* (please), *arigato* (thank you) and *ohayo* (good morning), all with a smile, can go a long way.

Association member *ryokan* have Western-style toilets; and if your room does not have its own private one, the separate facilities down the hall will be plainly labeled in English.

This specific reference to "western-style toilets" is made because many a first-time-traveler to Japan is quite startled by the differences in American and—whether it is shiny new porcelain or old stonework—Japanese plumbing. The latter usually consists of a hole in the floor which must be straddled by men and women alike.

Kan means mansion, and the *ryokan* is built of wood, usually two or three stories high, like a large and elegant home. The pretty roof lines, the sliding paneled doors and *shoji* and the landscaped gardens that adjoin the guest rooms are traditionally Japanese. You'll find delightful inns right in the heart of Tokyo or Kyoto that are so designed that their rooms and gardens are oriented to mask out the city, to give an illusion of being in the country.

Arriving at a ryokan

As you arrive, you will be greeted with positively startling enthusiasm amid a great deal of bowing. *Genkan-ban* (houseboys) in blue *happi*-coats, will open the car door, pick up your baggage, and pretty, kimono-costumed maids of the inn will welcome you and give you a pair of backless, fiber slippers to put on as you enter. When you go into the inn, you will say goodbye to your shoes. The *genkan* will be in charge of them, returning them to you cleaned and polished when you need them again.

You will be escorted along highly polished corridors to your room or suite. Here you must also give up the slippers, for no one is permitted to walk on the room's soft *tatami* (rush mats) in either shoes or slippers. A pair of warm socks may come in handy here.

Your room

You will enter your *ryokan* room through sliding doors and probably look right out other sliding glass walls onto a typical Japanese garden with its careful placement of rocks, a pond, a pine tree or bamboo, a lantern.

Rooms are measured according to the number of *tatami*

on the floor. The standard *tatami* is three by six feet. They are placed side by side over the entire floor.

A long, low gleaming table in the center of the room, with *zabuton* (cushions) in place beside it, is the main item of furniture. But there may be two Western-style chairs, with a table between them, on the balcony or kind of lanai overlooking the garden where you can sit in a more accustomed manner.

The *tokonoma*, an alcove a few inches above the floor, as in a Japanese house, is the room's ornamental corner. A long scroll, a painting or decorative calligraphy, will hang there, and it will contain a flower arrangement— perhaps a single flower and a green blade, graceful and beautiful in its simplicity. Your maid will take care of your luggage.

The best thing to do is to sit down on one of the big cushions at the table when you have taken off your coat, for the maid will soon bring you hot tea and small cakes, and she will wait for you to finish them. This is your official welcome to the inn.

After tea, the maid will bring you the hotel register to sign (there is no big lobby and no clerk's counter in most *ryokan*). At this time she will check on how long you

*WOODLAND RYOKAN (above, center) snuggles
in a ravine with a mountain stream just outside the
window. Each room has a* tokonoma *(above), an
alcove containing a scroll painting and flowers.
Shedding your city clothes, you don a kimono
(upper right), and tea is served to bid you welcome
(center right). Futons (quilts) are spread on the
floor (bottom right) when it's time to retire.*

THE HONORABLE BATH, ryokan-style, is for soaking but never for soaping. You sit on a small stool and wash and rinse before you are ready to get into the tub.

TYPICAL JAPANESE DINNER is served in your room if you stay in a ryokan. Sitting on cushions, eating with chopsticks may seem awkward at first, but you quickly catch on.

plan to stay and will inquire as to when you want your bath. This will be the time to order an American breakfast for the next morning if that is what you want, and to give any special orders for dinner. Breakfast and dinner are included in the cost of your accommodations. If you want lunch served in your room as well, order it now for the following day.

The maid will bring you a freshly laundered *yukata,* or cotton kimono. The most relaxing thing you can do is to get out of your travel clothes and into it. At the hot-springs resorts, the Japanese all wear these *yukata* the whole time that they are at the resort. Most tourists do, too, so don't feel foolish if you want to wander around in one yourself. The design of each robe reveals the identity of the inn.

The honorable bath

The bath in Japan is a before-dinner ritual (dinner is usually served at inns around 6 o'clock). It is intended as a prolonged relaxing and sociable time at the end of the workday. You don't have to be sociable, but your bath will certainly be relaxing. If you have a private bath attached to your room, and you come in, as you are likely to do, in the late afternoon, it will be ready for you—a great tub of clean, steaming water, quite likely to have come from a bubbling hot spring, sometimes covered with boards that keep the water hot until you're ready to start soaking.

The one rule you must remember concerning your first Japanese-style dunking is: no soap in the tub. Some inns provide hot showers, but the usual system is to sit on a small wooden stool on the tiled bathroom floor, soap yourself, and then slosh yourself with warm water dipped from the big tub by a small wooden tub. There are water taps in the wall and a drain in the floor. When thoroughly rinsed, you get into the deep tubful of hot water. The Japanese like it very hot indeed, so step in gingerly; then soak to your heart's content. The tub may be a sunken one of tile or a fragrant, high-sided wooden one. The *ryokan* furnishes a washcloth in a plastic case, a towel (generally skimpy), a big bar of soap, cologne and body lotion. There are usually toothbrushes and toothpaste in the dressing rooms.

Dining on the floor

Then in your *yukata,* you will sink onto a *zabuton* (if you want to be a little higher off the floor, ask for more cushions), and dinner will be ceremoniously served by the same attentive, *kimono*-clad maid. If you have qualms about trying new Japanese dishes, you can always order a *sukiyaki* or *tempura* dinner, as most Americans find these to their liking; and usually *beefsteak,* a word the Japanese know, is available for the asking. If you have ordered *sukiyaki*, she will prepare it on the table in front of you.

You might, on a typical table d'hote menu find the following: clam soup, small portions of *sashimi* (raw fish) perhaps combining sea bream and cuttlefish and served with mustard sauce; cold crab and slices of cucumber; lobster with sweet pickled cabbage and tomatoes; whole soybeans, cucumber and cream, which may well be served on a chrysanthemum leaf; and steaming rice.

If you want to be adventurous, order a Japanese breakfast. You will probably get one or all of the following: *miso* soup with bean curd, seaweed (in dried strips), raw egg, a dish of cold mushrooms and greens with sesame seeds, hot broiled fish, cold broiled shrimp, sweetened beans and sweet potatoes, radish pickles, rice and green tea. This may seem like an appalling way to start out the day, but it will a least make for conversation at home. If you don't feel you can enter into the Japanese spirit to this extent, request a Western-style breakfast the night before. You could probably get ham and eggs and toast. Coffee is usually available, but may fall short of expectations—so better settle for tea. Fruit is generally not served.

Sleeping on the floor

Though sleeping on the floor may not sound desirable, the soft quilts atop the tatami are usually more than conducive to restful sleep. Your maid pulls the *futon* (quilt mattresses) out of the closet and piles them on the floor in the center of the room, the table having been pushed aside. In some inns, sponge rubber mattresses are now used. She covers this with a sheet, then lays silk quilts on top. Whether you are long or short, the bed can be made to fit you. A small lamp will be set beside the bed, and your nighttime tea tray will be placed on the floor beside your pillow. Where else in the world will your room maid appear voluntarily at whatever hour you return in the evening with a tray of hot tea for you?

In the morning the maid may wake you with a gentle knock on your door; but if you want breakfast before she comes, call for it on the telephone. If your telephone communications aren't understood, the maid will appear promptly anyway. And if by now you have learned that her nods and smiles often cover up an inability to understand you, it isn't hard to convey by sign language that you want some breakfast. She will put away the *futon* and serve you once more, bringing whatever you have ordered in a charming assortment of colorful dishes.

Leaving the ryokan

It is the maid who will bring you your bill. A 15 to 20 per cent service charge which covers tipping will be included in the total. If you feel that your own maid deserves more and you give her perhaps another five per cent, she will divide it with all those who waited on you while you were at the inn. There are no strict rules about it, but a day at a *ryokan* is usually considered to be from noon to noon.

Leaving is almost as ceremonious as arrival. In the midst of all the *sayonaras* and *arigatos,* you may be presented with a souvenir of your visit, perhaps a travel towel in a plastic case, a folding fan, or block-printed cotton napkins that bear the insignia of the *ryokan.*

Rates at ryokan

Ryokan rates vary depending on location, on the popularity of the particular inn, the size and location of your room and whether you have private bath and toilet. You can generally figure that rates will be in the range of Y4,000 to Y8,000 per day per person, including two meals.

A book to read

If you have not read Oliver Statler's *A Japanese Inn,* which climbed to the top of the nonfiction best seller list in the United States several years ago, read it to glean some understanding of the traditions of *ryokan.* The inn of the title is the Minaguchi-ya, which stands on the great Tokaido Road that runs between Tokyo and Kyoto. The book spans 400 years and 20 generations. The history of the inn, from its founding to a climactic visit by the present Emperor, is the central thread around which is spun a tale of more momentous happenings that take place in the political and cultural life outside the inn in the evolution of Japan.

LEAVING A RYOKAN is a ceremonious matter with almost as much pagentry as royalty commands. After the bill is discreetly presented, you are bid goodbye with low bows.

A BLOSSOMING BOWER of cherry trees arches over a walkway on the grounds of the Imperial Palace. The chrysanthemum grower (right) uses chopsticks to curl petals. In June the iris garden at the Meiji Shrine in Tokyo comes alive as beds of iris burst into bloom.

The Order and Serenity of the Japanese Garden

Landscape gardening in Japan is a unique art and an ancient one, dating back to the sixth century when the idea was introduced to Japan from Korea. Its aim is to translate nature into a landscape composition as a painter transmits a scene to canvas.

The varying levels, winding streams and subtle placement of rocks in a Japanese garden make a small area look spacious, and they are called *shuku-kei* (miniature nature). What a garden architect attempts is to condense nature, using rocks, water and plants to symbolize an all-inclusive scene.

If you find no blooming flowers, it is because the artist wishes to express the unchanging essence of nature. Flowers bloom and die. Rocks and evergreens remain the same.

The extensive use of rocks may go way back to early Shinto practices when certain rocks were worshiped in the belief that the spirits of deities had entered them. And ancient gardens used rocks also to represent Mount Sumeru, the Buddhist King of Mountains, comprising all the world. You are immediately aware of the order and serenity in a Japanese garden, which expresses above all the Buddhist philosophy that rules out the unessential and seeks harmony with nature.

What to look for

Look for standing stones which may suggest a waterfall, rounded shrubs that may represent a distant mountain, a raised rock which indicates a bridge, raked sand that reminds you of the surf. In the garden of the Katsura Detached Palace of Kyoto, a reef of pebbles in a pond represents a sea cap, the stone lantern at its farthest shore a lighthouse.

Many of Japan's present gardens were originally designed hundreds of years ago, and if you make a study of them, you will learn to recognize the different eras that they represent. Long under the influence of China, Japa-

nese gardens began in the Heian Period (8th to 12th centuries) to expand into elegant locales for celebrations of the aristocracy. Then from about the 16th century, gardens designed specifically for tea pavilions developed.

Three main divisions of present-day gardens include the hill garden, the flat garden and the tea garden. The term *kai-yu* means a garden planned for strolling, and this style, which developed in the 18th century, is often used in a tea garden. The Koishikawa Korakuen, Tokyo's oldest garden, typifies this style. The winding paths through its 17 acres provide varying views of the planned landscape with its large pond and central island.

The hill garden may have several hills, a pond and a stream. Whenever there is a pond, there is an island, usually connected to the mainland by a graceful, small bridge. The Kiyomizu Temple's Jojuin Garden in Kyoto is a good example of this type.

Only sand and stones make up the flat gardens, most famous of which is the Ryoanji Temple Garden in Kyoto. It is a long, clean oblong of white sand, meticulously raked. Dating back to 1499, this flat garden (and it is very flat indeed) contains exactly 15 rocks, arranged in groups of twos, threes and fives. It is set off by the blue tiles of the long temple roof.

Tea gardens built around tea houses for observing the Buddhist tea ceremony always feature a sylvan path of irregular stepping stones leading to the tea pavilion. There is always a stone water basin where guests wash their hands before entering, and always a stone lantern in which a flame flickers at night. Often the stone basins, square-cut and rounded in the center to hold water, are very old. The tea house itself is designed with austere

RITSURIN GARDEN in Takamatsu (upper left) is skillfully laid out to harmonize with pine trees, fountains and rocks. Kiyosumi Garden in Tokyo (above) surrounds landscaped lake. Garden of Heian Shrine in Kyoto (right) is famed for its round stepping stones hewn from granite.

simplicity. The Kinkakuji (Golden Pavilion) Garden in Kyoto, originally laid out for a famous Zen priest of the 14th century, has a tea pavilion noted for its design. Usually the architect of a tea house and its attached garden was also a master of the tea ceremony, as in the case of the Katsura Detached Palace Garden.

Home gardens

Home gardens in Japan are planned for viewing from the living room. If you have an opportunity to visit one, you might look for such special stones as these: the *seat of honor stone,* the *pedestal stone,* a *perfect view stone,* a *guardian rock,* and, the most easily recognized and the most frequent, the *shoe-receiving stone* at the entrance to the house.

How to meet a gardener

If you are a landscape architect or a hobby gardener yourself and would like to meet some of Japan's garden designers, arrangements can be made through the Japanese Institute of Landscape Architects, c/o Faculty of Agriculture, Tokyo University, Mukogaoka Yayoicho, Bunkyoku, Tokyo.

Viewing blossoms

If you are in Japan ahead of the cherry blossoming season, perhaps you can see some of the other early fruit trees in bloom. The *Baien* (Japanese apricot garden) at Atami has a grove of 700 trees which start to bloom in late December and last until February. The plum blossoms at the Soga Plum Blossom Forest, between Odawara and Hakone, are best in mid-February. Minabe, two and a half hours south of Osaka, has the country's largest groves of apricots—some 300,000 trees extending over the hills and valleys of three villages. The blooming season here is from late January to the middle of February. Other resorts where you will see many blossoms are Shuzenji on the Izu Peninsula, Takarazuka, near Osaka, where the trees bloom in late February and early March; Ogose, where the blooms appear in March, and Mito, Nikko, which blooms in April.

Cherry blossoms

Japan, of course, is proudest of its cherry blossoms, which may be seen in most parts of the country during the first two weeks of April. The season differs slightly, however, according to the district and the species of trees, while the blooms are later, of course, in the northern parts of Japan.

The best blossoms in and near Tokyo are at Ueno Park where 1,500 trees, stretching for almost five miles along an aqueduct, break into full bloom in early April. The Imperial Palace and Shinjuku Gyoen Garden each has 1,000 trees. Koganei's 900 trees generally bloom around April 10, while the 800 of Tama Cemetery also bloom early in the month. Four thousand trees bloom early in April at Mukogaoka Recreation Ground near the Mukogaoka-Yuen Station of the Odakyu Electric Railway, not far from Tokyo. Higashiyama-toshi, about an hour north of Tokyo near Lake Tama, boasts a grove of 10,000 trees which bloom in early April.

In Kyoto extensive groves of cherry trees may be seen in blossom in late April along the Oi River in the vicinity of Arashiyama Park—trees that were transplanted from Yoshino near Osaka in the 13th century by order of ex-Emperor Kameyama who was living nearby. Maruyama Park, also in Kyoto, has such a magnificent display that the trees are illuminated at night during the blossom season—one of Kyoto's musts in April.

Yoshino, an otherwise sleepy little town about an hour out of Osaka, becomes the target for thousands of sightseers from all over Japan for about two weeks in the early part of April simply because of its cherry blossoms. More than 50,000 trees are spread out over the Yoshino hills, groves originally planted in the 7th century by a Buddhist priest.

Hokkaido, Japan's northern island, usually has blossoms in early May. The largest areas there are Goryokaku Park, near the city of Hakodate, with 6,000 trees, and Matsumae, near Goryokaku, with 4,000 trees.

Chrysanthemums

Viewing chrysanthemums may be the highlight of an autumn trip to Japan. The *kiku,* as the Japanese call the

ROCKS AND RAKED GRAVEL predominate in the Southern Gardens of the Abbot's Hall at Tofukuji Temple, Kyoto.

chrysanthemum, has been grown there for more than 1,500 years. Under the dextrous, patient hands of Japanese gardeners, the flowers take on some amazing colors, shapes and sizes.

There are the pompons in vivid yellows, purples and whites, and the spider-petal blooms of bronze hue. You can see them in proud, massed display in October and November. They are grown to prodigious size: single blooms six to eight inches across.

The *kengai-zukuri* (falling over a cliff) mums are grown singly in boxes and coaxed into a cascading floral spray like a waterfall of flowers. When put out for public view, it is a solid blanket of blossoms. Sprays five feet long and three feet wide are not uncommon. You will also see bonsai chrysanthemums, the floral cousins of Japan's miniature trees.

If you are in Tokyo in November and take an early walk some crisp morning in Hibiya Park, across the street from the Imperial Hotel, you might see gardeners grooming their blooms for display. Not content with nature's work, the perfectionist Japanese will take chopsticks and curl each petal of a pompon or spider mum until it suits his eye. And in some places—most notably at the Shinjuku Gardens in Tokyo and at Nagoya Castle in Nagoya —you'll see chrysanthemum sculptures: figures of *samurai* and other traditional shapes built out of blooms.

Hibiya Park in Tokyo has annual November chrysanthemum shows. While shopping, you may well find a superb display on the roof of a Tokyo department store. In Kyoto there are magnificent displays at Heian Shrine and Nijo Castle in November.

Bonsai and bonkei

Added to the long list of Japanese garden attractions that can be worked into a visit are exhibitions of *bonsai* (the art of growing miniature potted trees) and *bonkei* (tray landscaping).

Bonsai clubs and shops specializing in this art can be found in Tokyo and Kyoto. Some of Tokyo's larger de-

---

THE "MUSTS" AMONG JAPANESE GARDENS

As you travel through Japan, you'll find lovely gardens everywhere—in most cities, around temples, on castle grounds, some featured as major attractions at resorts. To single out a few for special recommendation would mean the risk of naming a few to the exclusion of many. But there are those gardens that have special significance to the Japanese.

The list that follows includes the well-known gardens that are within easy reach of most tourist routes. Among them are the three the Japanese consider the "most celebrated": Korakuen Park at Okayama, Kairakuen at Mito, and Kenrokuen at Kanazawa.

In Tokyo

Hama Detached Palace Garden. A large garden with a tidal pond spanned by three bridges, each shaded by wisteria trellises, leading to an islet; the pond is connected to Tokyo Bay by an estuary of the Sumida River. The garden was laid out to preserve a view of Mount Fuji.
Kiyosumi Garden. Particularly celebrated for its rocks gathered from all over Japan; typical garden of the Meiji period.
Korakuen Garden. Built in 1626. Contains a lake with a stone moon bridge, an island and a small temple— all with a marked Chinese influence.
Rikugien Garden. A stroll garden laid out early in the 18th century. Represents a landscape garden typical of the feudal era. Includes a pond with an island that consists of a large hill covered with ancient trees.
Shinjuku Gyoen National Garden. One of the best places in Tokyo to view cherry blossoms in April, chrysanthemums in November. Contains Japanese-style, French-style and English-style gardens. Its large greenhouse contains tropical and subtropical plants.

In Kyoto

Daitokuji Temple Gardens. Planned by Enshu Kobori (1576-1647), outstanding landscape gardener of his time. Dry-style gardens of white gravel, stones and background shrubbery. East garden utilizes the idea of "borrowed scenery" to extend itself to the distant horizon.
Ginkakuji (Silver Pavilion) Garden. Noted for its stone bridges, stone groupings and waterfall. The original features of the garden, dating from the 15th century, are preserved in their entirety. Considered by some the most beautiful in Kyoto.
Katsura Detached Palace Garden. A stroll garden with a pond and several teahouses overlooking the garden, laid out between 1620 and 1624. Example of simple elegance and the finest work of Enshu Kobori.
Kinkakuji Temple (Gold Pavilion) Garden. Features a brook running into a small lake with a fine grove of

---

partment stores hold *bonsai* exhibitions between June and October. The Tokyo Bonsai Club at Ikenohata near the Ueno Station has an exhibition of *bonsai* every month; and Bonsai-Mura (Bonsai Village) at Omiya, Saitama Prefecture, about an hour from Tokyo Central Station, has long been a famous haunt of Japanese *bonsai* enthusiasts.

Bonkei exhibitions can be seen in department stores almost anytime during the year, and every spring and autumn the Japan Bonkei Association holds exhibits featuring the works of various schools of *bonkei*. You can make arrangements to visit the studios of *bonkei* masters in Tokyo and even take some lessons from them in this art. Ask your travel agent or hotel or make arrangements through JNTO's Tourist Information Center (see page 9).

As an introduction to the intricacies and subtleties of Japanese gardens, read one of these: *The Art of the Japanese Garden,* by Tatsuo Ishimoto; *Japanese Gardens Today,* by Tatsuo and Kiyoko Ishimoto; *Japanese Gardens,* by Matsunosuke Tatsui (published by the Japan Travel Bureau); and *Sunset's Ideas for Japanese Gardens.*

BEAUTIFULLY GROOMED black pine bonsai (near Kyoto's Manshuin Temple) has windblown shape.

maples on one side. The garden's teahouse is especially known for its design. Dates from 1394.

Nanzenji Temple Garden. Laid out in the 14th century, it is an excellent sand garden, although less austere and less balanced than others.

Nijo Castle Ninomaru Garden. Meticulously laid out with numerous fine stones; originally designed without trees (because falling leaves were considered a sign of the mutability of life).

Ryoanji Temple Rock Garden. Contains only rocks and sand. One of the masterpieces of Soami (late 15th century designer), who was greatly influenced by the Zen philosophy. Extreme simplicity obtained with an economy of materials.

Saihoji Temple Moss Garden. Comprised of nearly 40 species of green and yellow mosses in a typical example of a stroll garden. Laid out in the 14th century.

Shugakuin Imperial Villa Gardens. At the foot of Mount Hiei where Shugakuin Temple once stood. Three spacious gardens, each containing a villa, with the largest and finest garden at the Upper Villa, from where there is a beautiful view of Kyoto. Permission to visit must be obtained from the Kyoto office of the Imperial Household Agency (arrange through your hotel).

In Kanazawa

Kenrokuen Park. Kenroku means "combining six features"—vastness, solemnity, careful arrangement, ven-erability, coolness (induced by running water) and scenic charm. Built in 1819, with three artificial hills, two ponds, a waterfall, a stone lantern on the lake shore, large beds of iris, groves of azalea, stands of cherry. (Kanazawa is 5 hours north of Nagoya.)

In Mito

Kairakuen Garden. Contains about 3,000 Japanese apricot trees (blossoming late February to mid-March). Built by Lord Narioki in 1842. Natural features create the beauty of this garden. Pavilion on the grounds is an excellent reproduction. (Mito is about 2 hours northeast of Tokyo.)

In Okayama

Korakuen Park. Situated on the Asahi River; designed as a stroll garden in 1700. Its graceful contours are enhanced by several ponds, waterfalls and a variety of trees that give it beauty at every season: pine, maple, cherry and Japanese apricot. (Okayama is about an hour and a quarter west of Osaka.)

In Takamatsu

Ritsurin Park. Laid out with fountains and huge rocks to harmonize with a natural forest of magnificent pines. Also has a zoo, art gallery and a commercial museum. (Takamatsu is on the northern coast of Shikoku, due south of Okayama.)

YASUKUNI SHRINE (above), a Shinto sanctuary, seems uncrowded by comparison with student groups at Imperial Palace courtyard (right) and shoppers in Ginza (far right) on weekend afternoons when vehicular traffic is barred.

Tokyo... Glittering, Garish, Sprawling Megalopolis

Even at first glance, Tokyo is not like any other big city you've ever seen. Keep in mind that it's the largest city in the world (more than 11 million people). But its skyline is lower than you expect it to be—because of a chronic earthquake condition, building heights were restricted for many years and the city sprawled out over an 800-square-mile area. It's a city of wood, with fences of bamboo and sliding walls of grass cloth. Almost all of the business signs, neon and otherwise, spell out their messages in Japan's handsome calligraphy—some of them looking more like ornaments than signs. Its traffic, foot and vehicular, moves seemingly without discipline.

Like all big cities, it's crowded—a city of people—busy, energetic, hard working. Like most old cities (Tokyo was founded in 1457), its streets are narrow and arranged rather heterogenously. "Greater Metropolitan Tokyo" is a megapolis that comprises 23 *ku* or wards (incorporated cities and towns), 1 *gun* or rural district, 26 cities and the 7 islands of Izu. When the population of these adjacent cities and towns is added to that of Tokyo proper, you find yourself entering an area with an estimated population of more than 11½ million.

Off the streets of cluttered confusion are quiet tea gardens where life moves with slow-paced tranquility. The city's modern hotels and glass and steel office buildings stand beside old Japanese houses, their serenity protected by fences and gardens and an invisible curtain of Japanese tradition. Step into a small shop, leaving the noisy, turbulent rush of traffic outside, and you'll be greeted by a bowing, quiet-spoken Japanese who will wait on you with unhurried courtesy.

Tokyo is glittering and garish, delicate and charming. And it's expensive. Prices are comparable to what you pay in San Francisco, Los Angeles, Chicago, New York. You can easily spend $30 a day for a room, $5 for lunch, $15 for dinner. But what you get in return is worth it—your room will be tastefully decorated and beautifully

CENTRAL TOKYO

TOKYO HARBOR

Note: Haneda Tokyu and Tokyo Air Terminals hotels are at Haneda International Airport; Hotel New Plaza is at Tachikawa in the northwest part of Tokyo.

COPYRIGHT BY PACIFIC TRAVEL NEWS

maintained, your meals served with such finesse and in such surroundings that eating becomes a fresh experience.

Here are some bits of information that will help you get acquainted with this East-West metropolis.

Where to stay

For the past 10 years, Tokyo has been on a hotel building spree that has provided the city with more than 40 "Western style" hotels, among them some of the newest and finest skyscraper hotels in the world. Some have more than 1,000 rooms; all provide a special brand of Japanese service that you won't find in many other parts of the world; and some are expensive—Y10,000 to Y12,000 for a double room.

Some Western-style hotels feature a few rooms done in the Japanese manner, where tatami mats cover the floor. You sit on cushions at low tables and have all the atmosphere (and the personal service) of Japanese life at its most luxurious.

Tokyo also has a number of *ryokan* (inns) within the city limits. The best ones are members of the Japan Ryokan Association. Inn reservations are usually even more difficult to get than hotels—six months in advance is none too early. See the chapter on *ryokan* (page 36) for details.

How to get around

Tokyo has superb subways, buses and taxis; but unless you speak the language easily and until you become oriented to the city's morass of nameless streets, stick to taxis. Cruising taxis are plentiful until about 11 P.M. and there's always a supply at the hotel. Taxi fares are reasonable when compared with those in most big cities in the United States, and tipping is not necessary.

If addresses of stores, restaurants, offices, etc., leave you completely baffled, here's why: the *ku* you see as part of an address indicates the ward in which the building is located, *cho* means the precinct and *chome* the block. Numbers, if any, merely mean when the buildings were put up; and if a couple of houses were built at the same time, they may have the same number.

Following World War II, some of Tokyo's streets were given simple number or letter names. Lately an effort has been made to name the streets, and you will see some street signs. But to date the Japanese have paid little attention to this Western notion. Their own system works for them. As a result, the only way you can be certain that your taxi driver actually understands where you want to go, unless you can speak Japanese, is to hand him a map on which your destination is marked. Get the hotel clerk to draw directions for you and write out your destination in Japanese. When you leave that place for a new

locale, get someone there to sketch out the next trip for you. The alternative is likely to be frustration. And it's always a good idea to carry a matchbox from your hotel or one of the cards that your hotel desk can give you which gives the hotel's name and location—an easy thing to hand the taxi driver when you want to get back to your hotel.

All cabs have green license plates, are clearly marked as cabs and have meters. The meters have "traffic-jam" buttons—which the driver switches from a mileage rate to a time rate if you get caught in Tokyo's heavy traffic. Fares are higher at night. If you are trying to hail a cab at night, remember this: a red light on the right side of the windshield means the cab is "for hire"; if it's green, it means he has a customer. You'll find Tokyo's taxi-drivers honest and efficient: you won't be taken the long way around or be short-changed.

You'll probably find taxiing in Tokyo a bit harrowing to start. Efforts are being made to calm down the average Tokyo taxi driver, referred to not without reason, as a *kamikaze*. You may be glad to know the Japanese expression, *"Yukkuri"*—it approximates our *"Take it easy!"*

A fine booklet, De Mente's *Taxi-Guide in Tokyo*, largely solves the communication problems with taxi

AT NIGHT a red light above windshield at right indicates that taxi is for hire. If you plan to rent a car, remember that driving on the left is the rule of the Japanese road.

BRINGING TOKYO INTO FOCUS... DISTRICT BY DISTRICT

Tokyo, like any large city, is composed of a collection of districts: financial, shopping, theater, warehousing, industrial, residential. But in Tokyo these districts carry names: the Ginza, Marunouchi, Asakusa, Shinjuku to name a few. A quick review of the brief description of each area will help you begin to feel your way about the city and gain some sense of direction.

The center of Tokyo is still the 250-acre Imperial Palace. All the major thoroughfares of the city radiate from this area, making it a good starting point.

East and across from the Palace is Marunouchi, which began as the main banking area of Tokyo around 1875. Today it is Tokyo's center of commerce —a district of finance, business, airline offices, and the central post office. Best described as 13 acres of office buildings, it has a daytime population of more than 120,000, with restaurants and shopping arcades to serve them. The Marunouchi landmark is the Tokyo Central Station through which a million and a half passengers pass daily. The giant station has five underground levels, several blocks of shopping malls, restaurants, coffee shops and a large department store.

To the south of Marunouchi are the areas of Yurakucho and Hibiya, the latter flowing into Hibiya Park across from the Imperial Palace. Some of the Marunouchi business feeling carries over into this area, but it's also where most of Japan's largest theaters are located: the Takarazuka Theater, the elegant Nesei Theater, the Imperial Theatre and a number of large movie houses.

The Ginza, to the east of the Yurakucho/Hibiya area, covers about a half square mile divided into eight blocks split by a four-lane avenue. Not as gridlike as it sounds, it's also full of small side streets and narrow alleys that invite exploration. Most people sum up the Ginza something like this: the greatest street in the world . . . color . . . masses of people . . . shopping . . . restaurants . . . bright lights and night life . . . action . . . girlie bars . . . continental . . . the pulse of Tokyo. All of which draws foreigners as well as Japanese. For more about the Ginza, see page 60.

To the north the Ginza merges into Nihombashi, a less crowded, less touristy, older district which locals recommend for some of the best quality department store shopping in Japan and for some of Tokyo's oldest and finest restaurants.

To the north of Nihombashi is Kanda, the book area and home of four universities, and Akihabara, said to be the biggest discount house in the world for electrical goods. Kanda is also an area of small publishing

THE BOUNDARIES of Tokyo's various districts are somewhat vague. Each blends into another without sharp definition, yet each has its own distinct personality.

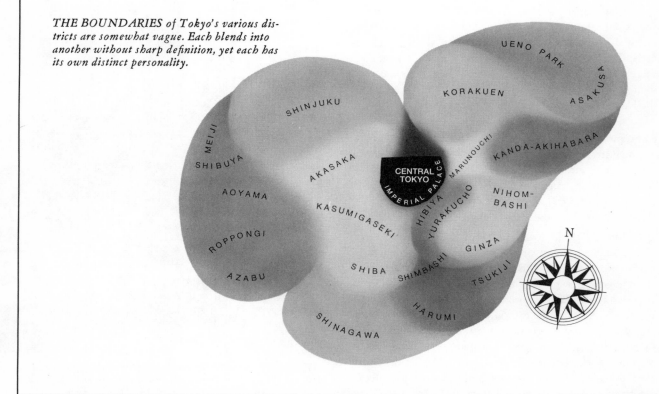

houses, printing works and streets lined with small shops selling new books, old books, foreign books, translations, rare editions and old prints at good prices. (An excellent place to find some true collector's items.) Akihabara is a noisy concentration of hundreds of wholesale and cut-rate shops that sell everything from electric back-scratchers to the finest of 4-track sound equipment, appliances, fans and other electrical products.

Northeast of Kanda is Asakusa, one of the most densely populated parts of the city. It combines a big amusement center that draws provincials on a spree with Asakusa Kannon Temple that draws crowds of worshippers. Surrounding the temple are a melange of movies, shows, bars, restaurants and souvenir shops. Nearby is Kokugikan, headquarters of Japanese *sumo*, with a stadium that seats 10,000 spectators, and 210-acre Ueno Park which surrounds the Tokyo Metropolitan Festival Hall.

To the south of Ueno Park is the little 17-acre 17th century garden that gave the district of Korakuen its name, and where iris are a big May display. As the home of organized baseball, the district is dominated by a sports and amusement center, including Korakuen Baseball Stadium. Nearby is Kodokan Judo Hall and, in another direction, the National Theatre.

Shinjuku, to the southwest of Korakuen, is a full fledged subcity. Called a 1970 town, it attracts the young for its relaxed atmosphere and freedom from tradition. Some compare it to Sydney's King's Cross or London's Carnaby Street. It's a good natured rival to the Ginza, though less touristy, quieter, more Japanese, and shopping and the swinging nightlife is less expensive. As a subcity Shinjuku has all the city atmosphere of crowds, large department stores, bars, coffee shops and night haunts popular with university students. For more detailed information on Shinjuku, see page 61.

To the south of Shinjuku is the airy, attractive district of Meiji, encompassing both Meiji Shrine and its Inner Garden and, across several boulevards, Meiji Shrine Outer Garden.

Somewhat to the south of Meiji is Shibuya, a milder, more compact version of youth-oriented Shinjuku and a good walking area. An eye-stopper here is the big department store that is combined with the main station, so that trains seem to run right through the second and third floors of the store.

Veering south of Meiji Outer Garden is Aoyama, with an avenue of sophisticated couturier shops and boutiques and a notable hundred-year-old cemetery, merging into Roppongi and Azabu. Roppongi, growing with business offices, is also the entertainment-pleasure center for young fashionables. Among its more than 600 restaurants are some of the finest in Tokyo. Some 300 nightclubs, going strong after the Ginza and other areas close up, attract visitors who like the late, late circuit. In Azabu (the greenest part of Tokyo) some of the great mansions of celebrated Japanese remain, but the district is mostly composed of embassies and posh residences and high-rises for the foreign community (apartment rents go as high as $2,000 a month). Behind the little Arisugawa Park (nice for strolling) is the National Azabu Supermarket, something worth seeing even though you may think that once you've seen one supermarket you've seen them all.

East and north of Azabu, toward the Imperial Palace, are Shiba, Akasaka and Kasumigaseki. The heart of Shiba is 50-acre Shiba Park which extends around Tokyo Tower and Zojoji Temple. Looming across a few boulevards from Shiba Park is the 38-story World Trade Center Building.

Akasaka is a gently hilly, sophisticated district with many of the major hotels, yet with many unexpected little streets and lanes for walking and exploration. The big tour focus in the area is the Versailles-style Akasaka Detached Palace. Akasaka's reputation is for some of the plushest and most expensive nightclubs and restaurants in Tokyo, a lot of small lively cabarets, bars and all night coffee houses—all within minutes of the major hotels.

Merging into Akasaka, Kasumigaseki District is headquarters for government buildings, dominated by the National Diet Building and nearby Kasumigaseki Building, one of Tokyo's first skyscrapers. From the 36th top floor you'll get a good bird's-eye view of the maze of government buildings below, the Imperial Palace Grounds to the north and Fuji on a clear day.

Between Shiba and the Ginza is Shimbashi, centered on what was the first railway station in Japan. The area is pretty much of an extension of the Ginza.

Along the Bay, southwest of the Ginza, are the less familiar names of Tsukiji, Harumi and Shinagawa where the emphasis is on industry. Tsukiji is home for the Tokyo Central Wholesale Market, where the action starts about dawn (see page 56). An anomaly is the 61-acre Hama Detached Palace Garden adjacent to the market. It's one of the less crowded and more peaceful of Tokyo's gardens, certainly worth visiting if you are in the area. The industrial-warehouse district of Harumi is the locale of the Tokyo International Trade Center, site of the big trade fairs and exhibitions. A bit farther to the south is Shinagawa, an industrial and residential area since the late Edo period, which also combines a couple of tourist sights—the Takanawa Art Museum and Seugaku Temple—several large hotels and Sony's main plant.

CULTIVATING SEAWEED, two women (left) stand knee-deep in the water of Tokyo Bay. Tokyo Tower (lower left) rises more than 1,000 feet and has two observation platforms. The Sumida River (below) is spanned by Kachidokibashi Bridge. Tokyo's Kanda Area is famed for its many bookstores (lower right).

drivers in Tokyo. It lists numerous stores, night clubs, movies, banks, airlines offices, etc., both in English and Japanese, with a small map of the area beside each entry.

You can rent a car—if you are the placid type and can cope with the traffic maelstroms of Tokyo streets and if you don't mind driving on the left hand side of the street—but it is not recommended. (See page 23.) It's easier if you have your travel agent arrange for a chauffeur-driven car which costs about Y11,000 for 8 hours.

Sometimes it's a great deal easier to get from one district of Tokyo to another by subway—and the Tokyo subway system provides an excellent transportation network and is very easy to navigate. Color-coded English maps are readily available at any subway ticket window. An outstretched hand and the word *chizu* covers the communication required. The subway, particularly during midday, off-hour periods, provides a convenient, inexpensive way to get around this rather crowded city. Your hotel desk can tell you where the nearest station is and where to get off. All the station stops are in English.

If you would like to get a commuter's eye view of Tokyo, you can take a loop trip that goes for about 20 miles, circling the city and stopping at 28 stations. It's the Yama-no-te or loop line, and it gives you a fast (about 1 hour) cross section of bustling Tokyo, as well as train window views of many of the Tokyo sights you would see on one of the standard city tours. At rush hour, commuters are crushed together in over-crowded cars, but you don't have to ride the loop at rush hour—try it during off hours under far less crowded conditions.

Sightseeing in the world's largest city

Sightseeing in Tokyo starts with the first shop window in your hotel arcade, the first step into the eternal parade of people on the Ginza, your first stroll beside a flower-lined walk in one of the city's lovely parks. Tour folders from your travel agent, your hotel or from the Japan National Tourist Organization Information Center, will help you decide on what to see and how to go about it. The following are some of the highlights.

Imperial Palace. Perhaps nowhere in Japan will you be struck so instantly with the contrast of East and West so closely intermingled as in the area of the Imperial Palace, residence of Emperor Hirohito and his family. The castle itself—surrounded by broad moats, high rock walls, pine forests and gardens—was first built 500 years ago for the Tokugawa shogun. It has been the royal residence since 1869 when Emperor Meiji moved the capital of Japan from Kyoto to Tokyo.

The traffic that swirls around the palace grounds is hectic and noisy. But swans glide slowly on the still water of the moat and gnarled branches of old pines droop above it. During their lunch hour, office workers from the nearby Marunouchi district linger on the green lawns of the Palace Plaza. The palace has been called "a paradox of stillness in the middle of the world's largest metropolis."

You may walk to the end of the double-arched bridge, the Nijubashi, and gaze through the feudal gates—or you may ask for permission to go into the Imperial Palace grounds. You must apply at least one day in advance at the Imperial Household Agency (fairly near the Imperial Hotel), or sign up for one of the tours that include the Palace. You won't actually be allowed into any part of the building, but you do get to see the grounds and gardens. The Emperor and royal family appear on the balcony in the Palace grounds twice a year: once on April 29 (the Emperor's birthday), and once on January 2. On those two days, the wooded and arbored grounds are open to the public without special permission.

Akasaka Detached Palace. Near Yotsuya Station, in the Akasaka district, this was the palace used by the Emperor Meiji while the main Imperial Palace was being rebuilt. Currently being completely renovated, it was for a while the residence of the present Emperor when he was Crown Prince. It looks more like an 18th century European palace than Japanese; and its luxurious rooms, which now house the National Diet Library and a few government agencies, are hung with paintings by French and Japanese artists. The palace will be open to visitors after renovation is completed in 1974.

Tokyo Tower. A wonderful place for an exciting view of the city (if you don't mind high-in-the-air platforms or waiting in line to get there). You zoom up via a 30-passenger elevator to an observation platform several hundred feet up in this steel spire that rises higher than the Eiffel Tower to a sky-piercing 1,092 feet. But count on lots of company—mainly Japanese. On weekdays 10,000 people usually visit the tower, possibly 15,000 on Sundays.

Parks. Tokyo's parks are a delight at any time of the year. They contain museums, temples, art galleries, stadiums, and always gorgeous gardens.

Ueno Park, Tokyo's largest (210 acres), is known for its Cherry Hill (Sakura-ga-oka), and is as fine a place as you'll find in Tokyo to see April's display of cherry blossoms. The park also has one of the largest zoos in the world where the animals are kept in areas as similar as possible to their natural habitats. A short ride by monorail takes you to Ueno's Aquatic Zoo on the shore of Shinobazu Pond. The Tokyo Metropolitan Festival Hall in the park is the scene of many of the city's finest musi-

DAWN AT TSUKIJI . . . TO SEE THE BIGGEST FISH MARKET IN THE WORLD

One of the most rewarding and unusual sights in Tokyo is the Tsukiji Fish Market, located on the Sumida River near Tokyo Bay and easily reached by taxi or on the subway (take the Hibiya line; get off at Tsukiji station).

The huge market (largest in the world) gets into full swing about 5:30 A.M. Large fish—such as tuna, swordfish and sometimes sharks—are laid out in rows, each of them with a large red number painted on its sides to help buyers identify them. These big fish are purchased individually. Long before the bidding begins, the brokers are out in the sheds with flashlights, scanning the rows of fish and busily making notes. They chip off tiny pieces of the flesh near the tail to judge its quality. Good tuna should be the color of the inside of your lower lip and should have no smell at all if it is truly fresh. The best fresh tuna goes for about $4 to $8 per kilo, making a hundred kilo fish worth a tidy sum of money. The finer quality tuna is much coveted in Japan for making the traditional raw-fish delicacy, *sashimi*. In addition to the large fish, you'll see a bewildering array of other varieties, including pink octopus, mackerel, cod, shellfish of various kinds and caviar.

You'll want your camera—with flash equipment— to catch still lives of the brightly numbered fish and candid, in-action shots of the fish porters as they hurry around inside the soaring sheds, carrying vicious looking iron hooks with which they handle the large fish. From time to time they pause to warm their chilled hands over bright fires fueled with wooden fish crates.

Part of the charm of the fish market is being at the pulsing center of part of the everyday life of the world's largest city, watching a real activity rather than something displayed especially for the benefit of the visitor. You may also find the gruff friendliness of the porters and fish buyers unique in a land where formal courtesy is so common that it sometimes becomes a strain.

BIG TUNA, *each one tagged with a number, await the buyers at the world's biggest fish market.*

cal and cultural events. The train to the new Narita Airport, to be opened in 1973, will leave from Ueno station at the edge of the park.

Hibiya Park faces the Imperial Palace across the moat. This, like the nearby Palace Plaza, is a green oasis for office workers during the summer; and its outdoor theater is a fine place to enjoy a pops concert on a weekend afternoon. Some of the city's finest displays of chrysanthemums are found in Hibiya Park in November.

The campus of the University of Tokyo in Hongo District has a lovely park with a small woodland lake and a handsome old brick clock tower. If you're willing to take the first conversational step, you probably will find it easy to strike up a conversation with one of the students— most would like to practice their English. Reports of their radical acivities to the contrary, you will find them to be like students around the world: thoughtful, opinionated, sincere and, since they are Japanese, polite.

In Meiji Park, more properly called the Meiji Shrine Outer Garden, are the big sports arenas, starting with the huge National Athletic Stadium, main stadium of the 1964 Olympic Games. It also has the big Chichibu Rugby Ground, a baseball stadium which seats 60,000 persons and a swimming pool around which 12,000 persons can be seated. Here, too, is the Meiji Park Iris Garden, one of the most famous, and certainly most accessible, in Tokyo.

Tokyo gardens. Uniquely Japanese landscaped gardens are a part of every Tokyo park, the grounds of every shrine and temple, an important aspect of most of Tokyo's inns. But there are certain gardens in Tokyo that you should see. They include the 61-acre Hamarikyu Onshi Garden, famous for its lovely tidal pool, which is spanned by three graceful bridges, each shaded by wisteria vines. The Kiyosumi Garden, typical of the Meiji period, is celebrated for its rocks, brought from all parts of Japan. The Korakuen Garden has a strong Chinese flavor. Its

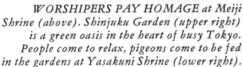

*WORSHIPERS PAY HOMAGE at Meiji
Shrine (above). Shinjuku Garden (upper right)
is a green oasis in the heart of busy Tokyo.
People come to relax, pigeons come to be fed
in the gardens at Yasakuni Shrine (lower right).*

stone bridge is called the Full Moon Bridge; built in a half circle, the bridge and its reflection form a circle.

At Shinjuku Gyoen you will see rare cherry trees, and in autumn, a bright display of chrysanthemums. Included in its 144 acres are a French-style, an English-style and a Japanese-style garden, the latter considered to be one of the most beautiful in Japan. The Rikugien Garden is another special one for strolling, with a pond as the center of the composition. Ueno Park offers one of the most lavish displays of April cherry blooms.

Temples and shrines. Although Tokyo is not as rewarding a place for visiting temples and shrines as Kyoto and Nara, there are some interesting ones to see.

The Asakusa Kannon Temple, or the Sensoji Temple, is in the midst of the Asakusa district which is Tokyo's liveliest amusement section. Dedicated to the Goddess of Mercy, the tall main hall enshrines a tiny image of the goddess, or Kannon. A fisherman, you will be told,

brought up the image in his net while fishing in the Sumida River (the river that flows through Tokyo). A festival in honor of the goddess is held on May 17-18.

Souvenir shops line the long approach to the Sensoji Temple. They indicate an age-old pattern of development in Japan, for once a market stood before the temple. In this same way, many a Japanese town has grown, beginning with a temple and its adjacent market. Another temple consecrated to the Kannon is the Gokokuji Temple in Toshima-ga-oka. Founded in the late 17th century, it is one of the city's largest Buddhist temples, and the hill in back of the temple has been the burial place for the Imperial Family for the last century. Here the image of the Goddess of Mercy is carved from amber.

The Meiji Shrine, near Harajuku Station, was built in 1920 as a memorial to the Emperor Meiji and is probably Tokyo's biggest tourist attraction. The trees within its Inner Garden, more than 100,000 of them, were gifts of

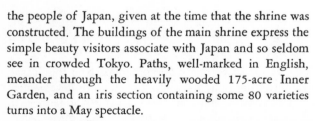

*SIDEWALK VENDOR (upper left) sells dolls
to young customers in Ueno Park. Banners
(lower left) in small off-street shrine indicate
that a festival is in progress. The fountains
in the Imperial Palace Plaza (above)
commemorate Crown Prince Akihito's wedding.*

the people of Japan, given at the time that the shrine was constructed. The buildings of the main shrine express the simple beauty visitors associate with Japan and so seldom see in crowded Tokyo. Paths, well-marked in English, meander through the heavily wooded 175-acre Inner Garden, and an iris section containing some 80 varieties turns into a May spectacle.

Museums and art galleries. New York may claim to be one of the largest art centers of the world; but running hard to equal and best this claim is Tokyo, which by sheer population count alone, has more artists per square mile than any other city in the world.

Among Tokyo's many fine museums, the Tokyo National Museum in Ueno Park is the most outstanding. Its exhibits include paintings, calligraphy and textiles, lacquer and ceramics, metal works and sculpture.

The National Museum of Sciences is next door to the National Museum, and nearby is the National Museum of

Western Art. In this very contemporary building is the Matsukata Collection, made up of the paintings and sculpture of famous Western artists, collected by a business tycoon of the 1920s, Kojiro Matsukata.

One of the world's finest collections of Oriental art treasures is available at the Toyokan Museum, a fairly recent addition in Ueno Park. It houses more than 700 exhibits including antiquities from China, Korea, India, Pakistan, Egypt and other countries of Asia and the Middle East.

The Memorial Picture Gallery within Meiji Park is a fine example of 20th century architecture, while the paintings that it houses all illustrate the life of the Emperor Meiji (1868 to 1912).

The National Museum of Modern Art in Nihombashi district is a handsome structure, open in design, its three floors housing a collection of paintings and sculptures by modern Japanese artists as well as changing shows that bring together fine art from around the world. For a cataloguing of Tokyo's museums, see the next page.

Minka-en. One of the loveliest and least crowded places to visit in Tokyo is Minka-en, a park in Kawasaki Prefecture reachable by the Odakyu electric train line. A selection of genuine old farmhouses have been reconstructed in the park, examples of rural architecture that are increasingly hard to find anywhere in the country since the thatch out of which they are made is being replaced by asbestos sheeting, and wood, by concrete blocks.

The houses come from all over Japan and at present there are sixteen in a finished state. They are set naturally around the wooded park, most of them with the open fireplaces and hanging iron kettles that are still used in rural areas, some with ancient looms or farm machinery.

Everything in the park is designed to fit in with the surroundings: the garbage cans are discreetly encased in wood, special areas are provided for smokers and one house has a small snack restaurant on the ground floor. Maps and descriptions of the houses are available, though unfortunately not yet in English.

Takao Mountain. Another excursion away from urban concrete Japan is to Takao Mountain. Any taxi driver can get you there, but by far the easiest way of making the 43-minute journey is to take any *Kyuko* train on the Keio Train Line out of Shinjuku and ride to the end of the line. Once there and after a 3-minute walk from the station, you have a choice: either a precipitous cable car or an enchanting open chair lift (Y150) up the side of the mountain. The ascent gives a wonderful view of wooded mountains, and Tokyo seems to have vanished into the mists. The ride is particularly spectacular in the fall when the leaves are turning.

Once at the top there is the inevitable small amusement park, but one activity there that you'll find attractive is a stand that will let you paint anything on an unfired piece of pottery which they then fire. If you prefer, they will draw an appropriate Japanese character on the piece. The result makes a very unusual non-mass-produced souvenir. A lantern-lined stone walk winds along the side of the mountain among giant pine trees to a Buddhist shrine perched on the very top of the mountain. The building is a National Treasure decorated with painted carved wood in the Chinese style and surrounded by storehouses and small pavilions. It is also an active temple, and there are often ceremonies being performed with accompanying conch shells and gongs.

The temple's popularity with the Japanese tends to make weekends a bad time to visit. If you have a little extra time and energy, you can descend the mountain on an easy trail through the woods and past an attractive waterfall. A small zoo on the mountain is worth a stop if you are traveling with younger family members.

Mingei-kan. There's a small folk craft museum, called *Mingei-kan,* about a 5-minute walk from the *Komaba* (Tokyo University) stop on the Inokashira train line, which leaves from Shibuya. Under the directorship of the potter Shoji Hamada, this museum has attempted to preserve and chronicle the true folk arts of Japan. Exhibits include pottery, furniture, cloth, including some woven from paper, and other artifacts. What makes this museum especially worth visiting is that it is housed in a very beautiful old traditional Japanese building which was once a wealthy private home, a kind of building you most likely won't have an opportunity to see anywhere else in the Tokyo area.

Shopping

Shopping in Tokyo is a delight. There is endless variety, and there are no pressure tactics. You can browse in tiny hole-in-the-wall shops or one of the huge department stores. The clerks are unobtrusive, courteous and helpful. And no matter what you buy or where, from a fine painting to a thimble, it will be presented to you carefully and attractively wrapped. The stores are so large, you will find it helpful to stop at the money exchange/information desk which each of the big stores has on its main floor.

DEPARTMENT STORES post attendants on first floor near escalator. They bow to customers, say irashaimase *(welcome) as they wipe the handrail with white cloth.*

This desk also has a detailed floor plan in English—most useful in familiarizing yourself with the layout and knowing where to go to make your purchase.

The Ginza. The world famous Ginza, stretching block after block through downtown Tokyo, is the main shopping center. It has all manner of specialty shops and about a dozen huge department stores. Ginza means Silver Foundry, a name that the area acquired when the ruling *shoguns* of Japan minted coin in the area.

The four major department stores in the Ginza are Matsuya, Matsuzakaya, Mitsukoshi and Komatsu. All have spruced themselves up in the last few years, added boutique corners, folk-craft corners, good design corners, art galleries, special exhibits and other attractions to keep shoppers interested in the city center. Girls bow a welcome to everyone mounting the escalators. Most of the department stores have English-speaking floor managers. The Matsuzakaya has a Cafe de Paris on the ground floor in the front of the store where you can get superb coffee and French pastries and watch the passing parade. The Komatsu has a good old-fashioned beer garden on the roof (under the huge Pentax camera sign).

The two most popular fashion centers in the Ginza are on Chuo-Dori: one is Meitetsu Melsa, around 2-chome on the east; its high-quality (and high-priced) merchandise is housed in an attractively designed building. The other is the Core Building, to the south of Yon-chome crossing and also on the east side of the street. At the latter, you should take the outside elevator to the top floor and ride the escalator down through the seven floors: Japa-

---

A CHECKLIST OF TOKYO'S MUSEUMS AND GALLERIES

Tokyo is richly endowed with museums. Exhibits range from art to astrological and theatrical displays, from ceramics and calligraphy to paper, swords and folk-craft collections. You'll find visits to some of the following will enrich your Japanese experience.

All but two museums—the Meiji Memorial Picture Gallery and the Metropolitan Fine Art Gallery—are closed on Mondays. Some, but not all, are closed on national holidays or the day after the holiday.

Bridgestone Museum of Art, 1, Kyobashi 1-chome, Chuo-ku. Exhibits of representative paintings and sculpture by Japanese and Western artists of the 18th and 19th centuries.

Gotoh Art Museum, 9-25, Kaminoge 3-chome, Setagaya-ku. Contains ancient objects, some classified as "National Treasures."

Gotoh Planetarium Astrological Museum, 8th floor, Tokyo Bunka Kaikan Building, in front of East Exit of Shibuya Station, Japan National Railways. Star gazing and related exhibits.

Japan Folkcrafts Museum (Nippon Mingeikan), 3-33, Komaba 4-chome, Meguro-ku. A superb display of old and new ceramics, dyed and woven fabrics, wooden objects and other folkcraft articles from Japan and Korea.

Japan Sword Museum, 25-10, Yoyogi 4-chome, Shibuya-ku. The only museum in Japan designed exclusively for study and preservation of Japanese swords and related materials.

Meiji Memorial Picture Gallery, in Outer Gardens of Meiji Shrine. Contains paintings showing the main events in the reign of Emperor Meiji.

Metropolitan Fine Art Gallery, in Ueno Park. Part of the Tokyo University of Arts, with changing exhibits, the most distinguished of which are in the fall.

National Museum of Modern Art, in Kita-no-Maru Park, Chiyoda-ku. Contains about 1,000 pieces of work by modern Japanese artists, both of Japanese painting (including woodblocks, copper-plate prints, lithography), and Western paintings. Exhibits are changed often. Each display represents the work of a specific school or period in Japanese art.

National Museum of Western Art, in Ueno Park. Contains the famed Matsukata Collection of famous works of Western painters and sculptors.

National Science Museum, in Ueno Park. Exhibits in the fields of zoology, botany, physical geography, physics, chemistry, astronomy, meteorology and oceanography.

Nezu Art Museum, 5-36, Minami Aoyama 6-chome, Minato-ku. A collection of ancient objects of fine arts, handicraft art from Japan, Korea and China. Closed during August.

Okura Museum of Antiques, 3, Akasaka Aoicho, Minato-ku (in the compound of the Hotel Okura). Contains ancient art objects and classic books of the Orient.

Paper Museum, 1-1-8, Horifune, Kita-ku. The only establishment in Japan displaying Japanese and Oriental paper products and utensils for making paper. Process of making Japanese paper (*washi*) is demonstrated.

Sumo Museum, in Kuramae-Kokugikan Hall. Displays material related to *sumo* (Japanese wrestling).

nese designers have created some fascinating adaptations for the country's very contemporary-minded youth.

Boutique Julien Sorel on Miyuki-Dori is another one of the top boutiques and has very "in" coffee shops on the second and third floors where tea-time fashion shows are frequently staged.

On Sundays the Ginza suddenly turns into a Pedestrians' Paradise: the wide main street is closed off to motor traffic from 8 A.M. to 6 P.M. Shop owners put out sidewalk stalls and provide stools for weary walkers, restaurants set up tables in the middle of the street, decorated carts along the way sell snacks and beverages.

Shinjuku. Though the Ginza or Akasaka are considered to be the shopping and nightlife centers of Tokyo, the area around the huge Shinjuku railroad station has become a not inconsiderable rival in recent years. As far as the younger generation is concerned—tourist and Japanese alike, Shinjuku is definitely where the action is. It's known as Young People's town; however, the recently opened Keio Plaza Hotel nearby has somewhat increased the number of middle-aged persons in the area—and they seem to enjoy the people watching as much as the shopping. Two large department stores are actually in the station building (Odakyu and Keio) and nearby is Isetan which is a favorite among foreigners in Tokyo because of its high quality merchandise and efficient tourist service for shoppers.

More important than the department stores, however, is the fascinating maze of tiny streets and alleys leading off Shinjuku-dori, the district's main street. Sometimes

---

Suntory Museum of Art, adjacent to Palace Hotel, Marunouchi. Displays classical arts closely related to people's daily lives.

Takanawa Art Museum, 10, 4-chome, Takanawa Minamicho, Minato-ku. Collections of Buddhist images of the 11th and 15th centuries, modern Japanese painting, lacquer ware of the 17th and 18th centuries.

Tokyo National Museum, Ueno Park, Taito-ku. The largest museum in the country. Contains about 86,000 exhibits relating to history and fine arts of Japan and the Orient.

Transportation Museum, 25, Kanda Sudacho 1-chome, Chiyoda-ku. Over 20,000 exhibits, including the "No. 1 Locomotive" manufactured in England in 1871.

Dr. Tsubouchi Memorial Theater Museum, Waseda University, 1-chome, Totsukamachi, Shinjuku-ku. Best theater museum in the country for displays of *kabuki, noh, Bunraku* puppet drama and other aspects of the theater.

Yamatane Museum of Art, Yamatane Building, 30, Nihombashi Kabutocho 2-chome, Chuo-ku. Contains modern and contemporary Japanese paintings.

TWO of Tokyo's many museums: Okura Museum of Antiques (left) and National Museum of Modern Art.

only six or seven feet wide and festooned with lanterns, these tiny streets give a clear idea of what Tokyo must have been like before the devastation of the war. Many of the stores are tiny restaurants or food stands that sell *tempura* or morsels of charcoal grilled chicken or squid. Usually clients stand outside or perch on little stools at the counter. The smell of cooking and the charcoal smoke is everywhere. Interspersed are tiny general stores, *kimono* shops and *pachinko* parlors (see page 64).

All day every Sunday, the congested traffic on Shinjuki-dori is closed off—and the street becomes a broad walkway thronged with young people.

On the wider streets is an amazingly wide variety of coffee shops, a Western institution that the Japanese have adopted and made entirely their own. Many of them play classical music or live folk music, and almost all of them have decors that are a mixture of medieval and Disney-gone-wild. Coffee is expensive, usually Y120 a cup, but one cup entitles you to sit for as long as you like, plan your itinerary, rest your feet or just watch the passing parade.

If it starts to rain, you can go underground—underneath the station and the whole surrounding area is a huge complex of small shops and restaurants leading off underground pedestrian passages. You'll find a surprising number of small coffee shops in this underground world —something that is unique to the Shinjuku area. Most of these are only a few square feet in width, lit inside by colored tungsten lamps that give off just enough light to read the menu and the list of the record music available. The young people who frequent these places sit in absolute silence, having coffee and listening to either pop or classical music representative of every part of the world. And the music comes forth *fortissimo*—flooding the coffee shop with sound transmitted through four-channel stereo systems.

When the weather smiles, Shinjuku Gardens, within walking distance of the station, are some of the loveliest in all Tokyo. Their cherry blossoms are so famous that the Prime Minister gives his cherry viewing party there once a year in the spring. In the autumn thousands flock to see the chrysanthemums. And Shinjuku is the site of Kosei Nenkin Hall, home of the NHK Symphony Orchestra, the best of the city's many symphony orchestras.

Besides the Ginza and Shinjuku, you'll find many shopping opportunities in the Akasaka, Marunouchi, Nihombashi and Roppongi districts.

Japanese cultured pearls, of course, are one of the country's best buys. There are a number of fine companies, the most famous of which is Mikimoto's, whose main store is in the Ginza district.

For kimonos try Hayashi Kimono in the International Arcade on Miyuki-dori (about 5 minutes from the Imperial Hotel). Beautiful, custom-made silk kimonos are also available second-hand in Hayashi's and at some department stores. These dressmaker-made kimonos, generally in fine condition, can often be bought for perhaps a fourth the price of the original. (Custom-sewn, silk kimonos, new, start at around $100.)

The specialty doll of Tokyo is the Yamato—which is dressed to represent children in elaborate and colorful kimonos. You'll find them in countless shops, in the hotel arcades, and in wide selection in the department stores.

If you're a collector, however, you'll want to visit the Iwatsuki Doll Making Village near Omiya, about 20 miles north of Tokyo. You'll find many shops there displaying a huge variety of dolls priced considerably lower than those sold in Tokyo.

Other things to do

Tokyo offers a number of lectures and short courses for tourists that add to an understanding of the Japanese and much to your Japan visit.

Flower arranging, or *Ikebana,* one of the famous arts of Japan, is taught in classes specially planned for foreigners. Both classical, or traditional, methods and the new modern styles are taught at three main *Ikebana* centers in Tokyo. They are the Sogetsu Art Center, the Ohara Center and the Ikenobo Ochanomizu College. The three schools are all connected with the international organization of floral arts known as *Ikebana International.*

You can take a quick course or a longer one, depending on the length of your stay in Tokyo. Private lessons are available too, usually at rates ranging from about $3 to $4 an hour. To find out what is available in flower arranging classes and also to learn about current exhibitions, inquire at the information room of *Ikebana International* office—phone (03) 293-8188.

Cha-no-yu, the famed Japanese tea ceremony, is taught in Tokyo in lectures and demonstrations at the Ura Senke School, Nibancho, Chiyoda-ku.

It is usually possible to arrange a visit to Tokyo schools —any level from the primary grades through senior high school. You will be required to have a guide along. Your travel agent can make arrangements for you.

Going to the theater

Three distinct brands of Japanese theater are available— *kabuki, noh* and some fantastic all-girl revues. See page 30 for a description of *kabuki* and *noh.*

Kabuki. It would be too bad to miss a performance of *kabuki,* Japan's ages-old classical drama. Tokyo's three main *kabuki* theaters are the Kabukiza Theater (Ginza

IN BUSY, bustling Tokyo: Central Station's Yaesu
Underground Shopping Center (upper left), largest
of its kind in Tokyo. A street in Asakusa (upper
right) decked out with flamboyant decor at year's end.
Nursery school children (above) learning English.
Flower arranging (right) taught
with meticulous precision.

PACHINKO: A JAPANESE PIN-BALL GAME

Pachinko is a Japanese game of chance that has become practically a national pastime. For all its exotic name, it is merely a Japanese version of the pinball machine—except that the *pachinko* machine sits vertically instead of horizontally. With more than 1,000 pachinko parlors in Tokyo alone, you often hear the unmistakable click-clack of the *pachinko* balls as you walk along the street. Many Japanese will spend as much as an hour a day at the machines; the line waiting to play reminds you somewhat of slot machine line-ups in Nevada.

This is how *pachinko* works: first the player buys 35 steel balls for about Y100. These are shot onto the *pachinko* board one after the other at each pull of a spring-loaded lever. When the ball drops into one of the holes on the board, the player wins a certain number of steel balls. When the player is finished, he takes all the steel balls (both those bought and those won) to the pay-off counter. For these, if he has been lucky, he receives prizes—food, cigarettes, candies and the like. Gambling involving direct pay-offs in money is prohibited in Japan except horse and bicycle racing.

A SOLID WALL or two of pachinko games has an almost irresistible lure for many Japanese.

Higashi, Chuo-ku), the largest, which is open the year around and devoted exclusively to *kabuki*; the National Theater in Miyakezaka where *kabuki* is performed from the 5th to the 27th of every month; and the Shimbashi Embujo Theatre (Ginza Higashi, Chuo-ku) where *kabuki* is performed during January.

The Kabukiza Theater is a huge, very attractive building—it seats about 2,500 on the main floor, has inside boxes (with Japanese-style seating), and two balconies. It also houses souvenir shops, a sushi bar, tempura and Western-style restaurants and a snack bar. It is very clean. Many of the Japanese will bring box lunches with them—to eat in the theater while the play is going on or to eat in the spacious lobby areas during intermission.

There are usually three or four plays on a program with two programs daily—one starting at 11 A.M. and one at 4:30 P.M. Although the performances last for many hours, it is quite acceptable to visit Kabukiza or any other *kabuki* theater for as long or as short a stay as you wish. People come and go throughout the performance. Usually an hour or two, broken by an intermission visit to the snack bar, is enough to qualify you as having seen *kabuki*. The visiting *kabuki* aficionado will savor three or four hours of the performance.

Noh. *Noh* plays, usually given on Saturdays and Sundays, may be seen at the Hoshokai Noh Stage (27, 2-chome, Moto-machi, Bunkyo-ku); at the Kanze Kaikan Noh Stage (Shyotoh, Shibuya-ku); the Kita Noh Stage (Kami-Osaki Shinagawa-ku); the Somei Noh Stage (Komagome, Bunkyo-ku); the Tamagawa Noh Stage (Denenchofu, Otaku).

All girl revues. Since the girl revues are generally given three times daily, it is easy to work one into even a short visit to Tokyo. Evening performances start at 5 o'clock. The big revue companies of Tokyo are the Shochiku Girls' Revue at the Kokusai Theater in the Asakusa district; the Takarazuka Girls' Opera Company, at their own theater across from the Imperial Hotel; the Nichigeki Dancing Team, which performs at the Main Nichigeki Theater; and the drama or dance performances at the Shinbashi Enbujyo Theater in the Ginza.

Visiting industrial plants

It's quite easy to visit factories in Tokyo—steel plants, ship yards, factories for manufacturing automobiles, transistor radios, watches and optical equipment. Arrange such a trip through your travel agent, or inquire at the Japan National Tourist Organization Information Center (see page 9).

Watching Japanese sports

Crowds numbering in the thousands throng the arenas to watch Tokyo's three annual 15-day *sumo* tournaments.

They are held in mid-January, mid-May and mid-September in the Kokugikan Stadium in the Asakusa district. You should also visit the *sumo* museum in the building. For more about *sumo*, see page 34.

Judo (see page 34) may be watched any day at the Kodokan Judo Institute, world center of this defensive art. A stop at the big gymnasium in the Korakuen district is on many sightseeing bus tours.

If you want to play golf in Tokyo, inquire at the Japan National Tourist Organization's Tourist Information Center (see page 9). Most golf courses in Japan are private ones, but often visitors may play them on weekdays.

During baseball season (about the same months as ours), you can watch Japanese teams play at Korakuen Baseball Stadium—where sell-out crowds of 40,000 are common (tickets are not easy to get).

Dining out in Tokyo

You could eat your way around the world without leaving Tokyo. Tokyo's restaurants, some 95,000 of them, are as famed for their international cuisine as for their strictly Japanese fare. You can, of course, also eat only American-style food all the time you are in Japan and never know that you have been out of the United States so far as eating goes. See page 14 for some notes on Japanese food and restaurants.

ON STAGE: Kabuki *actor (upper left) being readied for performance at Kabukiza Theater. Autumn dance at Tokyo's Nichigeki Theatre (upper right) where lavish shows are staged year around.* Judo *students (above) practice the art of self-defense at Kodokan Institute. Visitors are welcome.*

EATING IN TOKYO: trees and interior garden provide inviting entrance to Ryukyotei Restaurant (upper left). In Asakusa (lower left), restaurants are small, unpretentious, more like "old Tokyo." Noodle shops (below) selling soba *(buckwheat noodles) are numerous.*

Any list of restaurants in Tokyo will commit the sin of omitting many that are excellent—particularly some of the small ones that are tucked into alleys off the main stream of tourist traffic. The Tokyo resident will have to be your guide to these little discoveries; no guidebook can begin to compile them. But there are some that are better known and should be mentioned. Here they are, district by district:

Marunouchi. The hotels have some of the best restaurants in this district: the Palace Hotel's Wadakura (Japanese), Grill Simpson (steak and roast beef) and Crown Restaurant (continental and expensive), the latter at the top of the hotel has view windows looking out over the grounds of the Imperial Palace; the Marunochi Hotel's Mashiko (*shabu-shabu*), Peter's Steak House, Bamboo Grill and Sakura Room, the latter a sophisticated supper club; the Kokusai Kanko's Prunier. There's also a good Chinese restaurant, the Sansuiro, in the Kokusai Building; another good steak house, the John Bull, in the Asahi Tokai Building; and the Seiyoken, on top of the Old Marunouchi Building, is one of the less expensive but good Western-style restaurants in the area.

Hibiya/Yurakucho. An excellent Chinese-Thai restaurant, called the Keiraku, is in the alley that runs north and south just north of the Imperial Hotel Annex building. Order *yaki-soba* which looks a little like chow mein and comes with beef and oyster sauce. The Maya Restaurant specializes in country-style Japanese food. The *yakitori* and *sushi* stands to the east of the Keiraku (walk through the arch under the elevated tracks easterly toward the Ginza) are clean, the food even more delicious than it smells. For a relaxing mid-afternoon stop, try the beer garden on top of the Hankyu Department store.

Ginza. So many restaurants are located in the Ginza that you can have an international feast—almost anything you want from small *sushi* stands that charge a few yen to sophisticated restaurants that charge New York and San Francisco prices and then some. Here are some of the best: the Ashoka (above the India Government Tourist Office) for Indian food; Italy-tei, Belvedere or San Marino for Italian; Rengaya, Four Seasons, Maxim's de Paris and Rotisserie des Vosges for French/Continental; the excellent Korean restaurant in the all-Korean building just south of Julien Sorel; the Chinese restaurants in the Imperial, Dai-ichi and Ginza Tokyo hotels; the Indonesian Raya (three locations); Ketel's, Lohmeyer's and Alte Liebe for German food; and Benihana for a Westernized version of Japanese cooking that specializes in steak.

Among the Japanese restaurants in the Ginza, there are several very special ones: Jisaku follows the feudal style and guests dine wearing the *yukata* (cotton kimono) and choose from a menu specializing in *mizutaki*, fish and fowl dishes. Okahan, in the heart of the Ginza, serves variations of the famous Wadakin beef (another pampered breed)—grilled, roasted or in *sukiyaki*—in private rooms with *tatami* mats and low tables. For *tempura* there are several: Ginza Happo-en, Ten-ichi, Tempachi, Tenkumi and Hashizen. Suehiro (with two locations in the Ginza) is part of a chain of fine restaurants that specialize in Matsusaka beef. Torigin is a small, hard-to-find restaurant that serves excellent *yakitori* and *kamameshi*; and Chikuyotei specializes in eel.

You'll also find *sushi* stands and *sushi* restaurants almost everywhere you go in the Ginza. Three that are especially good are Nakada, Ozasa and Sushiden.

Nihombashi. For *mizutaki*, *sukiyaki* and *shabu-shabu* try one of the Zakuro restaurants—one near the Takashimaya Department Store, the other near the Mitsukoshi Department store. For steak, there's another Benihana in this district; and for *tempura*, try Hige-no-Tempei or Inagiku. The latter is generally considered to be the best (and most fashionable) *tempura* restaurant in Tokyo. The *tempura* is prepared while you sit around a circular counter, and you are served directly from the fryer. If you would like to try a Japanese-style box lunch, order from the Daimasu.

Shinjuku. For all of its rapid development, you'll find fewer restaurants in this district than you might expect.

The new Keio Plaza Hotel, however, almost makes up for it all by itself—boasting 225 chefs and about a dozen dining facilities including Chinese, Japanese, sea food and Western (from coffee shop to sophisticated supper club). The Japanese restaurants are branches of already famous restaurants: of the Okahan for *sukiyaki* and of the Inagiku for *tempura*. Others in the district include: El Flamenco for Spanish food and decor; the Kyubei for *sushi*; and for a variety of Japanese dishes, Jiman Honten, Kurumaya, Shinjuku Gyuya and Shinjuku Suehiro.

Shibuya. Tori Shin serves fine *yakitori* in a scrubbed pinewood decor; and Ogawaken, despite its name, is one of the oldest and among the best of Tokyo's French restaurants. Furasato Restaurant near the Folkcraft Museum is famous for its farm-house style Japan cuisine (but the "farmers" make it expensive).

Roppongi. A district with an estimated 600 restaurants, 300 clubs and bars. Out of the many good ones, you should especially note these: Castle Praha, a fine Czech restaurant; the Chardonnay and Donq for French cuisine; Chianti and San Marino for Italian dishes; El Senor, Mexican; Mon Cher TonTon, an excellent and very popular steak house with a good bar; the Swiss Inn; Gamlastan, Swedish; Wadakin for superb Japanese beef dishes; Anne Dinken's which may be Tokyo's only Kosher restaurant.

Azabu. Mostly a residential district, but at least three restaurants should be mentioned: Chez Figaro for Continental fare, Nicolas for pizza and other Italian dishes and Hasejin for Japanese. Hasejin, established more than 100 years ago, specializes in *sukiyaki* but the menu also includes vegetable rolled beef, milk roast, grilled roast and some superb boned beef dishes. The quiet, private dining rooms in the old wing of the Hasejin were designed in the style of the Bell House, owned by a famous authority on Japanese classics.

Shiba. The Crescent, housed in a new brick "Victorian" building, is one of Tokyo's best French restaurants with decor that includes the owner's display of his hobbies: archaeology and European antiques.

Akasaka. Here the list is long. Shido in the basement of the TBS Building is fine for French food as is Le Colonial. Zakuro, in the NBS Building is good for *sashimi* and *sukiyaki* with folk-craft trimmings; Liu Yuan, Sanno Hanten and the Tokarin in the Hotel Okura for Chinese food; Akasaka Misono for *teppanyaki* style cooking; Tsujidome, Kissho and Shinryu for some varied Japanese menus; Kani Kosen for superb crab dishes; Mano's for Russian coffee and borscht and a good menu. Vegetarians may want to try the Muryo-an where Buddhist-style meals are served. The hotels in the area have excellent restaurants to add to this. The Keyaki Grill at the Hilton is one of the better Western-style restaurants in Tokyo, and you'll find Japanese, Chinese and Western menus and a wide variety of decor at the other hotels in the area (New Otani, Okura, Akasaka Prince, Akasaka Tokyu, New Japan, Tokyu-Kanko, Toshi Center). The poolside barbecue at the Akasaka Prince is delightful on warm summer evenings.

Shimbashi. The Fujino Restaurant, just west of Shimbashi Station, features *okaribayaki* or samurai grill, which is like a Mongolian barbecue: vegetables, meat, fish, fowl grilled on an inverted-shield grill. Further south on the same street is the Indonesia Raya—excellent Indonesian food in a rather camp island decor. The mosaic of little *sake-sushi* bars in the area are popular—most of them presided over by a *mama-san* and one or two pleasant waitresses.

Shinagawa. Best dining in this district is in the Takanawa Prince Hotel including outdoor barbecue in the summer and inside a Korean barbecue and the Tempura House.

There are a number of guides to Tokyo's restaurant world. Your hotel will usually be able to provide you with one of the several recently published guides, and you can get the booklet published by the Japan National Tourist Organization, titled "Restaurants in Japan", which lists the 269 members of the Japan Restaurant Association, giving address, phone number, type of menu and an indication of which credit cards are accepted.

After dark

Tokyo by night is a dazzling display of neon—Japanese calligraphy, some English signs, plus every flashing and moving trick in the neon art. Beneath the lights, the streets are crowded with Japanese that maintain a nighttime intensity that equals their day-time industry.

The city boasts the most varied after-dark entertainment of any city in the world—and stands unchallenged on the claim. There's all the usual—ballet, symphony, opera, legitimate theater, motion pictures, bowling, hotel dancing, plush or intimate restaurants for dining. Night clubs and cabarets abound. There are literally thousands of small bars (one estimate says more than 20,000)—most of them preserving a certain private club atmosphere for the Japanese men that frequent them, some of them openly inviting one and all. All of them come equipped with a supply of smiling, solicitous hostesses.

The center of most of this activity is the Ginza, and you can get glimpses of the action on a walk through some of the alleys in the area which will be jammed with both foot and auto traffic and dotted with neon-lighted bars. The top floor revolving cocktail lounge of the Kotsu Kaikan Building offers a fantastic nighttime view of the Ginza district.

Some of the large and lavish cabarets have adopted such familiar if un-Japanese names as Copacabana, Papagayo, New Latin Quarter, Queen Bee, The Crown, and Show Boat to name just a few. These places feature floor shows—often with big-name entertainers from the United States or Europe—serve drinks, and provide excellent orchestras and small dance floors. The shows at some rival Las Vegas. One features entertainers in overhead gondolas; another has fountains with synchronized lights and music; another has five floors, 400 hostesses and a dance band that goes up and down on a center elevator from floor to floor.

Although the cabarets are principally planned for single, lusty males (Japanese or visitor) an American man and wife might enjoy going just to watch the sideplay—with the floor show, music, and dancing as a bonus. A couple of hours in a cabaret can run Y10,000 per person—including beverage, cover charge, snacks, 15% tax, and 10% service charge. If big-name talent is on the marquee, the tab may be half again higher.

Three big theaters stage lavish musical revues—the Kokusai, the Nichigeki and Takarazuka. These are Ziegfeld-scale shows with huge orchestras, hundreds of beautifully costumed precision dancers (some almost completely un-costumed), good singing and music, excellent vaudeville acts. For a refreshing bit of variety, some purely Japanese skits, pantomime or traditional acts are mixed in with the purely Ziegfeld-type acts. Three shows daily—two in the afternoon, and one in the evening. Tickets cost Y500 to Y1,800.

The Theatre-Restaurant (Imperial) in the Imperial Hotel is one of Tokyo's popular new night spots. It features excellent revue-type shows that blend some of the traditional Japanese entertainment with extravaganzas headlined by internationally known Japanese nightclub entertainers. The themes of the show are tied to the season (blossoms in spring). Shows are staged at 7 and 9:45 P.M. nightly. Dinner (with Western menu) and show costs Y2,100 to Y3,500 per person. The cover charge is Y1,500 per person. Drinks, 15% gratuity and 10% tax are extra.

To help you make your after-dark selection, check the English language daily newspapers available in Tokyo—the *Asahi,* the *Mainichi, Japan Times* and *Yomiuri.* A copy of *This Week in Tokyo,* available in your hotel, will give you a run-down on what is current in Tokyo night life; and you should get a copy of the *Toyko Weekender* which has extensive listings (particularly cinema), prints addresses and taxi directions in Japanese, and has a shopping section that seems to be less influenced by its advertisers than some of the other tourist guides.

REVOLVING RESTAURANT, Ginza Sky Lounge (below) affords a fine view from the top of a 15-floor building. View from 17th floor revolving cocktail lounge of Hotel New Otani (lower left). On the street (at right), the night-lighted Ginza, banked with a phalanx of neon signs.

FISHING BOATS (above) are beached for
the winter on shore of Lake Shoji near Mt. Fuji.
A pair of hikers observe an age-old custom
of watching the sun rise from atop Mt. Fuji.
At far right is Yamashita Park on the
waterfront in Yokohama.

Exploring the Fuji Area and Northeastern Honshu

Because of its location on Japan's string of islands and because it is Japan's most visited city, Tokyo is the country's most popular starting point from which to sample other nearby cities and some of the Japan countryside. Here are some of the places you can visit from Tokyo:

Yokohama

Yokohama is a major seaport, the gateway to Japan for ocean liners coming from all parts of the world, and an industrial city of steel mills and heavy industry. Technically, it's situated 20 miles south of Tokyo; actually it melds into Tokyo to make one massive metropolitan area.

Unless you arrive by ship or have business there, you most likely won't visit Yokohama. It simply isn't intended to be a tourist target. You quite likely will see some of the factories and office buildings from the train window if you use rail transportation to reach Atami, Nagoya or any of the other areas to the southwest of Tokyo.

If you do go there, you should visit Nogeyama Park which commands a fine view of the city and port, Sankei-en Garden which has a three-storied pagoda said to be more than 500 years old, and the local Chinatown. The two principal shopping streets are Isezaki-cho and Moto-machi.

The Chiba Area

Hanging off mainland Honshu directly east of Tokyo is the appendage of land called the Boso Peninsula. The area provides a protecting arm for Tokyo Bay and offers some fascinating close-ups of rural Japan only an hour or so out of Tokyo. You'll see pretty country villages, farmlands, fishing villages and lovely beaches along with an assortment of ancient temples and shrines.

Chiba, at the head of the peninsula, may be reached by

SHALLOW DRAFT BOATS ply the canals in the marshy areas of Chiba Prefecture, an area of farms, villages.

car, rail or bus from Tokyo. During the summer months, boats (including hydrofoils) operate out of Kawasaki and Yokohama to other points on the peninsula.

At several points—along both the bay coast and the ocean coast—you can see women pearl divers at work. The whole process of pearl farming is demonstrated at Pearl Islands near Katsuyama.

At Cape Inubo, east of Chiba at the mouth of the Tone River, there's a picturesque fishing village with a photogenic lighthouse built in 1874. The mid-peninsula is farmland, and some of the most beautiful little farm villages are off the main roads. So, if you're driving, take off on the untraveled country roads.

The peninsula also boasts two of what the Japanese call Quasi National Parks: Suigo to the north and South Boso at the south. Suigo lies along the Tone River, Japan's third largest, and is a vast area of waterscapes, lakes and river courses with sand dunes, pine forests and migratory birds. South Boso embraces a series of picturesque fishing villages along the ocean coast.

Kamakura

A feudal capital from 1192 to 1333 and now a popular bathing and sightseeing resort 30 miles southwest of Tokyo, Kamakura is noted for its Daibutsu (Great Bud-

dha). This 700-year-old bronze image is second in size (42½ feet, 103 tons) to the Buddha at Nara but is considered first in artistic merit. It was originally housed in a large building on the grounds of the Kotokuin Temple, but storms and a tidal wave swept the structure away and the statue has remained in the open since 1495.

Most tourists whip out of Tokyo, see the Daibutsu, and proceed to Hakone for the night. Kamakura deserves more of your time. Remember, it was the 12th century capital of Japan, and it's only an hour from Tokyo on a train trip that costs about a dollar (trains leave every 10 to 15 minutes). Once you leave the industrial complex of the Tokyo-Yokohama area, you ride through charming countryside and a panorama of rolling hills. Train stops are clearly marked in English, so getting off at Kamakura poses no problem. Finding your way around the city (population of about 140,000) is easy. The train station is in the center of the city, and walking in any direction from the station will uncover a variety of interesting things.

Kamakura is located in a picturesque valley, rimmed on three sides by hills. To the south are beautiful sandy beaches, attracting great crowds from neighboring towns each summer. This creates a more than Waikiki-like beach congestion that's usually a little too great for most tourists, but you probably didn't plan to spend your time in Japan swimming anyway.

The Kamakura Museum of Modern Art has one of the finest collections in the Orient—with very avant-garde architecture, sculptures and paintings located in an environment of ancient temples and shrines. Designed by a student of the great French architect, Le Corbusier, the building itself is worth seeing.

On the side streets, you'll find many little antique shops with excellent selections and prices far more reasonable than you'll find in Tokyo or Kyoto. The same is true of handicraft shops: many of them are scattered around the city selling native art at prices lower than those found in the big cities. The local handicraft is *Kamakura-bori*, intricate carvings chiseled from hardwood, then heavily lacquered in black and vermillion red. Very popular with the Japanese, most of the carvings are designed for their tastes—flowers, trays, mirror and picture frames, sandals. But among the variety of objects produced, you're sure to find something unique and tasteful.

Throughout the temple areas are many ancient burial mounds with stone carvings from the 12th, 13th and 14th centuries. Art students from Tokyo have been visiting Kamakura in recent years to make temple rubbings—something that you too can easily make as a most unusual souvenir.

Visitors to Kamakura are invited to participate in the

traditional Japanese tea ceremony: on the 4th of each month at Engakuji Temple, on the 10th at Tomoe-kai at Tsurugaoka Hachimangu and on the 15th at Kojitsukai at Jufuku-an in North Kamakura. (The ceremony is not conducted during the month of August.)

Altogether there are 65 Buddhist temples and 19 Shinto shrines in the Kamakura area. Besides the Daibutsu, among those of special interest are: the Hase Kannon Temple with its 11-faced Goddess of Mercy, a 30-foot high statue supposed to have been carved in 721 from a single huge camphor log; Zuisenji Temple, known for its *fucha-ryor*i (vegetable dishes in the Chinese style) which you can have served to you (by special request); and Tokeiji Temple, an early day temple for women libbers. Built in 1285 and tucked away in a peaceful corner north of city center, the latter temple was established by Imperial decree as a haven for mis-treated wives.

If you are willing to walk a couple of miles, get off the train from Tokyo at the Kita-Kamakura station immediately before Kamakura. The temple complex of Engakuchi, one of Kamakura's leading centers of Zen Buddhism, is near the station; and from there it is a pleasant walk along the winding road through forest covered hills to Kamakura. Numerous temples along the way give you a better idea of the contemplative side of the old Kamakura, as well as of the power and wealth of the city to build so many temples!

BLACK-ROBED MONKS *(upper left) making the periodic pilgrimage required of Zen Buddhists. The Kamakura* Daibutsu (Great Buddha) *weighs more than 100 tons; via stairs inside the* Daibutsu, *you can climb to the shoulders. In early morning in Kamakura, monks (above) go from door to door begging.*

SNOW-COVERED *Mt. Fuji is majestic in winter. In Kamakura, a lantern maker (below) will paint your name on the lantern you purchase. Archery on horseback (below left) is an age-old custom revived at annual shrine festival in Kamakura. Japanese arrive in busloads to skate on frozen Lake Shoji (below right) or fish through the ice.*

Most impressive of those you will pass is the great Zen temple of Kenchoji. This lovely group of buildings (some of which date back to the fifteenth century) is set among the hills and surrounded by serene Japanese gardens. From Kenchoji it is only a short walk into Kamakura where a long staircase leads up to the Tsuragaoka Hachimangu Shrine that dominates the city and is considered by temple-goers as a "must." The approach to the temple is along an avenue shaded by cherry trees. Adding to the especially impressive setting is the enormous ginkgo tree to the left of stone steps leading to the temple doors. When the annual festival of the shrine is celebrated on September 15 and 16, you can watch sacred palanquins being carried through the streets and can thrill to the sight of horsemen in the hunting attire of warriors of the Kamakura period repeating ancient contests with spears and targets and archery on horseback.

Mt. Fuji and the Five Lakes District

Mt. Fuji, the five lakes at its northern base, and the surrounding forests are part of the Fuji-Hakone-Izu National Park, perhaps the most popular recreation area in Japan.

It is an all-seasons recreation area packed with natural beauty, historical sites, hot spring spas and man-made attractions—all within a few hours of the bulging metropolis of Tokyo. A favorite area for the Japanese, city dwellers flock there for family vacations, honeymoons, business meetings, camping, hiking, spa life and weekend excursions.

Although a visit to this area deserves more time, travelers on a tight schedule should at least allocate a day and night for the trip or make a tour stop between Tokyo and Kyoto.

Scenically, this resort-land is a low-key melange of domesticated and natural landscapes—undulating green golf courses, tidy tree farm forests planted with conifers, resort gardens, wild gorges, and natural mountain grasslands, lakes, waterfalls and dense deciduous forests—all dominated by superlative Mt. Fuji. Highways into the area are narrow, relatively unobtrusive and wildly congested on peak travel days (weekends) when hordes of tour buses, taxis and private cars, all headed in the same direction at the same time, labor up the twisting grades.

The Fuji Five Lakes area is considered by far the best area from which to see Mt. Fuji. Crisp winter days perhaps offer some of the best viewing, although viewing on summer nights, when lights carried by climbers create a ribbon of fire on the mountain's slopes, is highly dramatic.

There are several ways to reach the Five Lakes District from Tokyo. The Japanese National Railways has a 1-hour, 30-minute ride to Otsuki where you change to the privately-owned Fuji Kyuko Co. train. This carries you to Kawaguchiko on the shores of Lake Kawaguchi, an hour's ride. There is also one direct Tokyo-Kawaguchiko train daily which takes 2 hours, 15 minutes. The Odakyu Private Railway connects with a bus at Gotemba which will take you to Lake Yamanaka. By hired automobile it is a two-hour trip from Tokyo. It is possible to make a one-day trip to the area (215 miles, 13-16 hours) but a stay of a few days is recommended to fully appreciate the district.

Fujisan (*san* means mountain) is the way Japanese refer to Mt. Fuji. This magnificent mountain occupies a special place in the hearts of the people, not only for its supreme beauty but for its spiritual significance. It is climbed by tens of thousands of pleasure seekers and pilgrims each year. The highest mountain in Japan, it rises 12,365 feet above sea level to form one of the most beautifully symmetrical cones in the world. From time immemorial Fuji has challenged the creative genius of the nation's poets and artists to depict its beauty and charm in literature, art, and song. Its beauties are inexhaustible, varying with the view, the time of day, the season, and the weather.

It is believed that the ancient inhabitants of the area, the Ainu, named what was then an active volcano for their goddess of hearth and fire, Huichi, or Fuichi. Its last eruption was in 1707 and covered Tokyo, 75 miles distant, with six inches of volcanic ash. Now, only occasional wisps of steam escape from the summit.

The five lakes—Yamanaka, Kawaguchi, Saiko, Shoji and Motosu—are surrounded by extensive forests and offer a variety of recreation throughout the year. A good road encircles Mt. Fuji and skirts the five lakes. Moving from east to west, you reach Lake Yamanaka first, then Kawaguchi, Saiko, Shoji and Motosu. By bus the complete tour around the lakes takes 6 to 8 hours and covers about 100 miles. If you can take your eyes away from Fuji, you'll realize why the drive between Kawaguchi and Motosu lakes is ranked as one of the "most gorgeous mountain dell roads in Japan." Between Saiko and Shoji lakes lies Jukai (Sea of Trees), a 23½-square mile expanse of virgin forest. Surrounding the lakes, the forests are noted for birds, with more than 170 species identified thus far.

In spring, the cherry trees and azaleas perfume the air with their beautiful blossoms; in summer, camping, swimming and fishing are popular. Autumn presents a vivid display of brilliant foliage while winter brings skiing, skating, duck hunting and fishing for surf smelt through holes cut on the frozen lakes. Lake Yamanaka, the largest of the lakes, is a year-round resort, offering camping sites in the summer and skating rinks in the winter. There is also an 18-hole golf course nearby. Lake Kawaguchi is also a fine recreation center, noted for the beautiful view of Fuji reflected on its waters. Powder snow attracts thousands to the lower slopes of Mt. Fuji each winter.

Other points of interest in the area are: Fugaku Fuketsu (Wind Cave), formed when molten lava from within the volcano was expelled by inner pressure, is now festooned with icicles and lava stalactites. Another such cave, Fuji Fuketsu was once used by villagers to preserve silkworm eggs because of its near freezing temperature—the floor of this 600-foot-deep cave is covered with perpetual ice. Fifteen miles from Lake Motosu are two lovely waterfalls, Otodome (Noiseless Waterfall) and Shiraito

(White Threads Waterfall), the latter 65 feet high and 430 feet wide. There are souvenir shops, restaurants and accommodations in the towns of Funatsu and Kawaguchiko both located close to Lake Kawaguchi.

The Fuji-View Hotel on the shore of Lake Kawaguchi is a delightful hotel of rustic and old-fashioned character. Facilities include tennis courts, miniature golf course, swimming pool, boats and extensive grounds. Hotel Mt. Fuji is so close to Mt. Fuji that its slopes seem to be part of the hotel grounds. Overlooking Lake Yamanaka, the hotel has a large swimming pool, bowling alley, golf course, boating facilities and winter ski facilities. It's an excellent base from which to climb the mountain.

HOW TO HUFF AND PUFF YOUR WAY TO THE TOP OF MT. FUJI

Six trails lead up the face of Fuji. And every summer, during the climbing months of July and August, you can see long lines of climbers on their way to the top of that splendid conical mountain.

Why do they climb it? The Japanese make the climb as part of a religious and spiritual experience. For them, it's a sacred mountain. Visitors from other lands do so because it's one of the great experiences in mountain climbing.

The Japanese usually start up the mountain in the afternoon, climb until dark and spend the night in stone huts or start in late afternoon or evening and climb all night in order to achieve the supreme experience: seeing the sunrise from the summit. Many of the climbers wear the long white robes of religious pilgrims.

Most of the visitors who make the trek start fairly early in the day and make a one-day trip of it, reaching the top in four to six hours and then making a sand-sliding descent in little more time than it takes to tell about it.

Each of the trails up the mountain is divided into ten sections, and each section ends at a station. At each station you'll find concession stands that sell food, soft drinks and water. The price goes up as the altitude increases—since all supplies come up on the backs of porters. The stations also have primitive stone huts that provide communal overnight accommodations, but most travelers avoid these. Each station, however, becomes a place for a brief respite: a good reason to stop, catch your breath, look back down the slopes of the mountain and out over the countryside, and watch the fascinating procession of hikers serpentine its way up.

Japanese and foreigners alike arm themselves with a Fuji-stick, a rounded walking stick about four feet long. It not only helps with the climbing but also provides a cherished memento of the climb. At each station there is someone to brand your Fuji-stick, giving you a visual record of your climb. You can buy one at the starting point.

Station Five (at 8,250 feet) is the usual starting point for hikers. You reach it by bus from any of the popular hotels around Fuji's skirts. From this point a 4,115-foot ascent is still ahead of you. If you're reluctant to try it on foot, you can rent a horse for the climb from Station Five to Station Seven. This leaves one last hard, steep pull up to the 12,365-foot summit, but it does give your legs a rest.

Funatsu Trail from Station Five is a relatively easy one: it starts out fairly gently, becomes a little steeper, and then near Station Six begins traversing a narrow route in a series of switchbacks up to the summit.

The crater at the summit is almost a perfect circle, its edges topped by eight peaks. A stone hut (used in 1895 by a Japanese meteorologist and his wife) and a concrete meteorological observatory cling to one of these peaks. The two-mile trail around the crater is an easy one.

From the summit the panorama is spectacular unless the peak is completely cloud-bound. Usually it's above the clouds, and it's often clear enough to see over vast reaches of countryside, other mountains, the coastline and the Pacific Ocean. And the sunrise is an experience you'll never forget: watching sky and clouds change from the black of night to dawn through a myriad of unbelievable colors.

The down-hill trek is relatively simple—harder on the knees, perhaps, but easier on legs and lungs than the uphill climb. The fastest way to cannonball down-

Another Western-style hotel in the area is the Fuji New Grand, and there are numerous *ryokans* at both Kawaguchi and Yamanaka.

The climb up Fuji is a unique and exciting adventure for the tourist, a pilgrimage for the devout, a challenge to the athlete, and the means to an end for the nature lover—sunrise on the summit (see below).

If you don't feel like tackling the summit, you can make an interesting trek on the 20-mile Ochudo-merguri Trail that links the 5th level stations of the summit trails. The trail moves through a region of twisted pines and alpine flora.

Hakone District

One of three districts comprising the Fuji-Hakone-Izu National Park, the Hakone District is noted both for its mountain scenery and for its hot springs resorts. The district, which is generally regarded as a second-best Fuji-viewing area, receives more foreign visitors than the Five Lakes area. It encompasses an area about 25 miles in circumference that is really the bowl of an old volcanic crater. A dozen or so hot spring spas, Lake Ashi (also called Lake Hakone), and Fuji (as viewed over the ridge lines) are its basic attractions.

The typical "tour" of the area enters the Hakone moun-

slope is to try a little *sunabashiri* (sand sliding) on the section of the Gotemba Trail which is covered with volcanic sand. You cover a lot of land in a hurry.

If you decide to join the more than 3 million others who climb Fuji every year, a few advance preparations will make the trek more pleasant. A warm sweater and a wind and waterproof parka are necessities because there's often a thick overcast or a biting wind, or both. Also you can expect daytime temperatures at the summit in August (the hottest month) to run below 50°. High topped basketball shoes or regular hiking boots are recommended (the round trip can just about wear out a pair of ordinary sneakers). A pair of gloves will be welcome protection for your hands. If you plan to do any night hiking, take along a dependable flashlight and extra warm clothing.

As a Fuji climber, you'll probably experience some of the same spiritual feeling that the Japanese get even without any religious significance attached. And, as in all mountain climbing, you reap those small priceless rewards of the sights and sounds along the trail: the blossoms of the dotted bluebell, Faurie's rosebay and the Fuji thistle, and the trillings and warblings of the tiger thrush, the meadow bunting and red-tailed shrike. Then there's the tremendous view from the top. And you come home with that souvenir prized by every climber of Fuji: your Fuji-stick, marked at each of the stations along the route and topped with the brand: *Top Mount Fuji Alt 12,365 feet.* It's something you're likely to treasure even when the warblings of the tiger thrush have become lost in the limbo of the past.

CLIMBER is on his way to the trail up Mt. Fuji, out-fitted in water-repellent jacket and carrying Fuji stick.

UNENDING LINE of hikers serpentines up steep slopes of 12,365-foot Mt. Fuji during July and August.

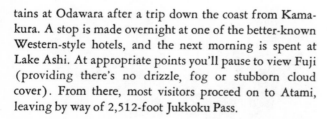

THE PIONEER (upper left) plies from one
village to another on Lake Ashi in the Hakone
area. The Fuji View Hotel (left) is one of
several excellent hotels in the Fuji area. Intricate
rice terraces (above) along the old Tokaido
Road have been cultivated since feudal days,
can be glimpsed from Tokyo-Kyoto train.

tains at Odawara after a trip down the coast from Kamakura. A stop is made overnight at one of the better-known
Western-style hotels, and the next morning is spent at
Lake Ashi. At appropriate points you'll pause to view Fuji
(providing there's no drizzle, fog or stubborn cloud
cover). From there, most visitors proceed on to Atami,
leaving by way of 2,512-foot Jukkoku Pass.

From Odawara the road (and rail line) twists up a
narrow, wooded gorge past the spas of Yumoto, Tono-
sawa and Miyanoshita. Farther along are Gora and
Kowakidani, joining Miyanoshita in reputation as the
most popular spas in the Hakone area and excellent bases
from which to make the climb up Mt. Fuji (see page 76).

Miyanoshita, 1,400 feet above sea level, is the largest
and most popular of the hot springs resorts. It can be
reached from Tokyo in about 1½ hours aboard an express
train or by bus. It also can be seen on one and two-day

package tours out of Tokyo. There are several excellent
hotels and inns in the area, the most famous of which are
the Fujiya and the Kowaki-en, both of which have Western-style rooms and excellent hot springs baths.

Opened in 1878, the Fujiya is still a leading resort and
retains its character, rambling willy-nilly over a forested
mountainside and boasting one of the loveliest gardens in
Asia. Guest rooms are in several older buildings and a
new wing. In the older buildings, renovation has brought
the bathrooms and all fittings up-to-date without destroy-
ing the old-fashioned flavor of the rooms. The Fujiya sets
an excellent table in the old dining room. Its wood panel-
ing and carvings and ceiling murals of mountain wild-
flowers add to the delightful atmosphere. Two swimming
pools are available for a refreshing dip summer or winter.
The one outdoors in the huge garden is fed by a mountain
stream; the one indoors is fed by hot springs. During
summer, there's dancing on the terrace.

A short way up the road, the Kowaki-en consists of two buildings—one on each side of the road. A modern mix of Japanese and Western rooms, it has extensive gardens and facilities that range from a gigantic Polynesian bath to a bowling alley. It also has two pools: a hotspring pool in the garden features pool-side summer barbecues, and the other pool has a tropical setting complete with jungle-like growth and waterfall in a huge hillside hothouse.

Other hotels in the area are the Gohra Hotel at Gora, the Hakone Hotel on the shore of Lake Ashi, the Fujiya's Sengoku Annex, Hakone Highland Hotel, Hakone Kanko Hotel, Hotel Kagetsu-en, and the Kowaki-en Sengokuhara annex. In addition, the Hakone district has numerous *ryokan* that range from the rustic to the fanciful, the latter category discriptive of the Hotel Ryugu-Den. Perched atop a bluff overlooking Lake Ashi, it has tiled and curly-edged temple-like roofs and its own "dancing waters" fountains spouting out of the lake.

If you have the time, the Sengokuhara Plain, just a few miles from Miyanoshita, has four top golf courses, including one owned by the Fujiya.

Hakone is criss-crossed by good, woodsy walking trails that lead to Fuji viewing points and, in addition, a variety of aerial rope-ways (of which the Japanese are so fond) that make getting around fun. You can take a 10-minute cable-line ride from Gora to Mt. Sounzan and then transfer to a ropeway for a 33-minute ride down to the north end of Lake Ashi. En route, you'll pass over Owakudani's sulphurous fumaroles and catch glimpses of Fuji as the gondola sways along. Worth a look at Mt. Sounzan is the Hakone Art Museum's excellent ceramics collection. Another long ropeway runs up 4,400-foot Mt. Koma on the east shore of Ashi. At the top, there's a big skating center. Still another aerial ropeway can take you on a 13,000-foot aerial experience to Togendai on Lake Ashi. En route, at Owakudani Station, you get a superb view of the Hakone area and Mt. Fuji.

Geologists claim that the district is located in the huge crater of an ancient volcano—thus the hot springs. The various spas offer a variety of mineral waters: iron, sulphur, manganese, salt, each claimed to be beneficial for a long list of ailments in addition to being delightfully relaxing.

You can see some rather dismal thermal displays at *Owakudani* (Valley of Greater Boiling) and *Kowakidani* (Valley of Lesser Boiling): boiling deposits of grayish mud curtained by sulphurous fumes, steaming hot springs and erupting geysers.

Lake Ashi (more popularly known as Lake Hakone) is seven miles from Miyanoshita. It nestles 2,372 feet above sea level and has a 13-mile shoreline. The lake is

HOTELS IN THE HAKONE AREA, *like the Kowaki-en Hotel (above), are surrounded by landscaped gardens.*

especially noted for its splendid reflection of Mt. Fuji, which dominates the scenery in the area. A variety of excursion boats scoot across Lake Ashi all day long, providing point-to-point transfers as well as views. Among the boats, you'll find speedboats, a twin-hulled catamaran ferry and the *Pioneer*—a replica of a 16th-century European sailing ship with dummy sails and diesel engines. You can rent boats as well. Fishing for black bass and trout is excellent.

Hakone Shrine, founded in 757, holds a particularly picturesque annual festival on July 31 (see page 154). Other festivals are: Diamonji-yaki on Mt. Myojo on August 16 when a huge bonfire, constructed in the shape of the Japanese character for "large" is lit on the mountainside; Daimyo-gyoretsu, held on November 3, when a grand feudal lord's procession, in ancient regalia, makes a regal tour of the Hakone District.

Izu Peninsula

This is a broad peninsula that juts out into the Pacific about 40 miles. It is a picturesque piece of geography—pine trees abound and there are orange groves, stands of bamboo, apricot orchards and small farms. The whole area abounds with hot springs—and, as a result, with many good resorts.

At the head of the peninsula is Atami, about 65 miles to the southwest of Tokyo and easily reached by rail or bus in a hour and a half or two. From Atami, a branch rail line stretches for more than 40 miles along the picturesque east coast to Shimoda at the southern tip of the peninsula, and roads wind their way to the southern tip along either coast and right down through the Amagi Range, the mountainous center of the peninsula. The drive down the center is on a beautifully paved road through very pretty country. Oodaru Spa at Amagiso along the way is one of the few Japanese hot springs with outdoor baths.

You can reach Ito on the east coast by rail from Tokyo in about two hours, or you can take a leisurely three and a half hour trip along the west coast on a coastal steamer that runs from Numazu in the north to Matsuzaki, a small resort on the west coast that is blessed with a delightful climate and a lovely beach. Ito can also be reached by sea —though, in a round-about way: you have to go from Atami or Enoshima (south of Tokyo) to Motomachi on Oshima Island and then from Motomachi to Ito.

The unofficial capital of the area is Atami, a seaside town that is a tangled assortment of hotels, inns and souvenir shops. In the summer, it's filled to overflowing by Tokyo residents seeking relief from the big city's heat. There are more than 300 hot springs hotels and inns from which to choose, many with a view of the ocean, some tucked away in charming gardens. It is at its most pleasant in the spring, ahead of the crowds.

Atami boasts baths of every size, shape, temperature, mineral content, and decor. The miles of shoreline, east and west of the town offer some lovely seascapes. The town counts among its attractions one of the hottest natural springs in Japan (over 200 degrees F.). This spring, called Oyu (Great Hot Water), was once a famous geyser; but the earthquake of 1923 reduced it to a bubbling spring. It's now marked with an enclosure in the center of town, and its waters, considerably cooled, are supplied to several local inns and bathhouses.

Transportation to Atami from Tokyo is excellent. By the New Tokaido train, it is a 55-minute trip; by bus about two hours along the Tokaido Highway via Yoko-hama and Odawara. It can be reached by three bus routes from Miyanoshita in the Hakone District. The loveliest is a 23-mile ride which takes you over the 2,500-foot Juk-koku Pass (Ten Province Pass), so named because on a clear day the view encompasses ten surrounding provinces (with Mt. Fuji as a magnificent bonus).

Many of the resorts in Atami are air conditioned, have private baths, television and radio. Some have pools and sun-bathing areas. Some have nightly geisha shows for after dinner entertainment. When you check in, the resort issues you a *kimono* and sandals; and it's not at all un-usual to see fellow vacationers strolling the streets in them. If you do decide to take a *kimono*-clad stroll, there's no need to worry about finding your way back to your resort—taxi drivers or local residents will know

where you're staying by the name on your *kimono*.

Next to Atami, the most popular resorts are at Shu-zenji, Ito and Shimoda. In the mountains south and west of Atami, Shuzenji is one of the oldest hot springs spas on the peninsula (its use as a resort dates back to the 9th century). Located in the lovely wooded valley of the Katsura River, the little town is dominated by picturesque Shuzenji Temple, built in the early 800's. Nearby Shu-zenji Park offers some sweeping viewpoints, particularly from the summit of Mt. Daruma. If you'd like to try some camping, you'll find an excellent, well-equipped camp ground at Heda Pass, about five miles from the spa.

Ito, with more than 200 small hotels and inns, is the peninsula's second largest resort area. Located at the mouth of the Okawa River on the east coast about 15 miles from Atami, Ito combines a little history with its hot springs: William Adams, the first Englishman to set foot on Japan, built Japan's first European-type ocean-going ships nearby in the early 1600's. A monument has been erected in his behalf, and the townsfolk stage a Wil-liam Adams Festival every August 10 in his memory.

The Kawana Hotel near Ito is one of the best in the area. Situated on a scenic stretch of coast, it has 148 rooms, 3 swimming pools, an excellent Japanese restau-rant as well as dining room, grill and snack bar serving American and European food. Kawana's two 18-hole golf

courses laid out along the sea—the Fuji Course, with
Mt. Fuji in the background, and the Oshima Course,
which looks across to Mt. Mihara on Oshima Island—
are probably the finest in Japan. Known throughout the
golfing world for their setting and their sporty layout,
the courses are also famous for the girl caddies that add
an unusual fillip to the game.

About 30 miles south of Ito, Shimoda is a busy steamer
port (for off-shore islands) and fishing center that is
remembered principally as the site of the first foreign
consulate on Japanese soil. Following Commodore Perry's
landing and the treaty that followed in 1854, U.S. Consul
Townsend Harris established his consulate office in a
nearby temple. The old consulate has been preserved for
its historical interest and is just about as Harris left it.
Memorials and statues to Harris and to Admiral Perry
make it an interesting town to visit.

In addition to the attractions of beaches and hundreds
of hot spring spas, the peninsula offers a host of other
activities: stream fishing throughout the mountainous
center; coastal fishing at Mito, Kawana, Shimoda and
Ajiro; hunting for wild boar in the Amagi Range; hiking—particularly the two-hour hike from Amagi Pass to
scenic Lake Hatcho hanging about 4,000 feet on the
upper slopes of Mt. Amagi, from Ito to islet-dotted Lake
Ippeki, and from Shuzenji up 3,200-foot Mt. Daruma.

Shiga Heights

Joshin-etsu Highland National Park, about 4 hours northwest of Tokyo, is one of the most popular high-mountain areas for residents of the Tokyo-Yokohama area. Within its boundaries are active volcanoes, wooded mountains, lakes, brooks and hundreds of hot springs. It's hiking and picnicking country during the late spring, summer and early fall and excellent skiing country from early December to late April.

The skiing centers around Shiga Heights, an alpine retreat on the skirts of 6,300-foot Mt. Shiga. The area is interlinked by 43 lifts and 2 cableways. The first of the cableways starts at Maruike, the heart of the Shiga Heights ski fields, and extends to Mt. Hoppo, where a second runs up Higashidateyama, a peak just a little lower than Mt. Shiga. One long chair lift linkage makes its way to the top of 7,800-foot Yokoteyama.

The Shiga area has about a dozen ski schools, in some of which you can find instruction in English and German, and there's an international ski center with a Japanese instructor formerly of Stowe, Vermont.

Nikko

FISHERMEN *cast their lines into mountain stream near Lake Chuzenji. They're fishing for* ayu, *a trout-like fish.*

Nikko, about 90 miles northeast of Tokyo, is a small town situated right in the heart of Nikko National Park. The park is a forested mountainland of more than 200,000 acres—but its shrines and temples are the big attraction.

Most visitors see it on a one-day round trip out of Toyko. Several good hotels in the area, including the 94-room Nikko Kanaya (the largest), offer comfortable overnight accommodations. The area deserves a stay of at least two days.

Japanese National Railways and the Tobu Electric Railway Company provide daily service on a two-hour run from Tokyo, and there are one and two-day bus tours from the capital, also leaving daily.

Of Nikko's several temples and shrines, Toshogu Shrine is the town's historic gem and architectural wonder. It is the mausoleum of Ieyasu Tokugawa who, in the 16th century subdued the warring clans and united the country under his control, thereby becoming the founder of the Tokugawa dynasty of military rulers. The finest craftsmen and artists of the day were taken to Nikko to build this magnificent tribute to the first of the shoguns. Completed in its existing style in 1663, twenty years after Ieyasu's death, the shrine is the most elaborate and lavishly decorated in Japan. The buildings are coated with vermilion lacquer and are decorated with precious metals, including enough gold leaf to cover six acres, and intricate

TOSHOGU SHRINE in Nikko, a short distance from Rinnoji Temple. Once inside, you walk through huge granite torii.

carvings of infinite variety that have been kept in a state of perfect preservation through the centuries.

The several structures of the compound incorporate a fine mixture of Buddhist and Shinto architecture: a *torii* gate, a five-storied pagoda, the Sacred Library, a belfry and drum tower and the *Honden* (Main Hall) of the Inner Court, to name a few. The Sacred Stable in the Middle Court bears among its carvings the original of the monkey trio "Hear no Evil, Speak no Evil, and See no Evil." Yomeimon Gate, a two-storied structure which is the entrance to the Inner Court, particularly enjoys international fame for the profusions of its exquisite carvings.

The Toshogu Shrine Grand Festival, held here on May 18, is one of the most colorful in Japan. Warriors clad in the armor of Japan's feudal days parade with spears, swords, and banners. The autumn festival of the shrine, held on October 17, is similar.

Eleven miles from Nikko by well-paved highway is Lake Chuzenji. The well-engineered toll road climbs 30 hairpin curves in less than five miles. Or you can reach Chuzenji by a combination of a short cable car ride and

TO MASHIKO . . . TO WANDER AND WATCH THE POTTERS

About two hours north of Tokyo and only a short distance from Nikko, the village of Mashiko is an ideal expedition if you are interested in pottery as a craft or simply want to get some idea of rural Japan without lengthy travel. Some 30 potters work in Mashiko the year around, producing the distinctive, unsigned (traditional for folk pottery) Mashikoware. Flecked with the spots of iron ore found in the local clay, the ware is particularly known for its water jars and salt pots, usually glazed in brown or persimmon. Of late the potters also produce Western-style cups and saucers, and their beautifully hand-painted plates are universally appealing. As soon as you reach the village, you will see the pottery stores, open to the street, with the diverse wares of each potter on display. It's both pleasant and quite acceptable to wander in and out of the stores with no more than a smile of introduction. On the same main street you'll find a number of antique stores where "finds" still exist.

The potters themselves are at work everywhere, often in a room just behind the stores. You can feel free to walk into any of these stores and on into the potting shed. Without any verbal communication, you will be made quite welcome—to watch and wander at will. Some men will be seated at their wheels throwing the pots, while women and apprentices work at the glazing and decorating, often using their finger tips to create the design.

Mashiko's most famous potter, and the man responsible for the flourishing community that exists today, is Shoji Hamada. He moved there about twenty years ago, and has devoted himself to improving and strengthening the tradition of folk pottery in Japan. In recognition of his work, the Japanese Government has awarded him the title of "Intangible Cultural Treasure of the Nation."

Of course, there are a large number of pottery villages in Japan, especially in the area around Kyoto; but Mashiko is very accessible from Tokyo, and the work for sale there is likely to appeal to Western visitors. The Tourist Information Center in Tokyo (see page 9) has a stenciled information sheet on how to get to Mashiko if you decide to make the trip on your own. Actually, it's an easy trip. Take the train from Tokyo to Utsunomiya. From there it's a short trip by bus or taxi. Several *ryokan* in the village provide adequate accommodations if you decide to stay in the area overnight. You can see a great deal in a few hours, but even a couple of days of leisurely wandering don't become tedious.

SHOJI HAMADA, a potter who is an "Intangible Cultural Treasure" of Japan, throws a bowl in his studio.

*KEGON FALL is a 316-foot cascade near outlet
of Lake Chuzenji in Nikko National Park.
From Zao Spa (above) a cable car goes to Lake
Dokko in 13 minutes. Area is great for hiking.*

a ten-minute bus ride. An aerial ropeway from Akechi-daira, the terminal for the cable car, can take you on a short ride to a lookout point that provides superb views of the lake, Kegon Waterfall and the entire surrounding area.

Lake Chuzenji, a clear, fresh-water lake nestling at the foot of Mt. Nantai, is about 15 miles in circumference and almost a mile above sea level. The district around the lake is a charming highland resort, rimmed with cherry blossoms in mid-May and vibrant maples and birches in the fall. A nice way to see the lake is on one of the sightseeing boat rides.

Kegon Waterfall, a 316-foot cascade, is the lake's outlet. You can view it from a platform at the bottom of the gorge, which can be reached by elevator.

Nikko National Park has a number of other lakes and plateaus for boating and camping, several ski slopes, skating rinks and two golf courses. Fish abound in the lakes and streams and hunting is excellent. There are several hot springs spas within the park boundaries.

The regional handicraft specialty is woodcarving in which a variety of woods is employed—cherry, birch, bamboo, willow, pine—to produce many attractive items.

North and east to Tohoku

Few tourists venture beyond Nikko to Tohoku, the northeastern portions of Honshu. Some go to see the famous festivals, a few simply to enjoy the magnificent mountain country, rugged coastline and uncluttered countryside. During the summer months, this is a popular area for Japanese tourists, and you'll find hotels and transporta-tion facilities hard to come by. Spring and fall are probably the loveliest seasons to visit the area. You'll enjoy a proliferation of blossoming trees in late April and early May and a tapestry of autumn foliage that begins in late September.

An excellent network of rail, air and bus facilities serves the area, much of which is about 4 to 6 hours out of Tokyo on express trains. The peninsula's extremity, Aomori at the northern end of Honshu, can be reached in about 8½ hours from Tokyo by rail, about 2 hours by air.

It's wise to convert plenty of your money into yen before leaving Tokyo (you won't find it easy to do this at towns throughout the Tohoku area, except in Sendai). Similarly, you'll find that English is seldom spoken or understood by the local people. So arrange for an English-speaking guide. Warm clothing is recommended for the mountain areas.

The big festivals in the Tohoku area are the Nebuta Festival in Aomari, the Kanto Festival in Akita, the Hanagasa Dance Festival in Yamagata, and the Tanabata Festival in Sendai. All are held during one week, starting August 3 in the northern town of Aomari. The first three will require your making seat reservations (through your hotel or a travel agent in Tokyo). The festivals begin about 7 P.M. and last for about two hours. It's wise to get to your seat well in advance to avoid the crowds often numbering up to 50,000. The Tanabata Festival in Sendai requires no seat reservations. You observe it by walking through the streets, and the best time for this would be for an hour or two after 7 P.M.

Other attractions of Tohoku are largely centered around

skiing resorts in the area and three national parks: Towada Hachimantai in the far northeast, Rikuchu Kaigan along the coast, and Bandai Asahi centered around Lake Inawashiro and the interior mountain ranges.

Towada Hachimantai. Lake Towada, in Towada Hachimantai National Park, is rimmed with mixed forests of evergreens and a variety of maples and other deciduous trees. In autumn the forests are a dazzling blend of reds, yellows and purples made even more intense by the deep green of the evergreens and the blue of the lake. Towada is a huge, water-filled crater, about 28 miles in circumference and dotted with pine-clad islets.

The terminus for buses and the lake's 20 launches is Yasumiya. In the vicinity are several country inns, a youth hostel and a new hotel along with souvenir shops and small restaurants. The town is usually bustling with knapsack-equipped hikers. Fishing is excellent, and there's a small aquarium behind the Towada Science Museum that displays the variety you might catch. (Lake trout is a standard part of the breakfast menus at the local hotels). The museum has an interesting display of the area's varied flora and fauna.

Of the several launch trips available, the best is from Yasumiya to Nenokuchi at the mouth of the Oirase River. It takes about an hour, and the shore along the way changes from gentle sloping hills and numerous inlets and coves to rocky cliffs that rise sheerly from the water. From Nenokuchi you can drive or hike (the latter recommended) along the Oirase River to Yakeyama and Ishigedo—a distance of about 13 miles. The forest-crowded stream alternates quiet pools with white-foamed rapids and waterfalls, some of which cascade 20 to 25 feet.

Aomori, on Mutsu Bay north of Lake Towada, is walled off from the rest of Honshu by the peaks of the Hakkoda Mountains. A lumber town and busy port, Aomori is the southern terminal for ferries operating between Honshu and Hokkaido. The surrounding area bristles with hot springs resorts. Some of the bath houses in the area are gigantic—accommodating as many as 800 bathers at a time. Nearby Asamushi Spa, with its rows of modern steel and concrete hotels facing a beautiful bay, is known as the Atami of the Tohoku Region.

Rikuchu Kaigan. Stretching for more than 50 miles along the Pacific in the vicinity of Miyako is the seacoast park, Rikuchu Kaigan. The coastline varies from rugged, rocky beaches to fiords to towering cliffs that rise nearly 1,000 feet out of the sea. On sightseeing boats, operating on weekends out of Miyako, you see grottos into which the surf surges, huge pillars of rock, sea-eroded terraces and reefs—all with the background of deep green pine forests. Rhododendrons grow wild throughout the area and add their special brilliance to the countryside in late spring.

IN HIROSAKI, just south of Aomori, remains of Hirosaki Castle soar above a bower of blossoms in Oyo Park.

ABOVE THE TREETOPS, a double chair-lift carries skiers uphill to the slopes of popular Mt. Zao during ski season.

MATSUSHIMA BAY is dotted with more than 250 islands providing spectacular seascapes, superb voyage opportunity.

standing runs accommodating all classes of skiers, about a dozen rope tows, and 20 or so chair-lifts. Chair-lifts in Japan are predominantly single and are slow moving by United States speed standards. There are also two cableway carriers, one of which goes up in two stages to the upper slopes of the mountain at an elevation of about 5,400 feet. Illumination is also provided for night skiing.

Zao boasts a mix of purely Western hotels, Japanese-style hotels (most of which have both Japanese and Western rooms), *ryokans* and *minshuku,* all for a total of some four dozen establishments. Advance reservations are a must—it is almost impossible to secure accommodations in December or on weekends. One other Zao attraction: it's an *onsen* (hot springs) town so you can take a hot bath at the end of a long day of skiing.

Another of Japan's good ski areas, Tengendai, lies south of Zao between Lake Inawashiro and the city of Yonezawa. Less frequented by foreigners than Zao, it's for the more adventurous skier. The ski slopes are at the top of a long cableway where there's an adequate lodge for overnight stays.

Matsushima

Another of Japan's officially designated "Three Great Sights", Matsushima lies to the north on the eastern coast of Honshu, a little more than 4 hours by express train from Tokyo via Sendai. (The other two Great Sights are Itsukushima Island in Hiroshima Bay, page 130, and Amanohashidate, page 123.)

Endless *Haiku* have been inspired by the vast sea park in Matsushima Bay which consists of hundreds of strangely shaped islands, often grotesquely eroded and covered with gnarled pines. Sightseeing boats make excursions among the islands, past oyster and seaweed collection beds. Some consider it the most attractive sea voyage in Japan, surpassing in beauty the longer, less varied (although more famous) trip through the Inland Sea. From April through October, you can take a four hour sightseeing voyage from the boat base at Matsushima Kaigan to Oku-Matsushima and Saga Gorge, and a one-hour sightseeing cruise from Matsushima Kaigan to Shiogama is operated the year around.

Although the area is seldom visited by foreigners, the village of Matsushima-Kaigan has a number of small hotels and *ryokan,* some with resort facilities such as boating, swimming and tennis. An hour's walk from the village takes you to some small islands that are tied together by charming little red bridges which lead to ancient caves and old temples. To give you some idea of how long this area has been cherished by the Japanese, there's

Bandai Asahi. The region around Lake Inawashiro is a mountainous, lake-dotted area that owes much of its spectacular beauty to 6,003-foot Mt. Bandai. The mountain blew off about a third of its mass in an explosive eruption in 1888. The north slope is a sprawling plateau with more than 100 lakes, each a different color: indigo, cobalt, green, emerald, turquoise. You'll see evidences of volcanic activity throughout the area.

This second largest park in Japan (next to Daisetsuzan National Park in Hokkaido), Bandai Asahi comprises nearly a half million acres and embraces not only the Lake Inawashiro and Mt. Bandai area, but extends north to the Asahi Mountains and west into a primitive area around Mt. Iide. There are a few rail lines through some of the area and a few roads, the best of these being the 18-mile toll road (the Bandai-Azuma Skyline) that runs from Tsuchiyu along the western slopes of 6,336-foot Mt. Azuma to Takayu. Small hotels and *ryokan* at Takayu, Tsuchiyu, Goshiki and around Lake Inawashiro provide the best accommodations in the area.

Ski country. Skiers throng to the Tohoku area in the winter—particularly to Mt. Zao, a dormant volcano that lies just south of Yamagata, about halfway between Tokyo and Aomori. The Zao ski grounds have nine out-a "wave viewing pavilion" on a rocky cliff near the village that dates from the 16th century.

Sado Island

Another trip that would take you up through some of northern Honshu's beautiful mountain country is the one to Sado Island, lying off Honshu's west coast. Boats to Sado Island leave from Niigata which can be reached by air in an hour and a quarter or by limited express train from Tokyo in about four hours. Rail routes also run from Akita (four hours) and from Yonezawa (three hours), both cities in the Tohoku District.

It's a fascinating boat ride to Sado. The boats have *tatami* cabins, and the passengers bring picnic lunches (usually with a supply of *sake*) and are most friendly to any foreign visitors. A number of sailings are offered each day for the two and a half hour voyage. You'll see frequent shoals of flying fish in the channel.

Sado, the fifth largest of Japan's islands, has two parallel mountain chains, between which lies an extensive plain with small rice farms. Ryotsu, the main town where your ferry docks, sits on the shores of Lake Kamo and is reached from the sea by a narrow inlet. The towering peaks of the Kimpoku Range rise above the city. You can get around the island easily in a day by bus or car.

Part of the appeal of Sado is the traditional dress: blue *kimono* and circular folded cane hat worn by the women. Supposedly this hiding of the face with a hat dates from the era when it was forbidden to look upon the emperor. These picturesquely dressed ladies paddle along the island's rivers in half barrels—more these days for the benefit of tourists than for fishing or transportation.

You may want to buy some of the red porcelain ware made at the village of Aikawa. Called *Mumyoiyaki*, it is made from a local clay taken from old gold mines.

The old palace made of rough hewn timbers at Izumi (about 6 miles from Ryotsu) is interesting in that it was a place of exile for Emperor Juntoku for 22 years in the early 13th century.

Apart from these points of interest, the island has several ancient temples, a pleasantly warm climate and an abundance of natural beauty including extensive bamboo forests, some Japanese crested *ibis* (a "special natural treasure") and groves of camellia trees that brighten the winter scene.

Oshima Island

The smoking volcanic island of Oshima, in the Pacific Ocean southwest of Tokyo, can be reached by regular ferries from Atami or Ito in about two hours. Noted for its active volcano, Mt. Mihara, the island is considered part of the Tokyo metropolis. The Oshima Islanders are quite different from Japanese you see in Tokyo. They wear plainer, more traditional dress, white *tabi*, and a characteristic headdress. The women carry their burdens —even pails of water—on their heads.

Lush with vegetation, the island is particularly noted for its camellia trees. Mt. Mihara trails smoke from its crater, providing a landmark that can be seen far out to sea. The crater can be reached by trail, a hike that takes about 45 minutes (or you can rent a horse). If you can ignore the tourist rubbish that defaces the area, you'll find the crater—with its clouds of smoke and steam— quite dramatic.

The Oshima Kowakien Hotel, an old hotel with a new annex, is built in such a way that the smoking peak of the volcano seems to be placed right outside your window for your own private pleasure. The hotel's big bath house has a glass wall that offers a sweeping view over the slopes of Oshima and across to Atami and Ito on the Izu Peninsula with majestic Mt. Fuji towering in the distance.

In addition to the Oshima Kowakien, there are some other smaller hotels and some charming *minshuku* (see page 14).

ON SADO ISLAND, *girls practice the* okesa *dance on the beach, wearing the costumes characteristic of the island. Folded cane hat is designed to prevent looking at Emperor.*

HIKERS PAUSE at Lake Happo in the Japan Alps (above). Cloisonné workers (right) incise a design on huge vase; cloisonné is chiefly made in Nagoya and Kyoto. A patchwork of crops (far right) is typical of farmlands in Nagano Prefecture, central Honshu.

Central Honshu ... the Nagoya Area and the Japan Alps

In the Nagoya area you may tour farms whose crop is pearls, see tame birds on leashes retrieve fish for men wearing traditional costumes, shoot the rapids on the Kiso River. And also in the locality are Japan's two most sacred shrines, repositories for precious relics of the Imperial Family. History, handicrafts, and heavy industry, castles, ships, parks, pottery and beautiful cloisonné—these, too, are part of the Nagoya scene. And to the north and east of Nagoya in this center section of Honshu lie the Japan Alps, towering mountains that provide a year-round playground for residents of Tokyo and Yokohama and for visitors who seek off-the-beaten-path experiences in Japan.

Nagoya

The super-express trains on the New Tokaido Line of the Japanese National Railways make frequent runs between Tokyo and Nagoya, the nation's third largest city, in just two hours. On all Nippon Airways it's an hour-long flight. Getting about in Nagoya is an easy matter as there is excellent bus service, a subway, and plenty of taxis.

Western-style hotels in the area include the Fujikyu Kanko, International Hotel Nagoya, Nagoya Kanko, Nagoya Miyako, the New Nagoya, and the recently completed Hotel Nagoya Castle. For those who prefer the Japanese inn, there is the Aoiso Fujikyu.

First stop on your city tour will probably be Nagoya Castle, a prime subject for your camera. Originally constructed in 1612 by Ieyasu Tokugawa, founder of the Tokugawa shogunate, it was destroyed during World War II. Reconstruction of the castle, topped by the famous "Golden Dolphins," was completed in 1959. The castle grounds and the five-storied donjon (inner tower) are now open to the public for a small fee.

Next on your itinerary might be the Atsuta Shrine, venerated because it houses the *Kusanagi-no-Tsurugi*

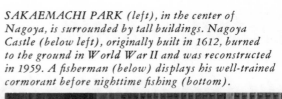

SAKAEMACHI PARK (left), in the center of Nagoya, is surrounded by tall buildings. Nagoya Castle (below left), originally built in 1612, burned to the ground in World War II and was reconstructed in 1959. A fisherman (below) displays his well-trained cormorant before nighttime fishing (bottom).

(Grass-mowing Sword), one of the nation's Three Sacred Treasures, the other two being the Sacred Mirror at Ise Grand Shrines and the Sacred Jewels at the Imperial Palace in Tokyo.

One of Asia's largest zoos is in Nagoya's Higashiyama Park; it has no fences to obstruct your view of the animals. It is open daily from 9 A.M. to 4:30 P.M. You will also find in this extensive park a botanical garden with its large collection of rare plants from all over the world, and a 33-foot wooden image of Kannon, the Goddess of Mercy.

Nagoya is the greatest center of pottery, porcelain, and cloisonné manufacture in Japan and a trip to one of these factories is fascinating. Tours through the Noritake chinaware factory and Ando cloisonné company may be arranged by your travel agent or through your hotel.

Cloisonné is an ancient art requiring the utmost patience, skill and delicacy. You will be shown how a design is outlined on a silver or copper base with fine ribbon-shaped silver or gold brass wires glued edgewise to the base. The sections are then filled with various enamels, created from formulas that are closely guarded family secrets. Further elaborate processing—vitrification, grinding, and polishing—is necessary to produce the exquisite plates, vases, bowls, and boxes typical of this art.

Riding the rapids

For a change from the passive pleasures of sightseeing in Nagoya, take a sidetrip to nearby Kiso River for an exciting ride down the rapids. There are several points of embarkation, reached by train or bus from Nagoya. Boats and boatmen may be hired, March through November, for the 6 to 7½-mile trip downriver to Inuyama. Boats vary in size, but all are perfectly safe. The trip is not dangerous as the boatmen are well-trained and experienced. Don't let the thrill of the ride keep you from noticing the scenery along the way, so lovely that this part of the river is popularly known as the Rhine of Japan. Inuyama, the terminus, is noted for its lovely white feudal castle perched on a hill overlooking the rapids. Transportation back is provided.

Gifu for cormorant fishing and parasols

Almost every night from May 11 to October 15, a curious spectacle takes place on the Nagara River at Gifu—cormorant fishing. From a lantern bedecked pleasure boat, you can see large tame birds, harnessed by long leashes, retrieve ayu (river smelt) for their masters by the light of fire baskets hung from the boats.

Cormorant fishing at night is an ancient industry still carried on at several places in Japan, but Gifu is considered the best place to see the remarkable performance of these teams of birds and men. Only thirty minutes by train from Nagoya, it is a gay excursion, particularly if you go with a group. Your travel agent or your hotel can make reservations for you. The boats, lighted with gay paper lanterns, are usually provided with food in the form of delectable snacks cooked over a hibachi, sake, samisen music, a geisha or two, and fireworks to add to the merriment. Spectators usually board their boats by 6:00 P.M. The fishing, which usually lasts about 40 to 50 minutes, takes place between 7:00 and 9:00 P.M. Despite the fact it is so well organized for tourists (around 100 boats go out each night), the atmosphere of ancient Japan—something that is getting harder and harder to find—remains untouched here.

Only a few families are entitled by tradition and law to carry on this industry which has been taking place for a thousand years. The famous poet Basho immortalized it in a poem in 1668:

> *After the brightest sight*
> *Of the cormorant fishing*
> *There remains a loneliness alone,*
> *The gaiety diminshing.*

The boat you ride to watch the fishing is a long, flat-bottomed craft with a canopy sheltering a tatami floor and a low table that runs the length of the boat. Unless you are with a group that has ordered food as part of the package tour, buy a picnic supper . . . it comes in an exquisitely decorated lacquer box accompanied by jars of sake and tiny sake cups.

Poled along the river by skilled, lithe boatmen, the boats are guided by other men who walk along the bank holding lines. Finally the spectators' boats are maneuvered into a line and chained together, there to await the coming of the fishing boats. During the wait an oblong barge, festooned with lanterns, drifts out of the darkness. As it drifts by the moored spectator boats, a dozen graceful girls in white kimonos and traditional hairdos dance to the music of the samisen. Other little crafts weave in and out, their owners selling fireworks.

Then come the noiseless fishing boats, with flaming beacons at their bows. Usually the fishing flotilla has from four to seven boats, four men to a boat. The usho (master) stands in the bow, dressed in the costume worn by cormorant fishermen for centuries: a type of straw skirt, rope sandals and a black cloth tied around his head. The master manages 12 birds, and his assistant takes care of four more amid ships. One man steers, and the fourth man keeps the fire flaming in the iron grate that is suspended from the bow of each boat. The fire attracts the fish and enables the fishermen to manage the cormorants.

Each cormorant (most are from Kushigata and trained for three years before they are used for fishing) has a ring around its throat, preventing the bird from swallowing the fish it catches. Each bird is tied to a hand string controlled by the fisherman. When the cormorant is pulled in, the fish are removed from its gullet and the bird is sent off again in search of more prey.

The parasol factory in Gifu is one of the few still active in Japan, its present prosperity due to a large extent to its export trade to the United States, where *bangasas* (Japanese parasols) have become somewhat of a fad. The factory makes both paper parasols (the special paper comes from a village to the north) and silk dancing parasols, each one individually painted. A cottage industry, the making of the bamboo frames is spread throughout the homes in the Gifu area. If you buy a *bangasa* at the Gifu factory, they cost from Y700 to Y2,000 and can be shipped direct from Gifu to your home.

Gifu is 20 miles north of Nagoya and may easily be included as a side excursion on trips between Tokyo and Kyoto. Western-style hotel accommodations are provided in the Gifu Grand Hotel and the Hotel Nagaragawa.

Porcelain making center

Seto, about 50 minutes by rail northwest of Nagoya, has been one of the major centers for porcelain production in Japan since the 13th century. It rose to fame after Toshiro Kato, the builder of the first kiln in Seto, went to China in 1223 to study the art of porcelain making. The skills he developed at that time have been handed down—with improvements and innovations—from generation to generation. Today there's a Tokuro Kato still active in the city's porcelain business; and in place of the single kiln, there are now more than 1100 kilns in more than 900 separate factories. You can go shopping for some of the locally produced porcelain at the Ceramic Center near Seto's city hall and see one of Toshiro Kato's masterpieces, the *koma-inu* (lion-like dog), at the Fukagawa Shrine in Seto.

Ise-Shima National Park

About two hours south of Nagoya by Japanese National Railways lies the Ise-Shima National Park, created in 1946 and covering the larger part of Ise and Shima provinces. Its mild climate, beautiful scenery and seascapes provide a lovely setting for two disparate but very interesting attractions: the Ise Jingu Shrines and the cultivated pearl farms of Ago and Ise Bays.

To get there, take the new Tokaido super express train to Nagoya and transfer to the Nagoya-Ise Shima Express. Trains leave Nagoya every half hour from 6 to 11 A.M. and every hour on the hour from 11 A.M. You get off at Ujiyamada Station, (a trip of about 90 minutes) and take the 10-minute bus ride to Naiku. Buses run every 20 minutes from 6 A.M. to 8 P.M. daily.

Located in a beautifully laid out park of more than 200 acres, the Ise Grand Shrines, as they are popularly called, are among the most venerated and ancient in Japan. The Geku (Outer Shrine) is dedicated to Toyouke-Omikami, the Goddess of Crops and the Naiku (Inner Shrine) to Amaterasu-Omikami, the Sun Goddess. The two shrines are about four miles apart but are easily accessible by bus or car.

Presenting a vivid contrast to the huge, ornately carved and decorated shrines found elsewhere in Japan, the two shrines are small, built of unpainted cypress with no ornamentation or decoration. The classic simplicity of their architecture represents a style that predates the introduction of Chinese architecture into Japan in the sixth century. These shrines are the purest examples of indigenous Japanese architecture. The buildings show very distinct resemblance to similar structures found in Indonesia and the southern Philippines. Built before the Iron Age, they were put together without nails or metals of any kind.

The Geku is only a short walk from the station. It stands in a magnificent grove of ancient Japanese cedars and is approached by an avenue which passes under the traditional three torii gates. Along the way you will see the Anzaisho (House of Sojourn) where the Emperor rests when visiting the shrine; the Sanshujo (Place of Assembly) for other members of the Imperial Family; and the Kaguraden where sacred dances are held. The Main Hall of the Shrine, 33½ feet long and 19 feet wide, is enclosed by four wooden fences of different styles. Between the first and second fence on the east side of the shrine is the Mikeden where food offerings are set out twice daily. There are several other buildings on the grounds, including a number of smaller shrines. One, Kaza-miya, is dedicated to Deities of the Wind.

Naiku resembles Geku in general layout. After crossing a small foot bridge and passing under the first *torii*, pilgrims go down to the bank of the river to touch the sacred water with their fingers, regarded as an act of purification before visiting the shrine. Naiku also has the beautiful setting of lofty, age-old cedars. There are several buildings within the four fences surrounding the shrine. Within the Naiku reposes the Yata-no-Kagami (Sacred Mirror) supposed to have been given to the Sun Goddess, ancient ancestress of the Imperial Family, when she came to reign on earth. The Sacred Mirror along with the Grass-mowing Sword (at Atsuta Shrine, Nagoya) and the Sacred Jewels (Imperial Palace, Tokyo) constitute the Three Sacred Regalia of the Imperial Family. The Sacred Mirror is said to have been enshrined on this site in about the 4th century.

To this day, it is a practice of the Japanese leaders to visit this shrine to announce to the Sun Goddess any

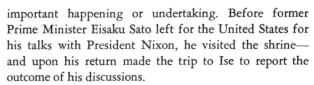

SACRED SHRINE (above) at Ise Shima, one of Japan's most venerated. Oyster divers (upper right) at a Mikimoto pearl farm bring up oysters to be seeded and then returned to the water. Craftsman at Gifu (right) is putting finishing touches on a parasol, one of Gifu's specialties.

important happening or undertaking. Before former Prime Minister Eisaku Sato left for the United States for his talks with President Nixon, he visited the shrine—and upon his return made the trip to Ise to report the outcome of his discussions.

The general public is not permitted beyond the first fence at either shrine, and courtesy calls for the visitor to remove his hat and overcoat in front of the shrines.

Pearl Farms

Japan's famous cultured pearl industry is centered around Ago Bay and five other bays off Ise-Shima National Park. On a tour of this area you may see the entire process involved in creating these lustrous gems. In addition, there are the lovely seascapes provided by the many island-dotted bays and inlets of the park.

More than 65 years ago a former noodle maker, Kokichi Mikimoto, developed the method of artificially stimu-

lating oysters to produce pearls by inserting an irritant (a grain of special sand) inside the oyster, causing it to secrete the nacre of which pearls are formed. The irritant sand, strangely enough, comes from the bed of the Missouri River near St. Louis. Over a period of several years this process was refined and perfected and Mr. Mikimoto became known as "The Pearl King." Today, K. Mikimoto, Inc., is the world's largest producer of cultured pearls.

Women divers collect the oysters which are then "seeded," placed in cages and suspended from bamboo rafts. The pearls are harvested anywhere from six months to seven years later, sorted and ground polished before being incorporated into myriad jewelry forms.

Toba, the rail terminus at Ise Bay, is approximately two-and-one-half hours by train from Nagoya and nine miles from the Ise Grand Shrines. Several travel agents run tours through the area from Nagoya to Ise Grand

Shrines and Mikimoto Pearl Island with overnight accommodations at Shima Kanko Hotel on Ago Bay. You can take a launch cruise on the bay that winds through the miles of pearl rafts and offers an opportunity to see the women pearl divers at work.

In addition to pearls, this area is famous for its delicious beef. Tours usually include a meal in Matsusaka whose restaurants have been famous for beef specialties for more than 90 years. Like the Kobe beef, the fine quality of the Matsusaka beef is believed to be the result of feeding beer to the cattle.

Cross-island to Kanazawa

Kanazawa, almost due north across the island from Nagoya, is a quiet, uncrowded city—an ideal setting for strolling. Untouched by war and unscarred by modernity, Kanazawa retains the flavor of old Japan in a physical isolation that contributes to recreating the feeling of times past. Kanazawa, home of the famous Kenrokuen Garden (see page 47), is also known for its row upon row of ancient *samurai* residences surrounded by earthen walls, all built during feudal times.

However unscarred by modernity it is, Kanazawa does offer Western-style accommodations. The Hakuunro, half-Western, half-Japanese style, is typical of pre-war luxury resorts. A short distance out of town, the Hakuunro overlooks a boating lake and a fish-stocked stream. The city's downtown hotel, the Kanazawa Miyako, is air conditioned and has 63 Western-style rooms as well as a dining room, cocktail lounge and a range of shops.

Kanazawa is the site of the Eiheiji Temple, a famous Zen Buddhist temple, where you can stay overnight—*if* you join in the meditation that begins at 3:30 A.M. The cost is about Y2,000 per person and includes a spartan bed and bath, but a superb *shojin* cuisine—an all vegetable fare that is a delightful epicurian experience. Brought to you by a novice, the food is served in lacquer ware bowls embellished with the distinctive Eiheiji crest.

The cultural city of the area, Kanazawa was a one-time capital of the Maeda clan that made its fortune in the 16th century. If you are on the trail of the officially designated Important Cultural Properties of Japan, Kanazawa and the general area make up a rich hunting ground. Typical of the city's treasures is the three-story high gate at Omaya Shrine near the city's railroad station. The rewards of strolling reveal interesting architectural details—details that bring to mind old woodblock prints and a feeling of antiquity.

Since ancient times, Kanazawa has been famous in Japan for its silk textiles, excellent lacquer ware and the world renowned Kutani porcelain (a factory is located conveniently close to the city). The traditional crafts are perpetuated in the local university's arts and crafts college.

Because it can be reached in about two hours by train from Kanazawa, the Noto Peninsula makes an easy day's excursion. The peninsula stretches some 85 miles into the Japan Sea and has a wild and picturesque topography of hills and mountains and a rugged, indented eastern coastline. An hour or so up its east coast lies Tsukomo Bay that partially encircles a knot of islands, some of which have fishing villages. Motor launches take off practically from the doorstep of the popular hot springs resort, Kagaya Inn, at Wakura on the bay, and cruise about the islands.

On the west coast of Noto Peninsula, you can again pick up the trail of Important Cultural Properties. One, the main hall of Keta Shrine, is set against a luxurious primeval forest facing the sea. Several buildings of the same cultural importance are a few miles farther along in the Myojoji Temple, one of the great Buddhist temples of the area.

The Japan Alps

In the center of Honshu, about half way between Tokyo and Kyoto, lies the "roof of Japan"—the Japan Alps. This spine of mountains lies north and east of Nagoya. You pass the fringes of these mountains if you take the Tokaido express between Tokyo and Kyoto. In the winter, the train will be alive with ski-garbed young Japanese on their way to Nagoya and from there to the alpine ski country. In the summer, the clothing of young people changes to blue jeans and knapsacks for the hikers headed for the clean air and the trails that lace this lovely mountain country.

If you choose the route between Tokyo and Kyoto that goes around the back side of Mt. Fuji and through Matsumoto, you ride right through this alpine country. It's a considerably longer way to get to Kyoto from the capital (so not many tourists use that route), but the scenic rewards make up for it. It's a striking contrast to the relatively flat, straight route followed by the Tokaido express. You can make the trip by rail or car.

These are the loftiest mountains in Japan—with many peaks soaring more than 10,000 feet. Mixed forests of evergreen and deciduous trees make for spectacular, displays of autumn color. If you want to stay overnight in the area, you'll find a number of Western-style hotels in such places as Ohtsuki, Kofu and Matsumoto and an abundance of *ryokan* throughout the mountains. Staying in one of these lovely mountain inns makes the trip more of a Japanese experience than simply a trip into the mountains.

In addition to hiking, horseback riding, swimming, boating and all the other normal mountain activities, you'll find castles, temples and shrines to explore. You can also ride rapids through the gorge of the Tenryn River south of Matsumoto. Not as well known as the ride on the Kiso rapids (see page 91), it is an exciting but not a dangerous trip.

Ski resorts abound throughout the Japan Alps, but the most celebrated in the area is at Happo-one, just north of Omachi. Noted as the "best alpine course in Japan," it has 20 lifts, a 6,000-foot cableway and night illumination. For accommodations, you'll find the usual assortment of *ryokan* and the Hakuba Tokyo Hotel with 44 Western rooms and 15 Japanese.

Probably the best base from which to climb some of the higher reaches of the mountains embraced by Japan Alps National Park is Kamikochi. Situated in a beautiful hidden valley about three hours by bus due west of Matsumoto, the area has a number of excellent *ryokan*, several well developed camping areas and the superb Kamikochi Imperial Hotel (with either Western or Japanese-style rooms). The Kamikochi Valley lies along the upper reaches of the Azusa River and is surrounded by towering peaks, several of them over 10,000 feet. Trails leading up into these highlands start from the Kamikochi area, some requiring six and seven hours of tough climbing. One relatively easy hike can be made to the summit of 9,800-foot Mt. Norikura, a conical volcano that has numerous small lakes near its summit. To get to the top, you take a bus from Kamikochi to Norikura Hut; the hike to the summit is a little less than two miles and takes about an hour and a half.

A small folklore museum near Takayama in the Hida District north of Nagoya is worth a visit if your explorations of the Japan Alps takes you into the area. Called Minzokukan, it's housed in a structure called a *gassho-zukuri* that is typical of the architecture of some of the remote valleys in the Hida Mountains. The structure appears to be a three or four-story dwelling. Made of wood, it has a towering roof thatched with grass. The design was developed in the late 16th century when silkworm culture was a livelihood in the area. The upper floors are actually bamboo slatted layers that held silkworm trays, the trays kept warm by the heat and smoke rising from the family living quarters on the ground floor. The spacious ground floor is large enough to have held *all* the members of several generations of a family—often as many as 25 or 26 persons. This particular house was moved from an area now inundated by the waters behind Mihoro Dam. More than a thousand folklore articles have been collected for display in the museum.

Takayama itself is an interesting old castle city that offers some beautiful views of the Hida Mountains. You'll probably want to buy some pieces of the locally-produced lacquer ware called *shunkei-nuri*.

SKIING ENTHUSIASTS will find plenty of snow in the environs of the Japan Alps all year long. To get to Nagano (above) takes about 3½ hours from Tokyo by train.

ALPINE HIKERS on Mt. Goryu in Japan Alps. Area abounds with hot springs, a welcome relief to hikers; many ryokan *and Western-style hotels afford bases for climbers.*

HEIAN SHRINE (above) on a winter's day. Built in 1895, it commemorates the 1,100th anniversary of the founding of Kyoto. At right is a billboard with a conglomerate of advertising for restaurants and bars. At far right, a narrow alley lined with handicraft shops is typical of many throughout Kyoto.

Kyoto...Ancient Capital, Living Museum

To many visitors, Kyoto's quiet and gentle ambience is the very core—the soul, if you will—of Japan. This city of almost a million and a half seems quite far from the madding crowd of Tokyo, even though on the surface (in the central section, at least) it is busy, somewhat drab, and dirty. You have to go beyond the clanging street cars and honking automobiles to find the quietness, the gentleness of this "living museum."

A city of imposing ancient palaces, temples, royal villas and shrines numbering more than a thousand, Kyoto dates from the year A.D. 794. That was when Emperor Kammu built this ancient capital of Japan, the city that of all Japanese cities remains the illustrious treasure house of the nation. The richness of these 1,200 years of history is on display.

The essence of Kyoto, however, is comprised of far more than a matchless collection of palaces and temples and shrines. It comes through in less tangible ways: the harmony achieved between the planned city and its unplanned natural features; the aspects of the changing seasons and how they relate to the daily life of Kyotoites; the sights and sounds (and the lack of sounds in places) that contribute a gentleness, a softness, a subtle gracefulness to the city.

Among Kyoto's fortunate attributes is its preponderance of straight streets, laid out in a checker-board pattern when the city was designed. For visitors, it's an easy place to get around without memorizing a complex street map.

The real beauty and charm of Kyoto can best be experienced by taking a stroll—or as many strolls as you can manage. Not too many tall buildings break the skyline, the main streets are wide and relatively unchaotic, and there are many trees. Off the main streets the city blocks are cut by small lanes, some so narrow that driving them in even a small Japanese car takes some tricky maneuvering. Many of these lanes are lined by simple and beautiful houses of one or two stories. For the most part Kyoto

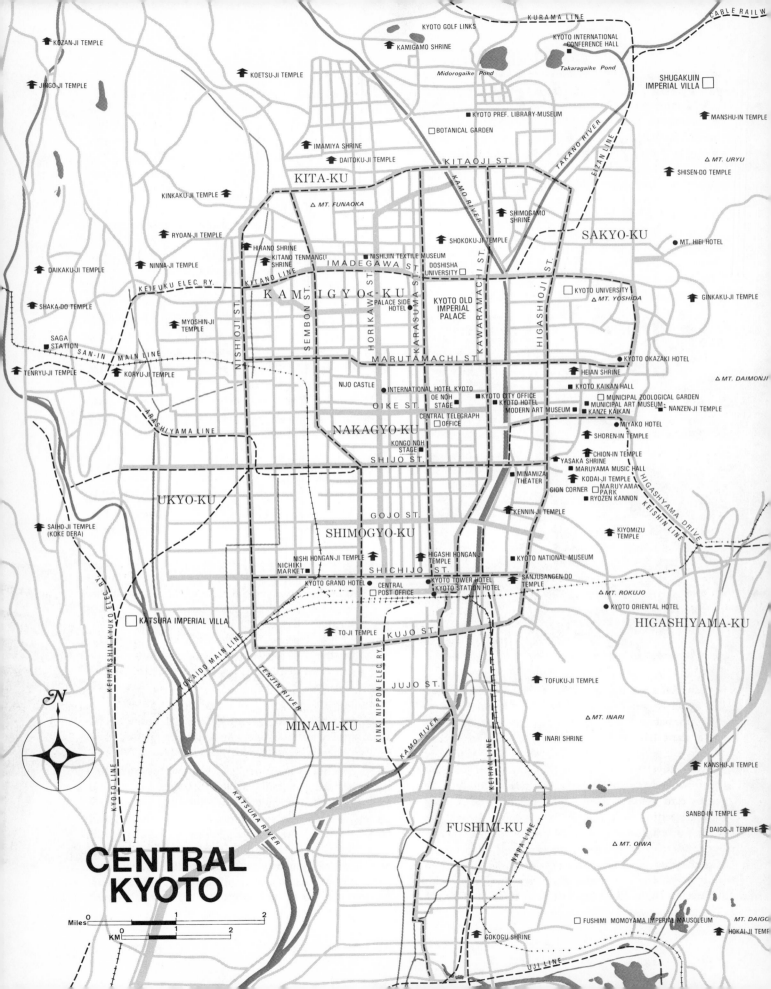

CENTRAL KYOTO

KURAMA LINE
CABLE RAIL W'Y

KYOTO GOLF LINKS

KOZAN-JI TEMPLE

KAMIGAMO SHRINE

KYOTO INTERNATIONAL
CONFERENCE HALL

JINGO-JI TEMPLE

KOETSU-JI TEMPLE

Midorogaike Pond

Takaragaike Pond

SHUGAKUIN
IMPERIAL VILLA

KYOTO PREF. LIBRARY-MUSEUM

MANSHU-IN TEMPLE

BOTANICAL GARDEN

IMAMIYA SHRINE

△ MT. URYU

DAITOKU-JI TEMPLE

KITAOJI ST.

SHISEN-DO TEMPLE

KITA-KU

KAMO RIVER

TAKANO RIVER

EIZAN LINE

KINKAKU-JI TEMPLE

△ MT. FUNAOKA

SHIMOGAMO
SHRINE

SAKYO-KU

RYOAN-JI TEMPLE

SHOKOKU-JI TEMPLE

△ MT. HIEI HOTEL

HIRANO SHRINE

NISHIJIN TEXTILE MUSEUM

NINNA-JI TEMPLE

KITANO TENMANGU
SHRINE

IMADEGAWA ST.

DOSHISHA
UNIVERSITY

KYOTO UNIVERSITY

GINKAKU-JI TEMPLE

DAIKAKU-JI TEMPLE

KEIFUKU ELEC. RY.

KITANO LINE

KAMIGYO-KU

PALACE SIDE
HOTEL

KYOTO OLD
IMPERIAL
PALACE

KYOTO OKAZAKI HOTEL

△ MT. YOSHIDA

HIGASHIOJI ST.

SHAKA-DO TEMPLE

NISHIOJI ST.

SEMBON ST.

HORIKAWA ST.

KARASUMA ST.

KAWARAMACHI ST.

△ MT. DAIMONJI

SAGA
STATION

MYOSHIN-JI
TEMPLE

SAN-IN MAIN LINE

MARUTAMACHI ST.

HEIAN SHRINE

TENRYU-JI TEMPLE

KORYU-JI TEMPLE

NIJO CASTLE

INTERNATIONAL HOTEL KYOTO

KYOTO CITY OFFICE

KYOTO KAIKAN HALL

ARASHIYAMA LINE

OIKE ST.

OE NOH
STAGE

KYOTO HOTEL
MODERN ART MUSEUM

MUNICIPAL ZOOLOGICAL GARDEN
MUNICIPAL ART MUSEUM
KANZE KAIKAN

NANZEN-JI TEMPLE

CENTRAL TELEGRAPH
OFFICE

NAKAGYO-KU

MIYAKO HOTEL

SHOREN-IN TEMPLE

UKYO-KU

KONGO NOH
STAGE

CHION-IN TEMPLE

YASAKA SHRINE

MARUYAMA MUSIC HALL

SHIJO ST.

MINAMIZA
THEATER

KODAI-JI TEMPLE

HIGASHIYAMA DRIVE

GION CORNER

MARUYAMA
PARK

GOJO ST.

RYOZEN KANNON

SAIHO-JI TEMPLE
(KOKE DERA)

SHIMOGYO-KU

KENNIN-JI TEMPLE

KIYOMIZU
TEMPLE

KEISHIN LINE

NISHI HONGAN-JI TEMPLE

HIGASHI HONGAN-JI
TEMPLE

KYOTO NATIONAL MUSEUM

NICHIKI
MARKET

SHICHIJO ST.

SANJUSANGEN-DO
TEMPLE

KYOTO GRAND HOTEL

KYOTO TOWER HOTEL

CENTRAL
POST OFFICE

KYOTO STATION HOTEL

△ MT. ROKUJO

KATSURA IMPERIAL VILLA

KYOTO ORIENTAL HOTEL

HIGASHIYAMA-KU

KEIHANSHIN KYUKO ELEC. RY.

TO-JI TEMPLE

KUJO ST.

TOKAIDO MAIN LINE

KINKI NIPPON ELEC. RY.

TENJIN RIVER

JUJO ST.

TOFUKU-JI TEMPLE

△ MT. INARI

KYOTO LINE

MINAMI-KU

KAMO RIVER

KEIHAN LINE

INARI SHRINE

KATSURA RIVER

KANSHU-JI TEMPLE

FUSHIMI-KU

NARA LINE

SANBO-IN TEMPLE

DAIGO-JI TEMPLE

△ MT. OIWA

Miles 0   1   2

KM 0   1   2

FUSHIMI MOMOYAMA IMPERIAL MAUSOLEUM

MT. DAIGO

GOKOGU SHRINE

HOKAI-JI TEMP

UJI LINE

houses are made of wood mellowed to a deep, rich brown, or of the warm, sandy stucco that is used all over Japan. Street windows and entryways are screened by airy, fence-like enclosures. One lane—the one your hotel is located on, for instance—may be the site of homes, a green grocer (busy very early in the morning, with big radishes, hens, and a variety of produce spilling into the street), an antique shop and several tiny shrines. This is Kyoto come to life—and each lane you pass seems more intriguing than the last.

Another fascinating quality of Kyoto is the juxtaposition of the old and the new in the downtown area. There is no city in or out of Japan where such contrasts quite compare.

A great many Kyoto visitors would find it difficult if not impossible to cite the most intriguing facet of the city. But visitors who have stayed for any length of time almost always include the gardens, along with the temples, palaces and shrines, as uniquely beautiful aspects of Kyoto. In all of Japan it would be hard to find a collection of gardens more esthetically and artistically pleasing. They play a strong part in creating the essence of Kyoto.

Where to stay

Kyoto's major Western-style hotels—Miyako Hotel, International Hotel Kyoto, Kyoto Hotel, Kyoto Grand Hotel, Kyoto Royal Hotel, Hotel Fujita and the Kyoto Station—are completely air-conditioned and enjoy a high reputation for accommodations and service. Most of the hotels have some Japanese-style rooms or separate cottages in addition to their Western-style rooms. So if you want to experience Japanese-style living in a Western-style hotel, have your travel agent reserve one of these. There also are some excellent Japanese inns (see page 37) in the area which are accustomed to catering to visitors.

How to get around

Taxis are plentiful in Kyoto, and you pay by the size of the cab. Rates are higher for U. S. cabs, but in general, taxi travel is inexpensive and convenient. Hotels maintain information booths from which you can call a taxi for a short trip or hire it for a day's sightseeing. It usually is a good plan to have a well marked map ready for your driver so that he will take you where you want to go without communication difficulty. Remember to carry a card with the name and address of your hotel to facilitate getting back to your starting point. Rather than hire a car, many foreign tourists utilize one of the excellent coach tours to get around the city—and this is especially advisable at the outset of your Kyoto visit. You get an overview that is a useful preliminary to more specific sightseeing jaunts. Bookings can be made at most hotels.

What to see

Since Kyoto offers so much, you must tailor your sightseeing to your time and personal interest. Historically important castles, palaces, museums, art galleries, shrines and temples, where art treasures and cultural properties are preserved, are located in many areas of Kyoto and its suburbs. Here are some suggestions for your itinerary:

Castles and palaces

Nijo Castle best displays Kyoto's many-sided nature. Here you will see masterpieces of art, buildings of splendid architectural beauty, gorgeous interior decoration, the celebrated Garden of Ninomaru, and gates with outstanding wooden carvings and exquisite metal work. If you visit Nijo Castle in the fall, you'll get to see the chrysanthemum exhibits on the castle grounds.

Originally built in 1603 by Ieyasu, founder of the Tokugawa Shogunate, as a residence for his visits to Kyoto, the castle now is owned by the city and open to the public. It is registered as a "Place of Historical Importance," and its buildings and art are "National Treasures."

The castle grounds of 70 acres are surrounded by stone walls with turrets at two corners. Its compound consists of five buildings. The most famous is the Ohiroma or third building, which contains the Great Hall, audience chamber of the shogun, which is decorated with "Paintings of Pine Trees Mounted on Walls" by Tanyu Kano (1602-74), official painter of the shogunate government and most influential artist of his time.

COMBINING old with new, the Kyoto International Hotel is typical of the excellent hotel facilities in Kyoto.

TEAHOUSE and garden at the Katsura Detached Villa. Above is audience chamber of Nijo Castle.

Old Imperial Palace, surrounded by high walls, is situated in the 220-acre Kyoto Imperial Park. Close to it is Sento Gosho, the palace for retired Emperors. In the southwest part of the park is the Office of the Imperial Household Agency where permits to enter the buildings are granted only to foreigners who apply directly or through their travel agent at least one week in advance.

The palace is open to Japanese only twice during the year and is closed to all visitors Saturday afternoons, Sundays, national holidays and the period between December 25 and January 5.

Emperor Kammu, who founded Kyoto as a capital city, built the original Imperial Palace in 794. It and a succeeding palace were destroyed by fire. The existing palace, which dates only from 1855, follows the same design as the original and is noted for its noble simplicity.

The Imperial Household Agency rigidly controls visits and may exclude you if you are late. As a visitor, you are expected to behave as though the royal household were in residence. Shoes are taboo, so be prepared with your own slippers or slip into a pair at the entrance.

You are admitted through one of the west gates. You sign the visitors' book and show your permit at the guardhouse. From here a palace guard, accompanied by an interpreter, if you are lucky, will admit you to the former royal palace through the "Honorable Carriage Approach." You first visit the rooms of dignitaries, then you enter the *seiryoden* (serene and cool chamber), so called because the stream from Lake Biwa runs under its steps. Before you enter the chamber you step on a squeaky or

"musical" floor known as *naruita* (alarm-board), placed there to warn the noblemen of a stranger's approach.

The main hall of the *seiryoden,* partitioned into three apartments, was used for minor ceremonials, and you will observe the matted dais, covered with elaborate hangings, upon which the Emperor of the time sat. He was protected by two wooden *komainu,* fabulous legendary animals said to ward off evil spirits, which still guard the steps to the dais. Sliding screens of the chamber are decorated with paintings of the Tosa school. Each painting has its own descriptive Chinese or Japanese poem and the imperial crest of the sixteen-petaled chrysanthemum is everywhere in evidence.

You will next visit the ceremonial hall used for more important functions of the state. Here the enthronement of the Emperor and the annual New Year's party took place. Rich silk draperies, stands for the sacred treasures (swords and jewels are absent) and sliding screens exhibiting paintings—representative of originals of 22 Chinese sagas—are fascinating.

Shugakuin Detached Palace. The detached palace of Shugakuin Rikyu, or Imperial Villa, is situated at the west of Mt. Hiei on the site of the Shugakuin Temple (Temple of the Ascetic Doctrine). To visit this palace you must show your permit from the Imperial Household Agency, remove your shoes, refrain from picture taking and bow when it seems indicated.

The park-like grounds cover 69 acres and are divided into three large gardens landscaped on different levels— uppermost, middle and lowest. Each garden contains a summer house called *ochaya*. The villa originally was constructed in 1629 by Iyetsuna Tokugawa, the 4th Shogun, as a reatreat for the ex-Emperor Gomizuno-o.

Entering the uppermost, considered the most beautiful of the three levels of gardens and pavilions, you go through the south gate and climb steps to a small two-room summer pavilion known as the Rin-untei which was the ex-Emperor's retreat. It is situated on Dragon Bathing Pond with Myriad Pine Trees Islet in the center. This is the highest point of the palace grounds and you get a superb view of the gardens, city and surrounding hills. The pavilion has two balconies. On the north side is the Poem Composing Balcony opposite the *odaki* (male waterfall) and a west balcony which faces the *medaki* (female waterfall).

You descend the steps and cross two bridges to another summer house located on an island. The name of this summer house is written in Japanese on a table. The three characters, written by the ex-Emperor himself, represent Kyusuitei. On another island, you find an arbor topped by a gilt bronze phoenix, and after a short walk you enter maple valley, particularly impressive in autumn.

The middle garden, Naka-no-chaya, contains the Rakushiken (house of bliss) originally a building of the Rinkyuki Temple established for Princess Mitsuki, daughter of the ex-Emperor. The ex-Emperor wrote the inscription over the entrance. The building is decorated with many art treasures, including a set of small paintings by Yuzen, inventor of the method of dyeing called *yuzenzome,* and a sliding door painting of the procession cars (*yama* and *hoko*) still used in the Gion Festival (page 154). Note the carp paintings on both sides of the wooden door. This has caused much Japanese amusement through the centuries. The original was done by Gukei (1631-1705), who did the sliding door, but there was no net. Okyo, a famous 18th century artist, added the golden net in which the carp are now enmeshed to prevent the realistic fish from "going out every night to join the carp in the lake outside."

The last garden, Shimo-no-chaya, contains two houses constructed primarily for the tea ceremony.

Shrines and temples

The shrines of Kyoto are Shinto and the temples are Buddhist. You can distinguish the shrine by its *torii,* a kind of beamed propylaeum or gate, and a temple by its Buddha or Buddhas. Shintoism and Buddhism have had profound effect upon each other and upon the customs and manners of the Japanese people.

Selection of the shrines and temples to visit depends upon the length of your stay and the areas in which you are sightseeing. Often you come across a temple or group of shrines when you are taking a leisurely stroll. You

KAMIGAMO SHRINE in Kyoto is a Shinto shrine built in 9th century. It's a short distance from the Botanical Gardens.

always are welcome to watch a worship ceremony if you show respect by being unobstrusive.

Kinkakuji, or Rokuonji Temple, popularly called Gold Pavilion because of the gold foil which covers it, belongs to the Shokokuji school of the Rinzai sect, one of the three main branches of Zen Buddhism. (Kyoto has temples of 30 different sects, each a headquarters.)

The pavilion, which is an exact reproduction of the 1397 original, stands in a lovely garden at the base of Kinugasa Hill in the north part of Kyoto. The landscaped garden is regarded as one of the finest in Japan.

Ginkaku-ji Temple, known as the Silver Pavilion, is even more lovely (and far older) than the Gold Pavilion. It dates to 1483 (the Gold Pavilion burned in 1950 and was rebuilt in 1955). The two remaining original buildings of the Silver Pavilion are in excellent condition, and the gardens are among the best preserved natural gardens of their period.

Buddhist temple of 1001 statues. Sanjusangendo is the Buddhist temple of 1001 statues of the Kannon Bodhisattva. One thousand of the gilt wooden images stand row upon row, 500 on one side of the main altar, 500 on the other, just as they have stood since 1266. All are alike. At the center of these phalanxes is the principal

KIYOMIZU: A CAPSULE DISPLAY OF MISTY GROVES AND PAGODAS

When you look at the hill you must climb to explore Kiyomizu Temple, you may be tempted to skip it, but this is no place to falter. The temple complex amounts to a capsule display of what you go to Japan to see, and its elevated position is ideal for viewing central Kyoto and musing on the misty groves and pagodas on the hills all around.

An hour is all you need to see the buildings and approaches. Add whatever time you wish for contemplation in the gardens and for shopping along the pedestrians-only extension of Gojo Street that ultimately becomes a series of short, stone staircases leading up to the temple grounds. The way is lined with souvenir stands and pottery shops—sort of a "Teapot Lane."

Among the structures—most of which were rebuilt in 1633, although the temple itself was built in 805—one of the most pleasing is a wide three-story pagoda flanked by mellow, old pavilions with gracefully upturned eaves. But the outstanding architectural achievement is the relatively plain but imposing open-air veranda of the main hall. Most of the veranda rests on a massive trestle of great timbers rising boldly from the pine and maple forest in the ravine to the south. The site is dedicated to the 11-headed Kannon, or Goddess of Mercy.

KIYOMIZU TEMPLE with three-story pagoda is part of a capsule display of old Japan. Above, massive temple veranda is supported by a trestle.

image of the temple, a solemn Kannon with 11 faces and 1,000 arms. With candles and long, thin aromatic sticks of incense, offerings by worshippers burn in stands before it. If luck is with you, you will see the morning mass, conducted by a priest wearing vestments of scarlet and deep purple. You can watch as he kneels and recites the mass and carries out the age-old rituals.

Kiyomizu Temple is a complex of buildings stairstepped up a hillside and famous for cherry blossoms in April, maples in November (see above).

Heian Shrine has no long history. It was built a mere 100 years ago when the government moved to Tokyo. It is a replica, 12 times reduced, of the original Imperial Palace of 794. Here tourists will enjoy the simple vermilion and green buildings; the impressive *torii* gate, largest in Japan; the magnificent gardens, pond and bridge behind the shrine; and in proper season, chrysanthemum displays, weeping cherry trees, azaleas, or "snow scenes."

At Heian Shrine you may have a chance to catch glimpses of one or several wedding parties, especially in autumn, as a Shinto ceremony is the most popular way of getting married. See page 24.

Kyo-Ogokokuji Temple, best known as Toji (East Temple), was established in 823 by Kobo-Daishi, founder of the Shingon sect. Original buildings, largely destroyed in the civil wars of the 15th century, have been rebuilt. The main hall of the temple is one of the largest buildings of the Momoyama Period (1573-1615) now extant. The temple's five-storied pagoda is the highest pagoda in Japan. It stands 182.6 feet on a raised base. The *azekura* (storehouse) is built of wood without nails, and contains a large collection of art objects considered unrivaled by any other Kyoto temple. Many of the works are registered as "Important Cultural Properties" and include fine Chinese and Japanese carvings and a 12-roll illustrated history of Kobo-Daishi.

Higashi Honganji Temple, a magnificent temple with massive roofs, is considered by some architects to be the best existing example of Buddhist architecture. Visiting foreigners have special privileges at this temple, so apply at the temple office if you wish to visit apartments and buildings not open to the general public. The junior headquarters of the Jodo-Shinshu sect of Buddhism, this temple is visited by thousands of believers. The pavilion is devoted to the presentation of Noh lyrical drama. The Chrysanthemum Gate (Gate for Imperial Messengers), a copy of a Fushimi Castle gate, is a point of interest.

Chion-in Temple is the headquarters for the Jodo sect founded by the priest Honen. Worshipers seeking to be reborn in Jodo (Pure Land) or the Western Paradise of Amida (Buddha Amitaba) have to recite, day and night, the prayer formula *Namu-Amida-Butsu* as many times as possible.

Fires often have ravaged the temple buildings, but of those now standing, several date back to 1633-39. The Sammon, two-storied gate, is 80 feet high and known as Japan's most imposing gate. Behind the main hall the corridor is so constructed that every step of a visitor or intruder emits a floor sound resembling the song of the *uguisu* (Japanese bush warbler). This architectural phenomenon, similar to that found in the Nijo Castle, is attributed to Jingoro Hidari.

Kamo Shrines at Shimogamo and Kamigamo, in the northern Kyoto district, are famous for the *Aoi Matsuri,* or Hollyhock Festival, held annually (see page 91). A historic horse race, started in 1903 as a form of prayer for a good harvest, is conducted at Kamigamo Shrine every year on May 5. Twenty horsemen dressed in court costumes worship at the shrine and perform other ceremonials; then they race on the track which is within the shrine precinct.

Kyoto walks

The real beauty and charm of Kyoto is best experienced by taking a stroll—or several. It's a rewarding way to get to know the city. Streets and various areas are filled with a special charm, and it is in these places that you will find the candid face of Kyoto.

One place to begin is at the end of Shinkyogoku Arcade, a roofed and popular amusement center paralleling busy Kawaramachi Street, site of the Kyoto Hotel and municipal offices. It is, of course, impossible to hurry to the arcade from your inn or hotel. There are so many shops to catch the eye—everything from a shop dealing in pickles to one selling religious goods (Buddhist rosaries with beads of various hues to represent the many troubles of man, simple and elaborate home altars, bronze candlesticks, lotus blossom stands, incense, figures of Buddha).

The arcade is lined with souvenir shops, theaters, cake and cookie stalls and restaurants. These last seem always to have a red, black or white chalk cat, its paw raised in welcome in a window. Movie houses display pictures of current *samurai* and American western epics. Tucked into a lot near a movie house is a tiny temple.

Shops that produce silver-dollar-size pound cakes have their baking machines right in the window, and at other open-to-the-street shops you watch girls making crisp rice flour and ginger cookies with a hot griddle top and two wooden blocks. You see little shops that sell personal seals, simple wooden ones and antique seals of ivory, amethyst, coral. There are shops selling *mah jong* sets, and a shop where a man patiently and carefully chisels house numbers out of stone.

At the far end of the arcade, where it joins Shijo Street, you find an apothecary's shop, its window full of herbs,

STURDY STEPPING STONES in a pond in the Heian Shrine gardens. Superb garden is a favorite of photographers. Pond is lined with iris in the spring.

TOGETSUKYO BRIDGE *spans the Oi River and reaches one of the beauty spots of Japan: the densely wooded ridge of Arashiyama, covered by maples, cherry trees and pines. A close-up view (lower left) of the Oi River and trees. Kyoto is the center for geisha training (below). Children (bottom) make a game of crowding into a hula hoop.*

roots and nameless things; dried and live salamanders; dried, powdered, pickled and live snakes.

You turn down Shijo Street toward the Kamo River. Almost across the street from the apothecary shop on Shijo stands one of Japan's ultra-modern department stores. "Super stores," such as this one, begin with a supermarket in the basement, where many types of seafood may be seen, and usually end with a zoo on the roof.

Other places of business will catch your eye: a shop selling geisha wigs and ornaments; a cafe specializing in eel, with cook and charcoal stove in view of the street; crowded pachinko parlors, offering upright pinball machines, prizes of candy, cigarettes and canned goods; a shop displaying nothing but *kokeshi* dolls, cute, cylindrical folk dolls with nodding heads; a shop selling lanterns and umbrellas and another dealing in old-fashioned wood combs; a theater fronted with lanterns and big signs advertising a modern comedy.

You cross the Shijo Bridge over the Kamo and see the many restaurants facing the river. Shijo Street ends at the gate of the Yasaka Shrine.

Other favorite walks include ones in Ohara (within the city limits but still called a village) where you touch the heart of rural Japan. Several easy walks lead to the small temple of Sanzenin, whose main hall stands virtually as it did in the 10th century, and to the hilltop Jakko-in-Nunnery, a small solitary gem of a building with a tiny garden breathing the sad story of a young empress dowager of the 12th century. The garden is considered one of the best places in Kyoto for maple viewing. Because the nunnery is always crowded, go there early in the morning or during the off-peak season for fullest appreciation. The whole Ohara area is planted with maples, and fall color from early November through the middle of the month is incomparable.

A walking area somewhat comparable to Ohara is that of Saga-Arashiyama, about a half-hour drive out of the city. Subject of poems and pictures, it was once an excursion place for emperors of the Heian period. Kyotoites today make annual excursions there to see the cherry blossoms in spring and maples in fall color and listen to the singing of the mountain frogs. And while you're in the area, you can explore Gioji Temple, associated in legend with a dancing girl turned nun, and Rakushisha, summer residence of a famous *haiku* poet.

For a pleasant in-city walk, try the one along the old canal lined with cherry trees between the Nanzenji Temple and the Silver Pavilion. Watch for the little alley that flanks the canal, called the Path of Philosophy by scholars.

Another city walk between sightseeing attractions is between Maruyama Park and Kiyomizu Temple, through an area that gives the visitor the best cross section of all the contrast that Kyoto offers. It's a favorite for Kyoto people because it combines cherry blossoms in the spring, maples in autumn color, large and small temples and shrines, a pagoda, a ceremonial gate, a charming stone stairway, parks with beckoning paths, a fine city view, picturesque small streets and curio shops, old houses and pottery shops.

For a look at another segment of Kyoto life, walk through Nishiki Market, a narrow 10-foot-wide street about a quarter of a mile long and lined with produce, poultry and fish shops, groceries and dry goods shops. The market dates back some 400 years. Today housewives and restaurant food buyers shop here for the best and the freshest produce—at the rate of some 60,000 shoppers a day who throng the market from early morning until late afternoon.

Other attractions

Kyoto is traditionally the center of the *geisha* art—the place where most of Japan's *maiko*, or apprentice *geisha* girls, receive their training. The two main *geisha* schools are the Gion-machi and Pontocho. You can see the girls on the streets in the area of the schools—especially in the evening—with their elaborate *kimonos*, special hairdos and elevated wooden clogs. For more on the *geisha*, see page 33.

The Minami-za Theater, in the area of Gion-machi, stands on the site of the first *kabuki* theater in Japan and *kabuki* is performed here much of the year. The colorful Miyako Odori or Cherry Dance is performed at the Kaburenjo Theater in Gion-machi from April 1 till about May 18. Before each performance you may take part in the tea ceremony which is presided over by a *geisha* who is highly skilled in this important art. Dancers are dressed in brilliant kimonos and the Cherry Dance consists of graceful posturing to the accompaniment of *samisen*, (lute-like musical instruments), flutes, drums and sometimes bells.

Kyoto National Museum was erected in 1897 by the Imperial Household as a repository for art objects and other treasures possessed by Buddhist temples, Shinto shrines and individuals. The museum has three departments—history, fine arts, handicrafts—and exhibits include some 1,000 rare and valuable examples of art in 17 rooms which include Chinese ceramics and archaeological displays of note.

Botanical Gardens are on the left bank of the Kamo River. Opened in 1923, the gardens commemorate the enthronement of the late Emperor Taisho.

Kyoto University, the second oldest national university in Japan, was founded in 1897 and has faculties of literature, education, law, economics, science, medicine,

A QUIET POND in the gardens makes a mirror image of Kyoto's Kinkakuji Temple, also called the Gold Pavilion.

engineering and agriculture. Its Yukawa Memorial Institute perpetuates the achievements of Dr. Hideki Yukawa who won the 1949 Nobel Prize in physics.

Ryozen Kannon, a 75-foot ferro-concrete, seated statue of the Buddhist deity, Kannon, Goddess of Mercy, stands at the foot of Ryozen Hill in the precincts of Kodaiji Temple. It was erected in 1955 as a monument to the world's unknown soldiers and to "console the spirits of those killed in World War II."

Maruyama Park is the principal public park in Kyoto and it is famous for its display of cherry trees which are illuminated at night when in bloom.

Standard sightseeing tours

A variety of bus tours is available, all accompanied by English-speaking guides. You can choose from morning or afternoon tours; after-dark tours that combine visits to a temple garden to hear music with a nightclub floor show; a garden tour and tea ceremony; a trip to watch the cormorant fishing on the Uji River; an art and craft route which includes visits to a woodblock printing studio, a tea ceremony and a silk dyeing factory; and a

village life tour which includes a bird sanctuary, a farmhouse, a *bonsai* village, along with craft demonstrations and a *tempura* lunch.

There are others, of course, or you can have your travel agent arrange for private car and an English-speaking guide for Y13,000 to Y15,000 per day for each person in a party of two persons.

Kyoto's gardens

Kyoto provides the setting for some of the finest examples of Japanese landscaped gardens classified into two general types, the *tsukiyama* (hill garden) of hills and streams and ponds, and the *hiraniwa* (flat garden), a flat area with stones, trees, lanterns, water basins and wells as the decorative elements. For a list of the Kyoto gardens of exceptional beauty, see page 46.

Home visit program

The Kyoto Municipal Government has made arrangements so visitors from overseas may visit a Japanese family and learn what real Japanese home life is like. Application must be made two days in advance to the Tourist Industry Department of the Kyoto Municipal Government or to the Japan Travel Bureau (your own travel agent can make arrangements for you). There is no charge for this program.

Gion Corner

Gion Corner, set up by the Kyoto Visitors Club at Yasaka Kaikan in Gion, offers foreign tourists a chance to glimpse various phases of traditional Japanese arts. Shown twice a day, at 8 P.M. and 9:10 P.M., are the tea ceremony, flower arrangement, *Bunraku* (puppet play), *Kyomai* (Kyoto-style Japanese dance), *Koto* music and *Gagaku* (court music). The visitor who fancies himself to be a aficionado of Japan may look upon this show as somewhat lackluster, but it does serve as a simple introduction to some phases of the Japanese culture. Tickets are available at Gion Corner or from your hotel. Admission is Y1,000 per person.

Shopping

Things of lacquer are among Kyoto's most beautiful handmade goods. Not only can you buy these fine pieces of lacquer ware, but you can see how they are made.

The famous Nishimura Lacquer Factory (established in 1657) invites visitors for a lesson in lacquer ware production. You are courteously escorted to a special workroom where you learn that the finest lacquer is made over a cypress base and that lacquer is tapped from trees just as latex is tapped. You are shown how it takes some 30 coatings, applied over two months, to make a fine item, and that some six months in all is required to apply both lacquer and design. The lacquer is polished during coating, with whetstone, charcoal and calcined deer horn and oil. Antique lacquer is sometimes cheaper than good new ware because of today's labor costs.

You can stroll through a museum-like series of display rooms. You can watch men laboriously applying designs to bowls, boxes and trays and repairing old lacquer. Then you can stroll through the beautiful display rooms.

Only in Kyoto can one find *Yuzen* cloth, a fabric whose dyes (a special process developed 300 years ago) must be washed in the clear running waters of the Kamo River to achieve the perfection of color.

In Kyoto, too, is the delicate *Nishijin* silk brocade intricately handwoven in the picturesque old Nishijin district where the sound of looms pervades the narrow back streets.

Pottery reaches a point of delicacy in color and design in Kiyomizuyaki which originated in the 16th century. Other things bearing the Kyoto stamp of tradition include Kyoto fans of delicate design, old folding screens, perfumed incense in sachets, stone art for gardens, boxwood combs, and elaborately costumed *Kyo-ningyo* dolls.

KYOTO'S FLEA MARKET . . . FOR SINGING CRICKETS

On the 21st day of each month in Kyoto the kaleidoscopic fascination of a flea market comes around. And kaleidoscopic it is—a vast and varied collection of stalls set up for the day at the Toji (East Temple), just a few blocks from the Kyoto Station and not more than a few minutes by taxi from any of the major hotels.

If you've ever been bitten by the flea market bug, you may find that Kyoto's Toji Flea Market eclipses most others in color, liveliness, and good humor—and, of course, bargains. You could spend the better part of a day wandering around and browsing at stalls that sell everything from singing crickets in tiny bamboo cages to seaweed and baby chicks. And there's much more, all under canvas awnings that cover bamboo frames in a village of multi-colored market stalls open from mid-morning until late afternoon. It's alive with bargain hunters and housewives, hawkers and occasionally tourists.

The gamut of goods runs from potatoes, peaches and pickles to live crabs, bean curd, crockery, readymade skirts, even umbrella handles, potted plants, and a multitude of shoes (rubber boots, sandals, scuffs, sneakers, wooden clogs), some new, some secondhand. You'll find such hardware items as hammers and adzes, chisels, saws, planes, and crowbars, nails, screws, hooks, braces, angle irons, and wrenches, right along with ready-made clothing, cushions, kimonos, bedding, and light housekeeping wares. There's food, too: spun sugar candy, noodles, chopped squid and cabbage fried in batter, and other delicacies.

Outside the gate is a Japanese auction. Theirs is the reverse of ours. Instead of the auctioneer taking one piece and raising the price as the bidding drives it up, the auctioneer takes a piece, sets the price, and raises the number of pieces at that price as the bidding progresses. One plate, for example, may be marked for Y500 and has no takers. The auctioneer raises it to two plates for Y500, then three, four, and so on. The buyer, in this reverse order of things, may wait as long as possible to bid, hoping to get ten plates for that Y500.

If you're lucky enough to be in Kyoto on the 21st of the month, you can sample this merchandising facet of Japan that is in dramatic contrast to the Japanese department stores—those huge, ultra-modern emporiums with standardized floor arrangements and a multiplicity of services. The Toji Flea Market, in the shadow of the tall wooden pagoda of the Toji, seems more like a scene out of ancient Japan.

SIDEWALK VENDOR at flea market does a brisk business selling a variety of colorfully printed fabrics.

If a venture into seeing things made whets your appetite, you can spend an entire day seeing Kyoto craft displays. The Tatsumura Silk Mansion has a display of several weavers as a courtesy. One makes *obis* of complicated patterns and colors, with silver and gold threads on a Jacquard loom that looks like a prehistoric IBM machine. The complicated patterns may take as much as two weeks to set up. The weavers who create the more complicated designs have been at this craft for more than 20 years. Their *obis* will cost as much as Y100,000. Few tourists are in the mood to purchase Y100,000 *obis*, so the mansion thoughtfully provides a display house packed with a wide variety of printed and brocaded silks.

Kyoto's makers of cloisonné, damascene and woodblock prints all have similar open-house policies. Travelers from the mechanized West are likely to be amazed when they compare the price of finished products with the amount of hand labor that goes into them. Damascene, for instance, involves the chiseling of numerous fine lines on a steel foundation, followed by the inlaying of a design (in the chiseled area) in gold and silver, the corroding of the steel by acid, the application of lacquer and polishing. All by hand.

Another place to look and linger is the Kyoto Handicraft Center. Here you can watch craftsmen at work and buy their products too. A very pleasant restaurant on the top floor has a lovely view of the surrounding area. Most big hotels run a bus service to the center.

When you start to shop, you will find you can buy dainty brooches and earrings of damascene for Y700 to Y2,000.

Silk scarves of varied hues and sizes can be had for anywhere from Y500 to Y2,000. Silk brocade cigarette cases start at Y500.

Dining—and after dark

You'll find a limited choice in Western-style restaurants in Kyoto. Your best bet is probably the Alaska and the Western-style hotels.

There are a number of good Japanese restaurants—with emphasis on the excellence of the surroundings and the elegance of the service. In comparison with Toyko-style cooking, Kyoto cuisine is less seasoned, less colored by soy, and much more subtle in taste. From the standpoint of price, dining in the best Kyoto restaurants serving authentic Kyoto dishes may not be inexpensive (a *kaiseki* dinner can run as high as Y9,000), but it is an uniquely aesthetic experience that goes beyond mere eating.

All of the more familiar Japanese dishes—*sukiyaki, tempura, sashimi, sushi*—are to be found in Kyoto, plus some of the best beef in the world. Kyotoites, however,

recommend the traditional dishes as another way of savoring the essence of Kyoto. Typical is *kaiseki*, a mixture of fish—raw, baked, steamed—with vegetables and special soups; *shojin ryori* or Zen-style vegetarian dishes (in unbelievable variety); *makunouchi bento*, a glorified box lunch where the box is lovely lacquer ware and the contents such things as fish, eggs, chicken, rice, prepared with special artistry.

Some 40 Kyoto restaurants are listed in the Japan National Tourist Organization's *Restaurants in Japan* guide. If you're looking for especially good ones for Kyoto-style cuisine, keep these in mind: Hyotei, which specializes in *kaiseki*, a 350-year-old teahouse that once served temple pilgrims and still preserves its rustic atmosphere; Kikusui, also specializing in *kaiseki*, one of the most luxurious of Kyoto's *kappo ryokan* or restaurant-inns, and situated in a lovely garden; Kitcho, another one that specializes in *kaiseki*, located on a wooded hillside with a view of Arashiyama on the Oi River, and probably the ultimate in elegance and artistry of food and service (even the traditional last course, bowls of rice and soup, are individually prepared for each diner); Nakamuraro, also a restaurant-inn, located at the foot of Yasaka Shrine, another one that began as a teahouse about 250 years ago; Isecho, dating to the 18th century, its main restaurant downtown, geared to large groups, and two branches, one in the Gion area and the other in the Kyoto Hotel; Oku-

ふぐ料理
てっちり 六〇〇
てっさ 三五〇
おみやげ持帰りできます
出前配達も迅速にいたします

KYOTO CRAFTSMEN at work (above, center) on block printing, a craft the Japanese have excelled in for centuries. Above, the street sign of a Fugu (blowfish) restaurant serving a delicacy favored by those with a sense of adventure. At right, the interior of a typical Japanese nightclub.

FAMED RESTAURANT, Ponto-cho in Kyoto
(upper left) features geisha girl entertainment.
Father and son (lower left) are dressed for
the Matsuo Shrine festival in Kyoto. Above,
a typical tea house at Katsura Detached Villa.

tan, in the Nanzenji Temple compound (serving both indoors and out), which specializes in Zen-style cuisine; Nishiyama Sodo, in the Ienryuji compound, which specializes in *yudofu* (cooked bean curd dishes) and other vegetable concoctions; Ikkyu, in front of the Daitokuji Temple, also specializing in Zen-style cuisine (with advance notice this restaurant will cater to tour groups in one of the nearby temples); Minoko at Gion, good for *kaiseki* and specializing in the lacquer box lunch; and Minokichi, in a farmhouse setting in the Okazaki area, also specializing in the lacquer box lunch. Other good restaurants include Jyunidan-ya, Dai-Ichi, Karafune and Hamamura.

Note: prices will range from as little as Y700 at Okutan and Nishiyama Sodo to highs of Y6,000 to Y10,000 at Kikusui, Kitcho, Jyunidan-ya and Nakamuraro—plus tax and gratuity.

Though considerably subdued in contrast with Tokyo, Kyoto has its own Asakusa District with motion picture theaters, *pachinko* parlors, a multitude of small hostess-equipped bars, and a few nightclubs and cabarets. The best of the big nightclubs are Bel-Ami and Gion.

Other nighttime diversions include the Gion Corner programs (see page 106) and a nightclub show with music at the Bel-Ami which features international entertainers and *kimono*-clad hostesses. Free limousine service is available between Gion Corner and the Bel-Ami, and it's possible to take in both attractions in one evening.

Unique to Kyoto is an evening exhibition of martial arts, a fast moving, hour-long performance which includes demonstrations of *karate, kendo* and *judo* by experts. It's held at the Nihon Seibukan, the largest martial arts academy in the Orient. Pickup service is available from major hotels, and taxis are called for you for the return trip.

Kyoto would probably be the best place to try a *geisha* party, and there are several teahouses where this can be arranged. This is apt to be a rather costly evening—Y10,000 or more per person. Both men and women are welcome at such parties.

Sound and light

Something new has been added to the usually rather quiet Kyoto nighttime scene: a sound-and-light show titled *The Heian Years*. Presented jointly by the Kyoto International Hotel and the Travel Center of Japan in the hotel's lovely Japanese garden, it's a 40-minute show given nightly, first at 8 and again at 9:15. The show recounts Kyoto life of 1,000 years ago as recorded in the diaries of Imperial Court ladies. Taped voices are those of the members of the Royal Shakespeare Company of England; the score is based on authentic music from the Heian period.

Seating capacity for performances is limited to 125 persons per show. Contact Kyoto International Hotel or Travel Center of Japan offices before you leave Tokyo to arrange for reservations.

Festivals

Kyoto is rich in festivals. There is probably no other place in Japan where they are such an integral part of the life of the people. The three main festivals are the Hollyhock Festival, the Gion Festival and the Jidai Festival.

The Hollyhock Festival takes place on May 15 at Kamigamo and Shimogamo shrines and has been celebrated for 1,400 years. Kyotoites, dressed in ancient court costumes, reproduce the imperial processions made to the shrines in feudal times. Starting at Kyoto Palace, they pull magnificently decorated chariots and offer hollyhocks to gods and goddesses of the shrines.

The Gion Festival, on July 17 and again on July 24, celebrates a 9th century legend of a religious parade that saved the old imperial capital from a plague that was ravishing the land. Scores of richly decorated floats, accompanied by gongs, drums and flutes, parade through the main streets in a two-hour procession.

The Jidai Festival, on October 22 at the Old Imperial Palace and the Heian Shrine, commemorates the founding of Kyoto in 794. A grand procession of people in costumes representing Japan's main periods of history takes place for three hours.

These are only three of more than a dozen festivals that take place in Kyoto throughout the year.

Flowers and tea

The placing of flowers in temples as an offering to Buddha was the beginning of Japanese *ikebana* or the art of flower arranging. With the development of the tea ceremony it became customary for the host to place a

SOUND-AND-LIGHT SHOW ("The Heian Years") unfolds nightly in the handsome gardens of Kyoto International Hotel; guests can watch the activity from this vantage point.

PROCESSION of white-robed participants is part of the Jidai Matsuri (The Festival of Eras) held at the Heian Shrine in Kyoto once a year in October.

flower arrangement in the tea room. From these traditions the art grew and was refined. Today Japan has some 3,000 different *ikebana* schools, and Kyoto is the ideal environment in which to study the art.

The Japanese believe that a tiny tearoom in the Ginkakuji (the Silver Pavilion) was the birthplace of Japanese *ikebana*—and that both *ikebana* and the tea ceremony originated here at about the same time.

Perhaps the most interesting introduction to *ikebana* is at the Ikenobo College and Institute and the Ikenobo Office at the Rokkakudo Temple. The temple holds its festival day on the 17th of each month during which exhibits of arrangements can be seen.

Department stores also have *ikebana* exhibits of the best works of leading students and teachers, with an exhibit to be seen at one place or another almost every month.

First introduced into Japan in the 7th century, the practice of tea drinking was subsequently refined under the influence of Zen. Seeing the tea ceremony is an important part of enjoying the refinement of Kyoto. The point of the ceremony is not the actual drinking of the tea but rather the acquisition of serenity and grace which comes in the participation in a series of rites in perfect harmony and in tranquil surroundings.

The three main schools of the tea cult in Japan have almost 2,000,000 members. Largest is the Ura Senke, which has numerous overseas branches. The visitor who would like to learn about and participate in the tea ceremony on a serious basis can contact the Ura Senke School headquarters, Teranouchi Ogawa Agaru, Kamigyo-ku, Kyoto.

In the suburbs

The final villa that must be seen in the Kyoto area is the Katsura Imperial Villa, also known as Katsura Detached Palace. It is situated in the southwestern suburbs and is celebrated for its garden. Completed in the early 17th century by Kobori Enshu, a master of the tea ceremony (which had a tremendous influence on landscaping in Japan), the Katsura garden is considered Enshu's masterpiece and is preserved today in its original state. The palace and garden, in quiet beautiful surroundings, have views of the Arashiyama and Kameyama Hills. The Imperial Household Agency took over the villa in 1883 and the original structure has been carefully preserved. To enter Katsura, permission must be secured from the Imperial Household Agency (these arrangements can be made by your travel agent or the clerk at your hotel).

Lake Biwa, shaped like the musical instrument of the same name, is 261 square miles in area, the largest freshwater lake in Japan. It lies 285 feet above sea level and is 314 feet deep. Geologists say the lake was produced by a subsidence of land. According to Japanese legend, it was formed in a single night in 286 B.C. by the earthquake which, at the same time, produced Mt. Fuji. Following a Chinese custom, eight views around the lake were selected as the most scenic way back in 1500. In taking a steamer for the lake trip, you have the option of going around the lake or making a trip to see the eight views. Each trip makes a stop at Chikubu Island where you can visit Hakouji Temple with its superb Karamon Gate, a National Treasure. The boats start from Hama-Otsu, part of Otsu city, and a trip takes about seven hours. Overdevelopment and smog from the Otsu factories have stolen much of the lake's beauty to the extent that it's a questionable way to spend a day.

Mt. Hiei (alt. 2,782 ft.) is reached from Kyoto via a 50-minute drive along the toll road running from new Tanoya Pass up to Shimeigadake, where a panoramic view of Kyoto, Lake Biwa and adjacent areas is obtained. To reach the peak, you take a thrilling 1,500-foot aerial ropeway from the highway stop. If you prefer to take public transportation, use the Eizan Line of the Keifuku Electric Railway, which stops at Yase, then connect with a cable car there for the ascent. A temple on the summit is located in a grove of Japanese cypress trees, where it was placed by Emperor Kammu to protect his new capital of Kyoto from evil spirits. In later years, the "protection" to the Imperial Government reversed when "turbulent monks clad in armor" from the great monastery made frequent raids on the capital and threatened the palace.

The Hozu Rapids. Shooting the rapids of the Hozu River in a flatboat will add a completely new experience to your itinerary. The best time for this trip is during the months of May to October. During the spring and early summer (May to June), wild wisteria and azalea blossoms are seen on both banks of the river. In autumn the foliage is crimson-tinted. It's about a 10-mile trip which takes two hours; your skilled boatmen, three or five depending upon the size of the flatboat, navigate around rocks, through torrents, shallows, pools and cascades. Your travel agent can make arrangements for you—as part of a tour, the fare is Y2,500.

Otsu, the administrative center of the Shiga Prefecture, is located on the southwest shore of Lake Biwa. The city was the home of the Imperial Court in the 2nd century and again in the 7th, and as a result it has many historical relics, villas and temples. The Otsu Youth Hostel Center attracts students and other young people to the ancient city.

Uji, easily reached from Kyoto by train, is noted for the production of good quality green tea. Also, you find here the famous Byodoin (Phoenix Hall), Japan's best existing example of 11th century religious architecture.

YUZEN CLOTH (below), a specialty of Kyoto; designs are stenciled on silk, then colors applied. Shooting the rapids (bottom) on Hozu River near Kyoto. Peasant women from Ohara Village (upper right) come to Kyoto to sell flowers. Small cruise boat (lower right) shares inlet of Lake Biwa with four-man scull.

RIDING AT ANCHOR in Kobe's port: a string of lighters and a cargo vessel (above). Osaka at night (right) displays a facade typical of many large cities. Tranquility is reflected in Nara's Kofukuji Temple pagoda (far right), built in the late 13th and 14th centuries.

Busy, Industrial Kobe and Osaka...
Quiet, Ancient Nara

There are three other major centers of interest in the general vicinity of Kyoto—they are the huge seaport of Kobe, the big trading center of Osaka and another ancient capital city, Nara. These constitute the major sightseeing targets out of Kyoto.

Kobe

Kobe, sixth largest city in Japan (current population more than 1,300,000), is 365 miles west of Tokyo, about 40 miles west of Kyoto and 20 miles from Osaka. The city spreads out along the shores of Osaka Bay for more than 20 miles and is backed by the densely forested Rokko Range, that rises steeply above the city.

With its wide harbor, Kobe is one of Japan's major ports, and thousands of ships from the Pacific Ocean and the Inland Sea ply the harbor each year. Kobe's development into an industrial center began in the last century during the Meiji era with the start of shipbuilding and iron and steel foundries. A large percentage of the country's import-exports is handled through Kobe, which ships out quantities of steel, machinery, chemicals and textiles (silks and cottons).

If the totem pole that stands close to the City Hall in downtown Kobe looks familiar, it should: it's a symbol of friendship sent by the people of Seattle, Washington to their sister city in Japan.

You'll find several Western-style hotels—the Kobe International, the New Port, the Oriental, the Kobe Towerside, The Rokko Oriental and the Rokkosan, the latter on Mount Rokko. Fine restaurants abound, serving traditional Japanese food as well as a wide variety of foods from around the world. The foreign fare is the result of a small but sturdy community that has existed in Kobe since the early days when Kobe was first opened to foreigners.

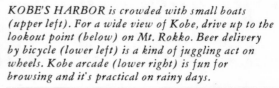

KOBE'S HARBOR *is crowded with small boats (upper left). For a wide view of Kobe, drive up to the lookout point (below) on Mt. Rokko. Beer delivery by bicycle (lower left) is a kind of juggling act on wheels. Kobe arcade (lower right) is fun for browsing and it's practical on rainy days.*

The best way for the tourist to get around Kobe is by taxi. The city is said to have 5,500 of them. Fares, as in other Japanese cities, are dependent on the size of the car, and are charged by distance, not per passenger.

Sightseeing

Best known by tourists as a starting point for tours and cruises into the Inland Sea (see page 125), Kobe has some attractions of its own in addition to an industrial complex and busy port.

Arcing behind Kobe, the Rokko Range offers some sweeping views of the city and harbor, of Awaji Island that cuts off Osaka Bay from the Inland Sea, and beyond to the Kii Peninsula that stretches south of Osaka. At night the view of Kobe Harbor is like looking down on a mini Hong Kong. The best view points—the summits of Mt. Rokko, Maya and Futatabi—are easily reached from town.

You can reach the top of Mt. Rokko (at 3,057 feet the highest peak in the range) by taxi in about 40 minutes, or you can take a taxi to the cable station and reach the summit by cableway. The mountain top is flat and large enough to support a resort complex of hotels, restaurants, ponds, open grasslands, an observatory, golf course and alpine garden. Oldest in Japan, the 18-hole golf course was opened in 1903. From the revolving observatory on a clear day, you are supposed to be able to see ten provinces.

Mt. Maya can be reached by cablecar and a ropeway trip of 5 minutes. Maya is thickly wooded with aged Japanese cedars, and cherries and azaleas bloom on the mountainside in the spring. If you feel like a little exercise, you can climb up a flight of 400 rather steep stone steps from the cablecar terminal to the ancient Toritenjoji Temple, established in 646. You'll probably find a number of Japanese doing the same. They are members of the Koyasan-Shingon sect of Buddhists making their annual pilgrimage.

Mt. Futatabi has a park at the top; and if you continue on north from the summit, you enter Kobe Municipal Arboretum, a huge tract with more than 1,300 kinds of trees brought in from all over the world.

A pretty waterfall (Nunobiki) is only a mile and a half from the port. And if you want to try the beaches, Suma and Maiko beaches west of Kobe are only about 30 minutes distant by car. Akashi, about 13 miles west of the city, has a planetarium, and you can ride a ferryboat from Akashi over to Awaji Island, the largest one in the so-called 1,000 islands of the Inland Sea and a place where you can see the whirlpools of Naruto Straits (see page 135).

Arima Spa, about 45 minutes by rail from Kobe or 35 minutes by bus from the Rokkosan Hotel on Mt. Rokko, is one of the oldest hot spring resorts in Japan. Visited by many for its curative spring waters, the spa is also popular because of the surrounding countryside: wooded, brightened by cascading streams, celebrated for its cherry blossoms in the spring and maple leaves in autumn. More than 30 *ryokan*, each equipped with its own hot spring bath, provide comfortable accommodations.

Shopping

The main shopping areas, like Motomachi Center, are quite near the docks where steamers tie up. Here you'll find the big department stores—Daimaru, Mitsukoshi and Sogo. You should also try Sannomiya Street, Tor Road and the Shopping Nook at Kobe International House. Pearls are a little less expensive in Kobe because it's a clearing-house for pearls. You'll also find some excellent small antique shops.

Other things to do

Kobe has a home-visit program for tourists by which you may meet and visit a Japanese family. Visits are made any time but early morning. Most families will show visitors their houses and gardens, chat for a few hours and entertain you (perhaps with songs accompanied on the *samisen*). Meals are not usually offered. The visits are free except for the services of an interpreter. A small gift (candy or flowers) for the hostess would be appropriate.

You need to apply at least a day in advance, and you can arrange for such a visit through the Tourist Section, Kobe City Office, through the International or Oriental hotels or through the Japan Travel Bureau's office in Sannomiya area near the harbor.

Osaka

Osaka is Japan's second largest city and her greatest industrial center (current population of about 3,000,000). Three hundred forty-four miles from Tokyo, the city sprawls about the mouth of the Yodo River. Osaka Harbor, indenting the central-western coast of Honshu, forms the easternmost part of the Seto, or Inland Sea, and opens southward into the Pacific Ocean.

Such a network of canals spreads throughout Osaka that there are approximately 1,700 bridges connecting its congested streets, and at night the myriad of neon signs reflected in the water turn the noisy daytime city into a maze of glowing color. Osaka used to be called the Venice of the Orient because of its many waterways. Now factories line the waterfront and smog often blurs any panorama of the city's mass of big buildings. Smoke and

OSAKA LANDMARK is magnificent Osaka
Castle (upper left). Shopping for fabrics at
Osaka department store (lower left). At year's
end Osaka residents hold rake festivals
(above) presaging good fortune.

snarled traffic mark your first impressions, but you'll find
havens like Nakanoshima Park in the city center.

Osaka is one of Japan's principal export cities.
The metropolis has big hotels, big theaters, big stores.
Five private railways have their terminal stations at department stores. Yet Shinto processions celebrating shrine
festivals are a common sight. Costumed marchers parade
through the streets at the foot of tall buildings that are
thoroughly Western in appearance. And in the midst of
the commercial hubbub, you can step into one of the huge
theaters in the center of the city to watch a long, slow performance of medieval *kabuki* or *Bunraku* (puppet plays).

The nucleus of the city, aside from the residential areas,
is divided into two main parts, the Minami, or southern
section, which has the chief entertainment centers, and
the Kita, or northern part, which includes the big shopping and amusement center around the Japanese National
Railways' Osaka Station. Terminals of the interurban
railways also are located in the Kita.

Osaka's most impressive street, wide Midosuji Boulevard runs for several miles north and south, linking the
two districts. Lined with gingko and plane trees, it's
worth just walking along it for several blocks to window-
shop. The Shinsaibashi-suji, in the southern part, is the
busiest shopping area, and the Sennichimae and Dotombori, also in the Minami, are the chief centers for theaters
and cabarets. Actually an island formed by canals, the
Nakanoshima section, has both the park by that name and
the civic center, with its imposing city and prefectural
buildings. The city is noted for its fine food (Osakans
have been given the name *Kuidaore* which means extravagant gourmets)—so you'll find a host of good restaurants featuring all the better-known Japanese dishes as
well as a good variety of Western-style restaurants.

Before Nara and Kyoto were chosen as capitals of
Japan, in the country's earliest history, Osaka, then called
Naniwa, was sometimes the seat of the Imperial Court.
It became Osaka in the middle of the 16th century, and

in 1583 the famed warlord, Hideyoshi Toyotomi, built Osaka Castle, the massive tower which still dominates the landscape in the eastern end of the city.

How to get to Osaka

Japan Air Lines and All Nippon Airways operate frequent flights between Tokyo and Osaka. Flight time is 45 minutes; allow about 30 minutes to get into town from the airport. Air services also connect Osaka with other major cities in Honshu, Shikoku, and Kyushu.

A number of international airlines land at Osaka with flights that originate outside of Japan: Cathay Pacific Airways, Civil Air Transport, Japan Air Lines, Korean Air Lines, Northwest Orient Airlines, and Thai International.

Super-express trains on the New Tokaido Line of Japan National Railways connect Tokyo and Osaka in 3 hours and 10 minutes. Express trains for Osaka leave Tokyo every 30 minutes. You can get to Osaka from Kyoto by Japan National Railways electric trains in approximately 40 minutes.

Where to stay

Osaka has a number of large, excellent Western-style hotels—the Hotel Hanshin, the International Hotel Osaka, the Hotel New Osaka, Hotel New Kankyu, Hotel Osaka Grand, Osaka Royal Hotel, the Plaza Hotel, the Osaka Castle Hotel, the Hotel Toyo, the Osaka Miyako Hotel and the Hotel Echo Osaka—and more than 20 *ryokan* that qualify for membership in the Japan Ryokan Association.

What to see

Bunraku and *kabuki* are the highlights of Osaka's stage entertainment. Skilled puppeteers perform at the Bunrakuza Theater in the Shinsaibashi sector. The theater is considered the home of this 300-year-old art. The classical *kabuki* plays are given in the nine-storied New Kabukiza, located on Midosuji Boulevard. April brings the cherry dances, the Ashibe Odori, at Dotombori. Japan's most famous girls' opera, the Takarazuka troupe, gives its revue at the Takarazuka Grand Theater in Takarazuka City, 40 minutes from Osaka by train. Train and theater reservations can be arranged for by your travel agent or through your hotel.

Osaka Castle is the city's most important sightseeing destination. Though dating from the 16th century, like so many of Japan's historical landmarks it was repeatedly burned and rebuilt. When Warlord Hideyoshi required his generals to bring him stones to build the castle, each tried to see who could bring the largest. Some of these enormous rocks (one called Higo-ishi measures 47½ feet long and more than 19 feet high) are still in place.

THE NEW KABUKIZA, a nine-story theater in Osaka, shows Chinese influence in design. Throughout the year the theater presents many performances of popular kabuki.

THE BUNRAKU PUPPET PLAY is one of the traditional stage arts in Japan. This close-up of puppeteer and puppet gives you an idea of a typical puppet's size.

The Shitennoji Temple, near Tennoji Station, was one of Japan's earliest Buddhist temples (originally built in 593). Though the building itself has often been destroyed, its stone *torii* has survived since 1294.

Sumiyoshi Shrine, dedicated to the guardian god of the sea, is characterized by a unique, ancient style of architecture. Designated as a National Treasure, it is one of the oldest in the area. You'll want color film in your camera to capture the bright reds and whites of the buildings, the high arched bridge and many stone lanterns given by the faithful. Sumiyoshi Shrine is the scene every year on June 14 of an ancient rice-planting festival, featuring a delightful folk dance performed by costumed children to the accompaniment of ancient music.

Keitaku-en, one of the finest examples of a Japanese circular garden, is in the northwest part of Tennoji Park. You may also go to the zoo and visit the Municipal Art Museum.

Mino-o Park, habitat of wild monkeys, is a good place to see autumn color because of the park's abundance of maple trees (half an hour by interurban railway).

Other points of interest: **Nintoku Mausoleum,** south of the city proper and built in the fifth century A.D., is a huge moated and wooded green belt. **Kanshinji Buddhist Temple,** at the foot of Mt. Kongo, is another of the earliest Buddhist temples in the country. **Yoshimura House,** south of Osaka, is the well-preserved residence of the family that ruled the villages of the Kawachi Plain during feudal times. **Hattori Green Park,** in the northern part of Osaka prefecture, is a huge open area with green hills and ponds, brightened by daffodils in the spring. Its collection of wooden cottages with straw thatched roofs, is typical of rural dwellings in many parts of the country. **Temmangu Shrine,** dedicated to a ninth century leader, is the scene on July 24 and 25 each year of one of the greatest festivals in Japan, the Tenjin Matsuri. It takes place on the Dojima River near the Minami-Morimachi subway station, and features a fleet of more than 100 sacred boats decorated with shrines and historical figures. Bonfires light the riversides, and lanterns brighten the boats, many of which carry dancers, singing groups and musicians. **The Fujita Gallery,** set in lovely gardens, is noted for its fine arts of the Heian period (897-1192).

Shopping

Shinsaibashi Street is known for its huge department stores—Hankyu, Daimaru, Mitsukoshi, Takashimaya—and a wide variety of excellent specialty shops. The department stores are open from 9 A.M. to 6 P.M. on a six-day week basis. Most of them close on Mondays; all are open on Sundays.

Industrial tours

An industrial plant inspection program enables you to visit any of some 20 factories. The industries vary: petrochemicals, pharmaceuticals, heavy machinery, appliances, ship building, textiles, railway equipment, auto and truck manufacturing, cosmetics and dental supplies to name a few. Two television plants and two sugar refineries are on the list. You can also visit the Osaka Stock Exchange (established in 1743) and the Osaka International Trade Center. At the latter, every two years (alternating with Tokyo), Osaka holds a mammoth International Trade Fair that attracts businessmen from all over the world.

You may arrange for plant visits through your travel agent before you leave home or apply to the Osaka Tourist Association, Daiichi Seimei Building, 2 Umeda, Kita-ku, or the Osaka Municipal Office, 4, 1-chome, Nakanoshima, Kita-ku.

Nara

Nara, which is only about 25 miles south of Kyoto, is even older than its sister city—and since the 20th century seems almost to have skipped this quiet city, the sense of antiquity and of Japan's ancient culture is more present here than almost anywhere in the nation.

For 74 years, beginning in A.D. 710, Nara was the capital of Japan, and seven Emperors reigned at Nara during these eighth-century days when it was called Heijo. It was in those years that art, poetry, craftsmanship, religion and politics flowered and, combining influences from China, India and Korea, formed the singular culture of Japan.

The Nara of 1,200 years ago was a far more extensive city than it is today. Now it is a soporific, pleasantly peaceful spot, and you'll probably find its pace a relaxing one after the confusion and excitement of Tokyo. Its crowds are made up of tourists, most of them Japanese, who come to look or to worship at Nara's temples and shrines and to view the ancient treasures within them.

The logical approach to Nara is from Kyoto or from Osaka. The quickest way from Kyoto is a 35-minute ride on the Kinki Nippon Railway. It takes about an hour to drive from either Kyoto or Osaka. Sightseeing bus tours operate regularly out of Kyoto for one-day excursions in Nara.

About halfway between Kyoto and Nara, you pass through Uji, the source of some of the finest tea in Japan. Ask your guide to arrange for a visit to one of the farmhouses in the area to see how tea leaves are gathered and prepared for the market (best in July and August).

Nara's one Western-style hotel is the Nara Hotel,

which is delightfully located in Nara Park overlooking a small lake, about a five-minute walk from town.

Sightseeing

The city's primary attraction is the Great Buddha of the Todaiji Temple. You may think that when you've seen one Buddhist temple you've seen them all. But the Todaiji Temple stands out from even the most confused recollection of the myriad sights usually visited in rapid-fire order in Japan's two ancient capitals. This headquarters of the Kegon sect of Buddhism strikes you with its bigness at once—especially if you approach the temple compound through the Nandaimon or Great South Gate, which was built in the eighth century, blown down in a typhoon in 962, and restored in 1199.

The next gate opens into a spacious enclosure around the largest wooden building in the world. But its proportions are such that you have to gauge its size by people in the doorways, and you have to remind yourself that all of the supporting structure is wood. Built in 1708, it is the most recent of a succession of halls begun in A.D. 745 and burned down in 1180 and 1567.

The building houses the Daibutsu or Great Buddha, not as famous (because not as easily photographed) as its outdoor namesake at Kamakura, but much larger—53½ feet high, with a head alone that is 16 feet long and 9½ feet wide.

The 452-ton Great Buddha of Nara—the largest Buddha in Japan and the largest bronze statue in the world—was designed by a Korean named Kuninaka-no-Muraji-Kimimaro. After eight unsuccessful tries, beginning in the year 745, the casting was finally completed in 749. As you see it now, it is not entirely original: The head was shaken off in earthquakes in 855 and 1567, and the head and right hand were melted in the fire of 1180.

Despite periodic dusting, the nearly black statue usually is highlighted with a mantle of pale dust that improves photography and makes the bronze indistinguishable from iron, stone or concrete. As you circle the Daibutsu, pause to look at the model of the first Todaiji Temple and to study the construction of the present building. The belfry, just east of the Hall of the Great Buddha, contains a huge bell that is more than 14 feet high and 27 feet in circumference and weighs 48 tons—Japan's largest bell.

The broad southern gate to the Todaiji Temple, with its 18 tall red pillars, is the largest such gate in Japan. Among other buildings of the Todaiji are the Nigatsudo (the second month hall) where the ancient Water Drawing ceremony takes place on March 12, and the Sangatsudo (the third month hall), which is the oldest of all the temple structures. Its architecture illustrates the style both of the Nara and the later Kamakura periods.

Another Nara attraction is the Kofukuji Temple, head-

TODAIJI TEMPLE, completed in 752, is one of "seven great temples of Nara." It was influenced by Chinese architecture, has ornaments on roof as charms against fire.

PLACID POOL reflects part of the Byodoin Temple in the town of Uji. It's about half-way between Kyoto and Nara.

NARA DEER PARK (left) shelters more than 1,000 tame deer, regarded as divine messengers. They roam through the 1,250-acre park and in the precincts of shrines and temples. A long line of stone lanterns (below) flanks the approach to Kasuga Shrine.

quarters of the Buddhist Hosso, sect. It is famous for its five-storied pagoda, 165 feet high, built in 1426 (to replace one just like it which had burned). The temple also has a three-storied pagoda dating from 1148. At the time of its greatest power in the eighth century, Kifukuji Temple had close to 200 buildings. Fire after fire leveled them, and now the pagodas and four halls are the only important buildings left.

Huge Japanese cedars, oaks and cypress mix with a variety of other trees to give Nara Park (Japan's largest) a woodsy character. Paths wind through the green expanse and still ponds that mirror the trees. More than 1,000 tame deer (called divine messengers) wander about the park during the day; at dusk, in answer to the call of a trumpeter, they return to their pens. The quietness of the park is even more emphasized by its approach: busy Sanjo Dori, Nara's main street which runs from the railway station to the park. The lovely willow fringed lake, just to the right of the park entrance, is Sarusawa Pond, Kofukuji Temple reflecting on its shimmering surface.

On the outskirts of Nara near Horyuji Station is Japan's oldest temple. It was founded in 607; its five-storied pagoda rebuilt after the war with the same timbers used in its original construction. There are about 40 buildings, but of chief importance are the Nandaimon, or South Great Gate, the Kondo, or Main Hall, the pagoda, the Kodo, or Lecture Hall (dating from 991)

and the Yumedono, or Hall of Dreams, built in 739.

The Nara National Museum has many works of art of the time when Nara was the capital. Hours are 9:00 A.M. to 4:30 P.M., March-October; 9 A.M. to 4 P.M., November-February; closed first and third Mondays of each month and from December 28 to January 4.

Kasuga Shrine, one of Japan's most celebrated Shinto shrines, stands at the edge of Nara Park. If you walk beneath its two torii (shrine gates) in Nara Park, you will approach the shrine by way of a long avenue of stone lanterns. Kasuga is renowned for its lanterns, approximately 3,000 of them, fashioned of stone and of bronze. This is the setting for the lovely Lantern Festival in February and again in August (see pages 90 and 93). Kasuga has four lovely small shrines, painted bright cinnabar, and each one is dedicated to a separate deity.

Close to the Kasuga Shrine is the Kasuga Wakamiya Shrine, thought to have been founded in 1135, and so-named because it is consecrated to the son of one of the deities enshrined in the larger place of worship.

North of Kasuga Shrine is high grassy Wakakusa Hill, which is burned off at 6 P.M. on January 15 every year to celebrate a festival held to expel demons from the mountain. It's a spectacular sight from the surrounding area. The burning is preceded by a procession of 15 priests from Kofukuji Temple, garbed in costumes of ancient monks and carrying lighted torches. During the rest of the year, the hill offers an excellent viewpoint from which to see much of the Nara Plain.

In a building off to itself north of the Todaiji Temple, much of the art of the late Nara Period (710-784) is preserved in the Shosoin Treasure Repository. Administered by the Imperial Household Agency, the repository is an excellent example of *azekura* architecture: a building made of triangular logs joined without nails, and with an elevated floor—resembling a log cabin on stilts. Sealed to preserve the ancient art works for most of the year, the buildings are aired in late October and early November.

As in Kyoto, you can soak up more of Nara and its charm if you go strolling. Nara means flat (the city is on a flat plain)—so walking is easy.

Most of Nara's main temples and repositories for art treasures are within walking distance of downtown. Tadaimi Temple and Kasuga Shrine are both within a mile of the railway station.

Shopping

Ningyo (carved wooden dolls) are a specialty of Nara, and you find them in shops along Sanjo Street. Other items typical of Nara are Indian ink and writing brushes, both of which are manufactured there.

Two other streets which intersect Sanjo-Dori, Higashimuki and Michiidono streets, also have fascinating shops for leisurely browsing. The Japan Travel Bureau, Yurakukaikan Bldg., near Kintetsu Nara Station, is a handy information center.

The Northern Coast

The north shore of Western Honshu—on the Japan Sea almost due north of Kobe—is rarely seen by foreign visitors, yet it is a beautiful stretch of coastline with lovely fishing villages, quiet inlets, rugged headlands with caves and grottoes, small islets, and extensive sand dunes. Several rail lines serve the area out of Kyoto, Osaka or Kobe. The principal attractions are Amanohashidate, where you can watch the Japanese do some upside-down viewing (see this page), and San-in Coast National Park.

San-in Park stretches for about 46 miles along the coast from Kinosaki to Tottori. Walled off from the interior by the Hakkusan Volcanic Range, the coastline is rarely flat, much of it dropping precipitously into the sea. But along the coast northeast of Tottori, a massive series of sand dunes stretch for about 10 miles, at places reaching back into the land for more than a mile. Thanks to the volcanic mountains that follow the coastline, the area has dozens of hot spring spas with small *ryokan* and hotels providing comfortable accommodations.

A "GREAT SIGHT" VIEWED UPSIDE DOWN

Amanohashidate, on Miyazu Bay about 2¾ hours out of Kyoto, is classified as an "Outstanding Scenic Place" by the Japanese and is known as one of the "Three Great Sights" in the country (the other two are Miyajima and Matsushima). Actually Amanohashidate is a sand bar covered with fantastically shaped pine trees. Literally the word means "Bridge of Heaven," and the Japanese have been making trips to view it for centuries.

There are those for whom Amanohashidate holds no special allure, but it undeniably provides an experience in viewing that is out of the ordinary. From special viewing platforms at various vantage points, the Japanese traditionally take an upside down look through their legs. This, it is said, gives the effect of a bridge in the sky extending toward heaven. Connections can be made in the Amanohashidate station for transport to one of the view points. Kasamatsu Park, half way up Mt. Nariai, is one of the best—however, several others will be championed by partisan groups of viewers.

Viewed right side up, Amanohashidate (the sand bar that it is) looks about two miles long and from 100 to 300 feet wide. The rail trip northward from Kyoto, however, is pleasant and relaxed. The Amanohashidate area is a fashionable resort for summering residents of Kyoto, Osaka and Kobe.

TRADITIONAL STANCE used to view Floating Bridge of Heaven (center of bay) at Amanohashidate.

CLASSIC VIEW (above) of the Inland Sea
from the port town of Tomo, between Okayama
and Hiroshima. At right, the Kintaibashi
Bridge, in western-most Honshu, is noted for its
unusual design. At far right, Miyajima is an
ideal summer resort with fine beaches. Tame deer
wander about the island as they do at Nara.

The Inland Sea and Western Honshu

Japan's Inland Sea—that long body of water that stretches for more than 300 miles east and west within the protecting arms of western Honshu and the islands of Shikoku and Kyushu—is one of the most picturesque waterways in the world. Actually a chain of five seas linked together and connected to the Pacific Ocean by narrow swift-flowing channels, the Sea is dotted with islands and edged by pine-clad shores along most of its length. It's a fascinating waterway for travelers and a great avenue of commerce for fleets of small freighters and fishing boats. You'll count a daytime voyage on the Sea as one of the great travel experiences in Japan. A train, bus or automobile trip along its shores will take you to a number of Japan's fascinating travel attractions including the gardens at Okayama, the old Edo-period town of Kurashiki, atom-bombed Hiroshima and the sacred city of Miyajima.

Cruising the Inland Sea

The ships that carry you from end-to-end of the Sea and criss-cross it in many places, range from 3,000-ton luxury cruise ships to hydrofoils and smaller cruise ships to ferry boats. A half-dozen steamship companies offer you a choice of more than a dozen routes. They take you on a watery thoroughfare through the Japan that you may have hoped to see but didn't really expect to encounter: a country right out of an antique Japanese print, in terms of natural scenery, architecture and the people and their manners and dress.

Most often taken by Japanese and visiting travelers alike, the route is the daylight trip that leaves Osaka shortly after 7 A.M. and arrives at Beppu shortly after 9 P.M., some 14 hours later. You can also board the ship in Kobe (where most passengers board) at about 8:30 A.M. Four trips a day are made, including an overnight voyage, but the early morning departure is the only one that offers most of the trip during daylight hours.

*THE INLAND SEA EXPERIENCE: passing
small fishing boats (above); inspecting the sleek
boat you'll soon be boarding (upper right);
tossing serpentine to shore-side friends who
came down to see you off (right).*

Operating four vessels on this route is the Kansai Steamship Company of Osaka. Each vessel is a 3,000-ton luxury cruise ship with space for more than 1,000 passengers. They're designed with a bulbous bow to reduce wave resistance and increase speed (to about 20 knots) and to provide more boat-deck and promenade-deck space.

Single or double first-class cabins have a wash basin, freshly made-up bunks, a writing table and chair and big picture windows. A special first-class lounge lies forward and has an unobstructed view three ways through picture windows.

Immediately below the lounge is the first-class dining room serving Western and Japanese food for all three meals. Dinner, which is served punctually in the dining room, consists of one sitting; if you are late, they come and get you. The service is superb, even though it is performed with a kind of dedicated speed and precision. Cocktails may be had in the Drinking Center (pronounced *drinkusenta* in the Japanese syllabary), which comes to life about 4:30 or 5 P.M. It is a round, domed room stretching the width of the upper deck with big side windows—a bar in the center and tables all around.

The ships are also equipped with movie hall, refreshment bar, an aft observation deck and ample promenade space. Spotless and modern, the ship's bridge has the latest navigation aids plus a tiny shelf-size Shinto shrine.

Many of the Japanese passengers (mostly honeymooners and a sprinkling of families on holiday) crowd into lower decks, leaving most of the higher-priced cabins for foreign tourists. One-way fare between Osaka (or Kobe) and Beppu is Y8,560 per person, first class.

Here are some of the sights you'll see:

Approaching Kobe from Osaka, you are treated to an incoming view of Kobe's harbor, lined with freighters from all over the world. Though land is indistinguishable from Osaka in the urbanization that has linked the two cities, Kobe has by far the grander harbor. This includes enormous ship building yards right across the channel from the boat dock.

Once under way from Kobe, your steamer joins a constant parade of coastal freighters, steamers and punt-sized open fishing boats. Sometimes you pass close enough to the fishing boats to look down upon them and exchange greetings with the crews. Coming to the myriad of pine-clad islands and islets, you see shrines with their graceful *torii* set on headlands, tiny fishing villages snuggled in coves, and sparse fields hacked out of the more level areas of rocky hillsides. Some of the villages look as if they had not had communication with the outside world in centuries. Lighthouses are high on promontories or low on rocks; an occasional channel buoy goes by. The water swirls by the ship as powerful tidal currents break through the chains of islands and channels. Sights along the way are narrated, first in Japanese and then in English (the Japanese, being a rather ceremonial language, takes about three times the number of words as the English version).

Express liners make their first stop after Kobe at Takamatsu on Shikoku Island. Docking at Takamatsu is a wonderful mixture of dockside sights and sounds: the noise, confusion and emotions as passengers get off and on, as cargo is thrown on the dock, as women vending tangerines and souvenirs come alongside, perhaps as a wedding party comes to bid goodbye to bride and groom. If the arrival of one of the hydrofoil ferries over from Kobe coincides with your arrival, it adds an extra dash of action to the scene.

The voyage takes you through Seto-Naikai, Japan's Inland Sea National Park—the only sea park in the world. At Beppu your journey ends in darkness with splashes of neon and bright lights reflecting in the black water. The ship docks rapidly. Leaving the exits, passengers are greeted by a swarm of people—some of whom have come to greet friends or relatives, some of whom are tour leaders brandishing their signs and tour names, and some of whom are flag-waving representatives from the local inns.

Before going on to Unzen, Nagasaki, Fukuoka or other parts of Kyushu, you can easily spend a day or so in Beppu. For more on Kyushu, see page 136. You can make the return trip by air from Fukuoka or Kagoshima, flying to Tokyo or on down to Taipei and Hong Kong.

Vary this trip, if you like, by debarking on Shikoku for a few days, then picking up one of the other vessels of Kansai Steamship—or by using one of the other smaller steamship lines. If you decide to stay over on Shikoku Island, take your camera. The area is considered by photographers to be one of the most photogenic in the Orient. See page 133 for more information on sights to see in Shikoku.

The other steamship lines run from various points on Honshu—Shimotsui (south of Kurashiki); Okayama; Kasaoka, Onomichi and Tomo (all west of Okayama); and from Hiroshima and nearby Ujina—to some of the islands in the Sea and to various small port towns on Shikoku. Vessels leaving Ujina squeeze through the Strait of Ondo which separates Kurahashi Island from the Honshu mainland and which was excavated in the 12th century.

You can get more information on the routes and schedules of the lines that ply the Inland Sea through the Japan

MEALTIME aboard Inland Sea ships gives you a choice of Japanese or Western cuisine. From Washuzan Hill you can see many of the Inland Sea's 950 islands (right).

HIMEJI CASTLE *(left) is a dazzling sight at dusk. Below, the Peace Arch, officially called the Peace Memorial Cenotaph, is in Hiroshima. At Kurashiki the Ohara Art Gallery (lower left) has an impressive collection of the great masters. From an overlook area (lower right) you can enjoy an expansive view of Hiroshima.*

National Tourist Organization. Your travel agent can arrange the itinerary for you.

Himeji

A 27-minute ride on the new super-bullet train of JNR's Sanyo Line from the New Kobe Station takes you to Himeji. This city is noted for its ancient feudal stronghold, a great five-storied structure atop tall rock ramparts. Finished in a white plaster from top to bottom, it is called the Egret Castle because its silhouette from a distance looks like the bird that is found in the nearby rice fields. From the top levels you get a sweeping view of the surrounding countryside and the waters and islands of the Inland Sea. The garden of the castle and much of the surrounding area are noted for their apricot blossoms in the spring.

Okayama

The new Tokkaido bullet express train that reaches speeds of 125 miles an hour has been extended west of Kobe as far as Okayama, considerably shortening the travel time to this castle town and its famous Korakuen garden (see page 47). Reconstructed in 1966, the castle was originally built in 1573, and is known as Crow Castle because of its black exterior.

Nearby Bizencho (about 45 minutes by train or road) is the home of *Bizen-yaki* porcelain ware, a rustic unglazed product developed centuries ago in the province of Bizen. You can visit the workshops in town to see how the ware is made (you can even design your own souvenir).

Uno, a small port town on an arm of the Inland Sea about six miles from Okayama, is a ferry terminal for services to Takamatsu on Shikoku Island.

Kurashiki

Kurashiki, just west of Okayama, is an old walled city that has moved into position as an important industrial center without losing the charm of being a quiet old town. In spite of the industrial zones surrounding it, the old town is a collection of tiny, winding streets, small shops, restaurants and canals.

Once a major shipping point for rice grown in the surrounding plain, the city still has several old rice granaries right in the heart of town. Four of these two-story wood structures have been converted into the Folkcraft Museum that houses displays of rugs, textiles, pottery, wood and bamboo and other handicrafts.

The Ohara Art Gallery in Kurashiki houses one of the best collections of Western art in Japan, including works of El Greco, Corot, Rodin, Gauguin, Picasso and many other masters. It also has a superb collection of ceramics and an extensive collection of block print masters, particularly of Shiko Munakata, a modernist of international reputation.

Hiroshima

Set on a bay of the Inland Sea, Hiroshima is about a 4-hour limited express train ride south from Osaka or Kobe. The stretch from Okayama (now the southern terminus of the New Tokaido Line) to Hiroshima is one of the most scenic train rides in Japan. Much of it winds along the shore of the Inland Sea, passing through picturesque fishing villages as well as ship building and repair centers. From Mibara, one route strikes inland on a single track through mountainous countryside, reaching the Inland Sea again at Hiroshima. Another route follows the coast through Takehara and Kure into Hiroshima.

The first thought one is likely to have about Hiroshima is that the first atomic bomb was dropped there. Some people may prefer not to see the site of such destruction; others out of conscience or curiosity may be attracted to it. If you go there, you will find that the place that people feared would remain an atomic desert for 75 years has been rebuilt, mostly since 1955, into a bustling, full functioning city, and has surpassed its pre-blast population of 400,000. Further proof of this amazing restoration are the brilliant flowers growing in the park not far from the center of the explosion. The city has become a leading center for atomic casualty research.

Where to stay

There are several good hotels in Hiroshima—the Hiroshima Kokusai Hotel, the Hiroshima Station Hotel, the Hotel Hiroshima Grand, and the Hotel New Hiroshima. If you prefer a *ryokan*, the Issaen Inn is recommended—it is situated on the shore of the Inland Sea with a splendid view of the island of Miyajima. The Issaen is small and charming with a flavor of times gone by. You may go there to dine even if you are not a guest of the hotel.

Festivals

Hiroshima is referred to as the "Peace City" now, and it holds a Peace Festival every year on August 6, the day in 1945 when the bomb fell. This is the city's most important event. On this day under the arch of the Memorial Cenotaph in Peace Memorial Park a stone box containing all the known names of the victims is opened.

A memorial service is held by Shinto, Buddhist and Christian leaders. At night many brightly burning red and yellow paper lanterns commemorating departed souls are cast into the river according to ancient Buddhist custom. A fireworks display is held the following evening.

On August 15 the O-Bon dance festival is held at the baseball stadium. Dance groups from all parts of Japan perform dances typical of their regions.

What to see

Peace Boulevard (Heiwa Odori) will take you to the Atomic Bomb Explosion Center south of Peace Park. This center includes the Peace Tower and a museum containing mementoes from the explosion with photographs of the bombed city and many of its victims. These exhibitions are not intended to be sensational and are soberly arranged. There is also the modern Roman Catholic Peace Memorial Cathedral standing in this area.

One building which survived the blast has remained standing. This is the Industrial Exhibition Hall which scientists believe was directly below the center of the blast which burst 1,800 feet up. All that is left of the building is its empty shell and ruined steel dome.

A large radiation center has been built on Hijiyama Hill east of the Atomic Bomb Center. Here American and Japanese doctors do research on the effects of atomic radiation. There is a lovely view from this hill of the city, the harbor and of Miyajima.

Miyajima

Perhaps the best reason for going to Hiroshima is to visit the enchanting island of Miyajima to see the famous Shinto shrine, Itsukushima. You can reach this beautiful island, 19 miles in circumference, by ferry. The ferry terminal is about 20 miles from Hiroshima—altogether, it takes about 40 minutes to get from downtown Hiroshima to Miyajima. Island and shrine have been famous for generations as one of Japan's three most beautiful sights (the others: Amanohashidate and Matsushima).

Itsukushima, the shrine, was founded by the Heike clan in the year 811. Most of it has been rebuilt many times and consists of a main building with several subsidiary shrines attached to it by long corridors of camphor wood which stand on stilts above the water. A huge vermilion torii, the characteristic gate symbolizing a Shinto shrine, stands about 530 feet from shore. Followers of Shintoism take a sacred boat which sails through the torii to Miyajima. When the tide is in, the whole shrine and torii look as if they were floating on the water.

The main shrine has three parts—the place where the goddesses live, the inner part where the priests enter, and the outer part which is for public worship. The ordinary dances of the shrine are performed here. For an offering to the shrine you can see the Shinto priests do the *kagura,* a sacred dance done for the general populace, and the *bugaku,* a fantastic, ritualistic dance done in extravagant costumes and in frightening masks, originally danced only for the nobility. Masks and costumes, swords, utensils and other curiosities are exhibited in the Asazaya or Morning Prayer Room near the east entrance of the shrine.

To the left of the shrine stand two pagodas, one two stories high, the other five, representing the Buddhist belief in the five necessary elements of life—earth, wood, water, fire and heaven. Near the pagodas is the Senjokaku, Hall of a Thousand Mats. It is said to be built from a single camphor tree. It is in this building that thousands of rice scoops are displayed around a small shrine. The name of the donor is inscribed on each one with a message of good fortune for some friend or relative. The custom of the rice scoop offerings developed in 1894 during the Sino-Japanese war when soldiers quartered on Miyajima gave prayer offerings for victory. The choice of rice scoops seems to have derived from the double meaning of the word, *meshitoru*—rice taking and to conquer.

A small stream, the Mitarashi-gawa, separates the Treasure Hall from the west gallery. This hall is a modern building containing about 4,000 pieces including more than 100 objects which are considered important cultural properties.

The Daiganji Temple, which stands west of the shrine, houses a number of statues of Buddha.

Other things to see

If you have the time, you might follow in the footsteps of many of the worshipers who visit the island. On their walk around Miyajima, they stop in at seven small shrines on the Nanaura or seven shores. The National Railway makes the trip around the island in about four hours, or you can go by boat (Matsudai Motorboat Company) in three hours.

April is the month for cherry blossoms in Miyajima; and in the fall the colors are vivid, especially in Omoto Park, west of the shrine, and in Momiji-dani (Maple Valley). The crowds are the greatest in spring and fall. In summer there is very good swimming and the days are pleasantly warm and the evenings cool.

For a lovely view of Hiroshima with the mountains in the distance and of the Inland Sea with its islands and boats, take the ropeway from Momiji-dani behind the Itsukushima Shrine to the top of Mt. Misen, the highest peak on the island. As a bonus, near the summit you can see Daishoin Temple, built in the ninth century.

There are teahouses at various places on the island and several inns if you wish to stay overnight.

THE SHINTO SHRINE, Itsukushima (upper left)
on the beautiful island of Miyajima, was founded
in 811. From Hiroshima you can reach the island in
gaudily emblazoned boats (above). Miyajima torii
(right) is Japan's most famous torii.

A COVEY of Japanese cranes wings its way south for the winter. At right, a hydrofoil ferry runs between Hiroshima and Horie on the island of Shikoku. At far right, drying octopuses hang above women repairing nets at Amakusa-Jima on Kyushu.

Japan's "Other Islands"
... Skikoku, Kyushu, Hokkaido

Only a small percentage of the tourists who visit Japan ever see the country's three other main islands—Shikoku and Kyushu to the south of Honshu and Hokkaido to the north. But if you have the time to visit any or all of them, you'll come home with a picture of Japan that is not nearly so Westernized, not nearly so geared to the 20th century, and not nearly so full of tourists.

Here briefly are a few highlights of those islands:

Shikoku

Bull fights, long-tailed roosters, fighting dogs, celebrated gardens, ingenious puppets, relative seclusion and unmatched scenery are the major visitor attractions of Shikoku. To ardent Buddhists of the Shingon sect, Shikoku is a land of pilgrimages, with pilgrims taking their choice of 88 holy temples, many of which are situated in mountainous areas. Kompira-San in Kotohira City near Takamatsu is the second most popular shrine in Japan. The shrine is dedicated to the god of the sea.

Shikoku is the smallest of the four principal islands—though it is the big island in the Inland Sea. Many tourists see some of the cities on Shikoku from the ship while However, you can reach Takamatsu by air from Osaka in 40 minutes or by boat from Osaka or Kobe in about 4 hours, by ferry in about 1 hour from Uno (near Okayama). Air and boat services also go into Kochi, Matsuyama and Tokushima.

Though it is a scenic island and the southern boundary of the well-known Inland Sea, Shikoku is somewhat off the main tourist routes of Japan. As a result, it retains much of the quaintness of rural Japan preserved in widespread ancient customs and folkways. Numbered among its major attractions are a wealth of beautiful land and seascapes, but much of the island's charm is due to its relative lack of modern production technology. Basic and traditional Japanese arts and crafts—for the most part

FEATURES OF SHIKOKU: *a curved bridge across a pond in Takamatsu's Ritsurin Park; a bulldog in elaborate trappings for the contest in which two dogs are pitted against each other in Kochi; parasols drying in front of Ishiteji Temple near Matsuyama; and a Kochi rooster with 20-foot-long tail feathers.*

hand-produced by families and small factories—are a major source of island income. You can find bargains in such things as bamboo products (carved and woven baskets and trays), varieties of decorated tissue paper and papier-mâché folk dolls, lanterns and mythological figurines and masks, paper streamers and traditional, earthy, unglazed pottery. The bulk of the weird and humorous kites exported from Japan are also made on Shikoku.

Although the island has four major cities—Takamatsu, Tokushima, Kochi and Matsuyama, each of which have more than 200,000 population—little English is spoken. Because of this, the island offers a travel experience for those who can cope with (and even enjoy) the adventure of going into an area with a serious language handicap. Obviously, the best way to see the island is with an English-speaking guide, and your best means of transport on the island is the train.

What to see

Takamatsu. Originally a castle town, Takamatsu's tourist attractions include Ritsurin Park, Yashima Plateau for a panoramic view of the Inland Sea and Kotohiragu Shrine, revered from early times by seafarers. Ritsurin Park, considered one of the three best landscaped strolling gardens in Japan, covers about 134 acres of natural pine forest. Its 7 ponds and 13 hills should be seen by following the paths in a counter-clockwise direction. The garden also has a handicraft exhibition hall where artisans consign many of the island's folk products for display and sale.

About 60 miles from Takamatsu is Kotohiragu Shrine, one of Japan's most popular places of worship and home of the patron deity of fishermen.

Kochi. The southern seaport of Kochi—about 100 miles from Takamatsu—is accessible in 2½ hours on a train that is comfortable enough but not exactly modern. However, the beautiful rural scenery makes up for any minor inconvenience. Kochi, a marketing center for folk art, is famous for its long-tailed roosters (birds sporting feather trains that reach 20 feet in length) and its *Tosa* breed of fighting dogs. Like *sumo* wrestlers, prized *Tosa* champions wear *mawashi*, a kind of ceremonial loincloth, about the neck. The mastiff-size dogs, bred and trained for hundreds of years as bodyguards, are matched in ferocious fights.

Kochi is also a good place to see paper being made by hand. And for hikers interesting scenic areas are waiting to be explored. Two such areas are the jagged-cliff headlands of Muroto Point and Ashizuri Point, both known for their rugged scenic beauty.

Matsuyama. West from Takamatsu is Shikoku's largest city, Matsuyama, also a seaport and one of the oldest spa areas in Japan. In addition to numerous old inns, one of its major attractions is Matsuyama Castle, designated by the government as an Important Cultural Property. The three-story castle dates from 1603 and contains numerous fine specimens from Japan's feudal era, such as swords, armor, palanquins and other artifacts. Among the Japanese, a major tourist spot is Dogo hot spring resort. It's situated on a hillside and reached by cable car.

Tokushima. Smallest of the island's four main cities is Tokushima, on the east coast 1¼ hours by train from Takamatsu. The city's annual 300-year-old Bon Dance festival (*Awa Odori*) held each August attracts throngs of visitors (see page 126). While in Tokushima, you should also see the famous puppet plays performed in the area's shrines and temples.

Uwajima. A form of bullfighting in which two bulls are pitted against each other can be seen at Uwajima in western Shikoku. Farmers enjoy the sport in a small open-air ring on several occasions during the year.

Naruto. A 45-minute train ride from Tokushima takes you to Naruto, where you can see one of the world's most unusual sights—the whirlpools of the Naruto Straits. Twice a day, the waters of the Pacific roar through this one-mile-wide channel and rage in swirls of angry foam. The turbulent nature of the whirlpools is caused by a difference in level between the Inland Sea and the ocean, a difference as much as 5 feet in some places.

Shodo Island. You can get from Takamatsu to Shodo Island in about 23 minutes via ferry boat. With a circumference of only 89.5 miles, the small island is noted for

BULLFIGHTING the Japanese way draws enthusiastic crowds to Uwajima to watch two bulls pitted against each other. No matadors, no picadores, just angry bulls.

THE ROLLING WATERS of the Inland Sea create treacherous Naruto whirlpool; boatsmen give it a wide berth.

BONSAI are grouped by size for interesting display on a hillside above the town of Takamatsu on Shikoku Island.

its seasonal bloom—in the autumn the play of color in the turning of the maples and other leaves is dramatic. Cherry blossoms are abundant in the spring, wild azaleas in early summer. The coasts of Shodo have been eroded by wind, rain and waves, making them superbly scenic. A horde of trained wild monkeys gather on the rocks and paths of the island to beg food.

Where to stay

You'll find at least one sizable Western-style hotel in each of Shikoku's three biggest cities. In Takamatsu, the Takamatsu International Hotel offers 76 Western-style rooms and five Japanese style. The Hotel Oku-Dogo in Matsuyama has 167 Western-style and 94 Japanese-style rooms. The Hotel New Kochi in Kochi offers 14 Western-style and 38 Japanese-style rooms. Each of the hotels is air conditioned and centrally heated, and each has restaurant or dining room and snack bar facilities and cocktail lounges. You'll also find excellent *ryokan* in and around the main centers of tourist interest.

Kyushu

Kyushu, twice as big as the state of Hawaii, is the southernmost and third largest of the four major islands of Japan. Its bubbling hot springs, active craters, national parks and other tourist attractions are popular with the adventuresome tourist as well as the Japanese vacationer.

Facing the China Sea at the southwestern end of Japan's Inland Sea, Kyushu is the closest Japanese island to the Asian continent and for 300 years was Japan's principal gateway to foreign culture and trade. This was accomplished through Nagasaki, the country's oldest international port on the northeastern coast of Kyushu, which from the 16th century harbored foreign trading ships.

The first of the European visiting ships were those from Portugal, Spain and the Netherlands which not only introduced Western goods but Christianity to Kyushu. In 1637 the Portuguese and Spaniards were expelled by the Japanese government and only the Dutch (confined to the small island of Dejima) and traders from nearby China were allowed to trade at Nagasaki. All through the period of expulsion, however, foreign learning filtered into Japan through Nagasaki, particularly in the fields of medicine, botany, geography and military science. When the country was reopened to foreigners in 1859, Nagasaki attained temporary prominence as ambitious Japanese youths flocked there to acquire Western learning. The city is the setting for *Madame Butterfly*.

Much of Kyushu's scenery is straight out of the old wood block prints: misty mountains and small coastal islands, thatched farmhouses tucked into narrow green

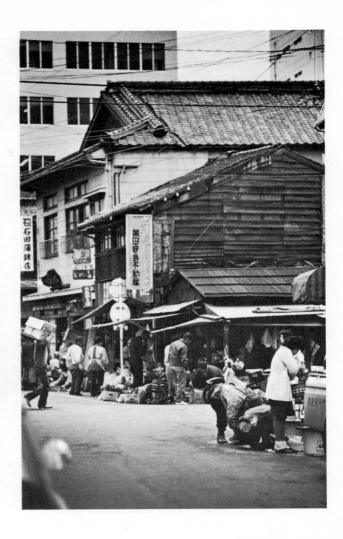

TO KNOW NAGASAKI is to wander among the old buildings and see the streetside marketplace (right). In the legacy of old buildings, Urakami Church (above), designated as a National Treasure, has a prominent location.

valleys, farmers and wives tilling their fields, fishermen poling their sampans—all in an uncluttered and uncrowded land.

There is also a virility to the land that is best expressed by the impressive and often awesome chain of volcanic mountains that snakes its way from mid-island to the southernmost tip, thrusting up stark, dormant cones, active but slumbering peaks wreathed in smoke and misty mountains green to their tips. Along miles of picturesque coastlines, rocky cliffs and spuming seas give way to long white sandy beaches, some warmed by hot springs under the sea. And all of Kyushu has great appeal to the gardener and nature lover. Of Japan's 25 national parks, four are on Kyushu along with a number of other areas designated as quasi-national parks.

The cities of Kyushu (most in scenic settings, with mountains never far away) are impressive for their cleanliness, their leisurely pace, for the warmth and friendliness of the people, and for local attractions that are easily encompassed without running into crowds of sightseers.

Another important plus factor is Kyushu's mild year-round climate. Spring and fall are the ideal seasons, but summer is never as humid as in other parts of Japan and summer-cool mountains are never far away. Winters are milder than elsewhere in Japan with snow virtually unknown.

Since the tourist has not "found" Kyushu, you may be looked upon in the more remote areas as somewhat of a curiosity. And since you'll find only a few who understand English once you leave the main hotels in the big cities, you may find language somewhat of a barrier. Furthermore, most of the tours operated on the island are geared only to the Japanese with all commentary in Japanese. So an English-speaking guide is pretty much of a prerequisite. But if you want to try it alone, you can get a good road guide in English at the Japan Travel Bureau offices in Beppu, Fukuoka or Nagasaki.

Fukuoka. A silk-producing center and major industrial city, Fukuoka straddles the Naka River. This location led to Fukuoka becoming a two-name city: the old town, east of the Naka was Hakata, and Fukuoka grew up as a castle town west of the river and in time dominated Hakata. Fukuoka has been the official name of both cities since the late 19th century, but many still refer to the old section as Hakata.

If time allows, you should visit some of Fukuoka's parks. Ohori Park, toward the west end of town, is a vast open space around a big tidewater lake (created from the moat of the former castle). The park is crossed by bridges to islands, ringed by paths and playing fields and backed by trees and the remnants of the old stone walls of the castle.

Nearby Nishi-koen (West Park) is reached by a cherry-tree-lined avenue and staircase at the top of which is a *torii* and shrine and another grove of cherry trees that creates a canopy of blossoms overhead in the spring. At the foot of the park's stairway is the workshop where the world famous Hakata dolls are made. The dolls are marvels of detail and authenticity of costume. Though the method of creating them has been kept secret through the centuries, you can see some of the process if you make a reservation to visit the workshop (your travel agent or your hotel can arrange this).

Across town is Higashi-koen (East Park), where a gigantic bronze statue of Nichiren (the priest who founded the Nichiren sect of Buddhism) dominates a vast expanse of lawn and pine trees. Beyond and to the east is a truly remarkable bit of Japanese Shinto architecture: the Hakozaki Hachiman Shrine. Its monumental, two-story, thatched-roof gate was erected toward the end of the 16th century without benefit of nails. There's a serenity and timelessness about the simple, subtly-detailed buildings that compel you to look in hushed silence.

Fukuoka was always considered the largest city on Kyushu, until the advent of Kitakyushu. By combining five major industrial cities at the northern tip of Kyushu in 1963, Kitakyushu became the largest city on the island (more than 1,100,000). Though not particularly interesting from a tourist standpoint, the city sits on the narrowest stretch of Kammon Strait which separates Kyushu from Honshu. The two islands are joined by both rail and road underwater tunnels. Expect an ample supply of comfortable hotels in both Kitakyushu and Fukuoka.

Routes to the west from Kitakyushu cut along a stretch of coast embraced in Genkai Quasi-National Park. The coast's long stretches of white sand beach are broken by fantastic rock formations and green pine groves. Between Fukuoka and Nagasaki, you pass broad flat fields, more often of barley than of rice. In the little isolated farmhouse groups, old thatched-roof houses and barns sit alongside more recently built tile-roofed buildings. Small villages nestle at the base of foothills—not built on precious flat land as they might be in the United States, but

just where the slopes begin. There are fields below and orchards above where the slopes level out. Here is rural Japan probably as unspoiled as any left in the islands, and the scene is entertainment enough, prompting you to make the drive a leisurely one.

Nagasaki. One of the most visually and historically interesting cities of Kyushu, Nagasaki curves around a busy port and spreads upward into the mountains. Immediately apparent is a European patina in brick buildings, old forts, canals and curving cobblestone streets—a legacy of the 16th century when the port was first opened to trade with the Portuguese and Dutch. For centuries before that Nagasaki had been a major port for trade with Korea and China; and remnants of this influence remain today in a famous Chinese temple, a large Chinese colony and restaurants that offer some of the finest Chinese cuisine in Japan.

It was in Nagasaki that Christianity was first introduced into Japan and became firmly entrenched throughout Kyushu, only to be forced underground for some 200 years. Monuments to martyred Christians add an unexpected facet to the city. (The theme of the hidden, or underground, Christians is a thread that can be followed all over Kyushu.)

Here are some of Nagasaki's highlights: The Western-style Glover Mansion, high on a hilltop overlooking the bay, is typical of the fine homes wealthy foreign residents

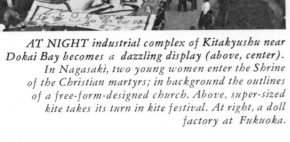

AT NIGHT *industrial complex of Kitakyushu near*
Dokai Bay becomes a dazzling display (above, center).
In Nagasaki, two young women enter the Shrine
of the Christian martyrs; in background the outlines
of a free-form-designed church. Above, super-sized
kite takes its turn in kite festival. At right, a doll
factory at Fukuoka.

SHRINE ENTRANCE at West Park (right) at Fukuoka is framed by spring blossoms. View from train window (above) is typical of the Kyushu countryside.

built when the city was a great trading port. (The mansion's association with *Madame Butterfly* is as lengendary as the lady herself.) Directly across the street from the mansion is No. 16 House, displaying a museum-like collection of European antiques and authentic paraphernalia used in Nagasaki's major festivals. Also on the sightseeing route is Oura Catholic Church, erected in memory of 26 Japanese and foreign saints crucified in 1596, Suwa Shrine and park, the Ming period Sofukuji Temple built in 1629 and the Peace Park and museum.

A day might well be spent in poking about the city, exploring the cobbled hillside streets (locally called Holland slopes), seeking out small shops for Nagasaki's famous tortoise shell souvenirs, getting a closer look at the great Mitsubishi shipyards (where some of the largest ships in the world have been built) and trying some of the variety of seafood for which Kyushu is famous. Recommended: The small Ten Hiro for one of the best tempura meals in Japan.

Two hotels, Nagasaki Grand and New Nagasaki Hotel, can cater to the foreign visitor, but for the tourist already familiar with *ryokan*, the Suwa-so is a good recommendation. The inn, on a hillside overlooking the city, is often used by members of Japan's royal family. While the inn is run in the real tradition of the *ryokan*, rooms with Western-style bathrooms (but with *furo*, or Japanese-style tubs) are available.

To Sasebo. A good example of the sightseeing as-you-travel qualities of Kyushu is the express bus trip from Nagasaki to the naval base of Sasebo—a two-hour comfortable bus trip with five or six stops (all commentary in Japanese only). It's scenery all the way, with glimpses of blue bays and tiny inlets, little villages, farmhouses, tobacco and rice fields. The route crosses the famous-in-Japan Saikai Bridge, traversing the spot where ebb and flow tides meet to create a great maelstrom. The phenomenon attracts hordes of spectators who come to watch from the heights of the bridge, from picnic spots on the forested hillsides, and from small restaurants along the water's edge. The restaurants specialize in seafood so fresh that it is alive even while the order is being given. (In the case of the specialty—raw lobster—it's still alive when served!)

Sasebo, though a naval station, has the charm of a miniature Nagasaki. It offers the same hillside vantage points, narrow curving streets and attractive hillside homes. You'll find comfortable accommodations in the tasteful Hotel Matsukura.

Hirado. The real objective in this corner of northern Kyushu is the island and town of Hirado. From Sasebo, it's about 1½ hours by taxi plus a 15-minute ferry ride. (Or it can be reached by small excursion boat.)

Hugging a strait, the little town of Hirado marches up the surrounding hillsides in a parade of willy nilly little streets seemingly too narrow for even the smallest taxi to negotiate. Here again you'll find traces of those 16th century Dutch traders who set up a trading post and settled in for some 30 years. Aside from the picturesque quality of the town and the little water-front shops and the pleasant feeling of being far, far from the beaten track, you'll find just two things to see: the castle and the museum. Hirado Castle, from whose ramparts one looks across the sea, is small and intimate enough to explore. In some ineffable way, it sharpens the perspective of Japan's feudal days. In a hillside garden mansion, the small museum houses not only European relics and objects of the Christian "underground" but also some outstanding treasures of the feudal past.

The quiet countryside—gentle mountains from whose tops a world of islands comes to view, farmhouses and orchards, rice terraces, an occasional pebble beach at the sea end of the valley—can all be sampled just a few minutes out of town on pleasant, unpaved country roads where traffic is confined mostly to bullock carts and farm folk on foot.

Though Hirado has no truly Western-style hotels, there are some Westernized Japanese hotels, such as the Hirado Kaijo. It has a Western-style lobby and Western bath, but sleeping, meals and service are Japanese-style.

Hirado is especially noted for seafood unique to the area. You should try some of the strange little sea creatures plucked out of the seaweed beds in the waters below the hotel.

Island Cruising. Hirado is one of the largest of the 99 Islands (in this case 99 merely means "many") stretching southward along this coastal area and supplying one of the most satisfying touring-sightseeing trips in Kyushu. Small excursion boats make the Hirado-Kashimae (Sasebo) run in 2½ hours, steering a course past faintly misty, pine-forested islands, some so tiny they may succor only a lone tree. Here and there you'll catch a glimpse of an isolated thatched farmhouse on a hillside, an occasional fisherman guiding a sampan toward the open sea or a few sports fishermen casting off the smaller islands. Often the boat threads through narrow inlets that give the effect of gliding through a forested gorge or sweeps around pearling markers that pattern quiet bays. Happily, commentary (and that only in Japanese) is held to a minimum to avoid marring the sheer pleasure of watching a landscape scroll slowly unfold.

Run by the Hirado-guchi Transportation Company, the small boats carry about 30 passengers in a comfortable compartment fitted with view windows; 10 to 12 persons can be accommodated on portable camp-style seats on the roofed-over open rear deck where the view is best. The boats depart Hirado for Kashimae at 9 A.M., 1 P.M. and 3 P.M. and leave Kashimae for Hirado at 9 A.M., 11:05 A.M. and 3:05 P.M. on a daily schedule.

This coastal excursion is so scenically rewarding that the round trip from Sasebo (Kashimae) could well be made going both ways by excursion boat. Or, if you are on limited time, it could be done as a full day's round trip that would allow about an hour for taxi sightseeing in Hirado. If you are doing it as a two day's round trip, the small but modern Hotel Matsukura in Sasebo would make a pleasant overnight stop.

OLD AND NEW: kimono-*clad women in predominantly Western-clothed group stroll through Suizenji Park, Kumamoto, carrying up-to-date shopping bags.*

ON ROAD SERPENTINING down toward Kumamoto, buses and car wind away from a volcano belching steam.

KUMAMOTO CASTLE, built in 1607, has an unusual right-angled entrance designed for defense against enemy assault.

Unzen Amakusa National Park. Offering contrast to the scenic coastal area of 99 Islands is Unzen, on the Shimabara Peninsula in the heart of Unzen-Amakusa National Park. Mt. Unzen is reached from Sasebo via train to Isahaya in about an hour and then by taxi from Isahaya (about another hour). The roads are excellent, so the drive is a pleasant, untiring trip. Much of the route skirts inland waters and then climbs over an easily graded highway through a forested landscape to the cooler, 2,400-foot heights at the town of Unzen.

Unzen proper is a quiet little mountain resort of small hotels, many with landscaped gardens, clustered about sulphur-misty, bubbling, boiling hot springs. A somewhat staid and old-fashioned feeling pervades this town that somehow has escaped the gaudy souvenir stall atmosphere associated with many such resorts. For the Japanese, Unzen is a year-round resort visited for the hot springs baths and the springtime displays of azaleas and cherry blossoms, for a cool summer retreat, for the spectacular displays of fall color and, in the winter, for the phenomenon of ice-rimmed, bare trees. The panoramic views out over the unusual scenery of the Shimabara Peninsula are spectacular at any time of year. The imposing chalet-type Unzen Kanko Hotel is an excellent place to stay.

Amakusa Islands. A variation on the route to Unzen described above would be to approach it by way of the Amakusa Islands, the most attractive of which are now tied together by five new bridges. Take-off point for the Five Bridges route is Misumi, about 20 miles southwest of Kumamoto. The trip across all five bridges takes about two hours, providing some pretty spectacular views enroute. The route is also called the Pearl Line because of the pearl diving activity in the area, and the next to last island in the chain has a showroom for pearls from cultivated beds right off shore. Prices are quite reasonable compared to those in the cities.

From the last island, the Kyushu Shosen Company runs a ferry service (five departures daily) to Shimabara, a good stopover point by virtue of the Western-style wing of 51 rooms at the Nampuro Hotel and a good base from which to explore the Mt. Unzen area. The 1½-hour ferry trip takes you through island-studded waters with views of distant mountains. Large and comfortable, the ferries have first-class quarters equipped with a large lounge, padded reclining seats and a covered deck space aft with tables for tea.

Shimabara is a small, photogenic port town with a castle and museum (Shimabara Castle, built in 1626) that contain many early Christian relics.

Kumamoto and Mt. Aso. In Shimabara you can make connections with ferry service that will take you to Kumamoto in about 18 minutes. What was formerly a three-hour ferry crossing is now an 18-minute trip by hovercraft traveling at 75 miles an hour. The craft carries 35 passengers in plane-type seats. This new routing makes it possible to see the main attractions of Kumamoto without necessarily making it an overnight stop.

Two attractions in the "famous" category here are Kumamoto Castle and Suizenji Park. The castle, an exceptionally striking building on a rise in the center of the city, is considered one of the three great castles in Japan. Massive stone walls line maze-like walks that lead up to the castle. You may be satisfied with exterior views (if climbing tires you) since, once inside the castle, you must follow a designated route up six or seven flights to the castle ramparts. For the energetic, the climb is worthwhile because of the varied museum displays of the feudal period on each floor. The grounds have handsome trees and provide a pleasant open space on an eminence that looks out over the city.

Kumamoto's other main attraction, 300-year-old Suizenji Park, is one of the most famous landscape gardens in Japan. The park is ready-made for easy strolling. Landscaped in 1632 to reproduce some of the features of Honshu from the old Tokaido Road (Tokyo to Kyoto), its most striking feature is a cone-shaped mound that evokes Mt. Fuji. Castle and park can be toured leisurely in an hour or so, leaving time for lunch before moving on. The Kumamoto Hotel Castle, across the street from the castle, is a first-rate, well-appointed hotel.

About an hour and a half by taxi or bus covers the route from Kumamoto to towering, smoking Mt. Aso—sentinel of Aso National Park and the largest active crater in the world, with more than 90 recorded eruptions. A toll road takes you almost to the top, and you can get to the rim by foot or ropeway. Trees give way to grassy plains and gradually to stark volcanic country as the excellent highway curves and snakes upward to the ropeway station. Seismologists keep constant watch on the volcano's activity. If the activity borders on the dangerous, the final access to the living crater is closed off. However, adjoining dead craters and cinder cones can still be seen, and you are still excitingly near the smoking crater. If you get to the rim, you'll find it impressive for its classic configuration but even more so for the rumbling you feel beneath your feet and for the roar as great spurts of white smoke and gases burst furiously out of fissures from the bottom. A number of concrete pillbox shelters are set a little back and below the rim, in case rocks should come blowing out with the discharge. Their presence is anything but reassuring. This is a real volcano.

A delightful stopover place in the area is the new Kuju Lakeside Hotel, about an hour and a half drive part way down the mountain from the ropeway station. The hotel is sited well back from the expressway on a large lake

STEAM BELCHES forth from one of the "eight great hells," an eerie sight in the popular spa of Beppu.

rimmed with pines. All rooms of the hotel either overlook the lake or a hilly 18-hole golf course. The hotel is one in which expense has not been spared, and amenities would satisfy any foreign visitor.

Beppu. Spilling down a hillside to the sea, Beppu looks at first as if it were one vast factory spewing forth steam. But there are no factories. The steam is coming from hillsides, gardens, back yards, cracks beside the road and out from under buildings. The steam, of course, is just a symptom of the real reason for Beppu's existence: hot springs. This is a spa resort—the largest in Japan.

You'll find baths under nearly every hotel—hot baths, tepid baths, carbonated baths, iron baths, sulfur baths, as well as an enormous hot spring swimming pool. And north of the ferry dock there's a section of the beach with hot, wet sand where Japanese hot sand enthusiasts bury themselves up to their necks.

The springs also account for the "Hells"—a variety of places where steam or hot water breaks through in odd ways: through fissures, through water, in the form of great blooping pools of mud. Many of these sites are landscaped as gardens and operated as tourist attractions. One even has a greenhouse where steam makes possible the growing of orchids and other tropical plants. Altogether there are eight "great hells" and a number of lesser ones.

Sightseeing in Beppu is limited to the various hot springs phenomena, a visit to Monkey Hill (if you dote on monkeys), and to the seafront aquarium (which is surprisingly good). The town looks less Japanese than most Japanese towns—more like a resort town in some other country.

To Miyazaki. If the hot-springs of Beppu are not appealing, it's possible to arrange an early morning taxi departure from the Kuju Lakeside Hotel, connecting with a morning train out of Beppu direct to Miyazaki. A comfortable first-class train makes the trip in four hours along the highly scenic east coast, following a route that tunnels through mountains and then skirts the ocean. Glimpses of the ocean are seen now and then through a forest of pines or bamboo, or as the background to a cluster of tile roofed houses or again in unobstructed view, with wide white sand beaches and rolling surf running for miles. Palm trees begin to mingle with showier stands of azaleas in season, a variety of annuals and more tropical flowers. Miyazaki's slogan as the Hawaii of Japan sums up its semi-tropical climate and leisurely pace.

In Miyazaki you'll be struck by the absence of billboards and extraneous signs and by the exceptional cleanliness of the sun-washed city. You could easily spend two or three days in and around the area. It's rich in history and legend: the home of the first Emperor before he set out to conquer Japan, and supposedly the site of the first Imperial palace. Ancient and sacred burial mounds, the beautiful Miyazaki Shrine where the first Emperor is enshrined, Haniwa Garden (dotted with replicas of pottery figures and artifacts of some 2,000 years ago dug from old burial mounds) and a Peace Tower commemorating the 2,600th anniversary of the founding of Japan—all these speak of the city's ancient origin.

Garden enthusiasts will revel in the wealth of flowers planted along city streets and in patterns on hillside parks, phoenix palms along the riverside esplanade, the show of azaleas, cherry blossoms and flowering shrubs in great concentrations, ancient wisterias, towering cedars, cryptomerias and smaller pines shading the pleasant walks in every park.

A morning can be spent motoring south of the city along the spectacularly scenic Nichinan Coast. Stops along the way include Children's Land, an attractively landscaped park adjacent to a wide white beach. A large area of the park is given over to a contoured garden of tropical trees and plants. Similar displays of tropical plants in a jungle of betel-nut palms is good reason for seeing nearby Aoshima Island—an easy walk from the mainland across a causeway over some strangely eroded rocks.

Farther along on the more rugged portion of the coast is a vast hillside cactus garden (some 2,000 varieties). A few miles farther south the charming Udo Shrine nestles against perpendicular cliffs that are washed by the surging sea.

In the opposite direction out of Miyazaki, there's another easy drive that can fill an afternoon. This samples the charming rural countryside en route to Saitobaru, site of the largest group of burial mounds in Japan. (It's in-teresting to note the similarity of these to the burial grounds of Kyongju in nearby Korea.)

Most of the hotels in Miyazaki offer Western-style, as well as Japanese-style, rooms with Western bathrooms and Continental cuisine. One of the best is the attractive 118-room Phoenix, with 22 Japanese-style rooms, the remainder Western. Completely air-conditioned, the Phoenix has two dining rooms, bar and swimming pool. Golfers can try their skills at the Aoshima Country Club golf course 10 miles away.

Kagoshima. About 100 miles southwest of Miyazaki lies Kagoshima, the self-styled Naples of the Orient (and now Naples' sister city). The resemblance is striking and the reason obvious in Mt. Sakurajima, the always-smoking volcano that looms 3,700 feet high across the bay from the city.

The city itself is worth a look by taxi, first for an overall view from a hillside park forested in bamboo and camphor trees, then for climbing the narrow hillside streets to stop at a small porcelain factory where ancient kilns are still used to turn out Satsuma ware.

Even though the city has numerous statues of famous persons, the statue of St. Francis Xavier comes as an anomaly. But it was in Kagoshima that the Saint first landed in 1549 in his attempt to Christianize Japan.

A very short drive out of the city proper gets you to Iso Park, a beautiful seaside villa noted for its landscaped gardens dating from the 17th century. Adjacent to the village is an old textile-mill-turned museum where the displays concentrate on relics of the city's past as the first place where guns, steam engines and glass were made in Japan.

Highlight of the Kagoshima stop is the trip across the bay to Sakurajima (15 minutes by ferry). A good road circles the island (about 35 miles around) and climbs to various stations toward the smoking mountaintop. As at Mt. Aso, the close watch kept on the volcano's activity determines how far up you may drive. You traverse areas completely denuded of vegetation where fingers of black lava have poured down the mountainside to the sea and cross other parts already softened by new growth of pine and shrub. Here and there the highway crosses a mad jumble of giant lava rocks spewed from vents that blew up from under the sea.

Kagoshima is also a base for visits to Kirishima-Yaku National Park, extending over both Miyazaki and Kagoshima prefectures. The park contains 23 volcanoes, 15 craters and 10 crater lakes. Ebino Plateau, in the Kirishima Volcanic Range extending 10 miles between the parks two outstanding peaks, is Kyushu's highest hot spring resort. It's especially popular with Japanese vacationers in the summer.

For an overnight stay, the Shiroyama Kanko Hotel on Castle Hill overlooks both the city and bay and the big volcano. It has 83 Western-style rooms, is air-conditioned, and has a dining room, grill, two cocktail lounges and a nightclub that features traditional Kagoshima music and dances. Also worth considering is an easy detour about 30 miles south of Kagoshima that combines overnight accommodations with the experience of sampling the most popular resort on Kyushu—Ibusuki.

Ibusuki is a typical beach and spa resort town. Dominating the beachfront where *ryokan* line the seawall is the huge Ibusuki Kanko Hotel that looks out at Sakurajima volcano. A large Western-style lobby is the nerve center from which a maze of corridors and stairs (and even an escalator) lead to a confusing number of levels, not only of bedrooms but of public rooms, restaurants, game rooms, *pachinko* rooms and a shopping section of department store dimensions and variety. Biggest attraction for the Japanese guest is the gigantic conservatory-like jungle bath—actually six or seven pools "landscaped" into a jungle of tropical trees and vines. Here men, women and children share the delights of the bath, along with small talk at all hours of day or night. Mixed bathing, like sand bathing, is becoming rare in Japan, but Ibusuki is the place to sample both. Underwater springs along the

ROADSIDE VIEWS: A winding road skirts the ocean en route from Beppu to Miyazaki (upper right). Seascapes abound near Kagoshima (above). Melons, mandarin oranges and Coca-Cola for sale—in the rain—at a roadside stand on the route to Mt. Aso.

BROAD BOULEVARD provides city center park for busy Sapporo (left). Noribetsu Spa (below), 2 hours from Sapporo, offers winter visitors variety of hot spring baths. Hokkaido farmers (lower right) becoming mechanized. Panorama from Sapporo area ski jump (lower left).

coast heat both the swimming beach and the water, and in special spots along the beach (there's one below the Ibusuki Kanko) attendants dig holes for the bathers who lie down in *kimonos* to be covered from chin to toe by warm sand (which is said to bake out aches and pains).

The most popular spot in the hotel at night is the immense glass-roofed theater-restaurant where you can loll in comfort in your *kimono*, dine and watch a floor show of local folk dances.

Hokkaido

Hokkaido, the "wild west" of Japan, is at the northernmost end of the Japanese archipelago, and its 30,334 square miles make up nearly one-fifth of Japan's total 142,338 square miles but only about 5 per cent of the population. The name, Hokkaido, is applied to a group of islands—one large and several small—separated from the Honshu mainland by the Tsugaru Straits and from Sakhalien Island (U.S.S.R. territory) by the Soya Straits. The area is largely mountainous with active and inactive volcanic cones in the central area. The highest volcanic peak is Asahidake which rises to 7,513 feet. In the southwest there are many hot springs, and the Ishikari River drains an extensive fertile plain in the West-central area.

For the foreign traveler, Hokkaido's appeal is probably greatest to the return visitor hunting for offbeat Japan, to the sportsman interested in adding new names to his collection of slopes, and to the traveler who'd like a refreshing break from the temple beat.

The climate of the island differs from that of other islands of Japan—with seasons about one month behind. The months to visit Hokkaido are from May to October, with the summer months the best. Winters are severe. Snow begins to fall in late autumn and lies on the ground from five to six months, making Hokkaido a favorite place for skiing and other winter sports. In summer, there is good hiking and camping in clear mountain air; excellent lake swimming, good salmon and trout fishing, and numerous government and railroad camp sites with cabins and tents for rent for adventurous outdoor enthusiasts. All the flowers—cherry, crocuses, primroses, iris, lily of the valley—seem to burst out at once in late May. September and October (sometimes rainy) usually have warm days, cool crisp evenings, especially in the mountains. These latter months see intense burst of fall colors across the countryside.

Tourists today can see in Hokkaido the results of United States guidance in large-scale farming, city planning and educational methods introduced nearly 100 years ago. American engineers and agricultural experts were sent to the islands at the invitation of the Japanese government to convert wilderness into farms and modern cities. This activity created a Japanese island with many Western-type dairy farms, sheep and cattle ranches, New England homes and a capital city, Sapporo, planned with broad boulevards. The teaching of English was also pioneered by an American, Professor E. G. Clark. His final words to his pupils upon his departure from Japan in 1877 were "Boys, be Ambitious" which now appear on a plaque halfway between Chitose airport and Sapporo. The school in which Clark taught has become the University of Hokkaido.

Sapporo itself is a city of more than a million. Its attractions add up to a rather modest list: Hokkaido University; the Botanical Garden with a stand of virgin forest and 6,000 species of local and imported plants; a university museum and the Ainu Museum; Hokkaido shrine, dating back to 1869 and good for cherry blossom viewing in late May; and the virgin forest at Maruyama, a government designated "national treasure"; as well as the clock tower building, one of the few remaining Russian-style structures in the city.

The Ainu Museum is housed in an English-style house, built in 1891 by Dr. John Batchelor, an English minister who was an enthusiastic student of the island's early inhabitants. It contains some 20,000 items, including Ainu and Gilyak costumes, canoes and harpoons.

Among Sapporo's hotels is the Sapporo International, a nine-story structure with 100 rooms, located in front of Sapporo railway station. Other hotels include the Royal with 89 rooms, the Sapporo Grand with 247 rooms and the Sapporo Park with 225 rooms.

Skiers added two new names to their lists of internationally great ski areas following the winter Olympics in Hokkaido: Teine, where the slaloms were held, and Eniwa, where the downhill races took place. Both are in the beautiful, birch-forested mountains that ring Sapporo.

Most skiers stay in a downtown Western-style hotel and do as the locals do: commute to the slopes via taxi (equipped with ski rack) or join the school kids at the bus stop. Hotels provide locked storage racks for skis and poles in their lobbies, and such major hotels as the Park, Royal and Sapporo Grand have equipment rental counters.

You'll probably do most of your traveling in Hokkaido by either train, bus or guide-driven car. It is one place in Japan where you could feel relatively at ease with a rental car. The roads are well maintained and the traffic is relatively light.

Tours may be arranged to give you an opportunity to see the Ainu, members of an aboriginal race of Hokkaido, who vie with the scenery as a main attraction of this northern land. These fast disappearing primitives are gentle farmer-fisher folk who are unlike other Asians.

THERMAL ACTIVITY on island of Hokkaido is a continually fascinating phenomenon to those visiting the area.

They have Caucasian features, light skin and hairy bodies. The men grow thick, colossal beards and the women have blue tattoos around their mouths. Their religion is a primitive-type nature worship which influenced Shintoism. With less than 16,000 Ainus left (as shown by a recent census), they now are seen in much the same way we visit American Indian reservations. Easiest to get to and "best staged" is the small colony in Asahikawa, Hokkaido's second largest city, and the display village in Shiraoi near Noboribetsu spa.

If you have a day or two to go to Akan National Park, which is reached by train or plane from Sapporo, you can see the Ainu under more natural conditions. They will pose for photographs, but they expect you to reward their efforts with tips. Live bears are caged or tied up for tourist attractions throughout the area. The Ainu consider bears as the repositories of the souls of men, and the souls are joyfully released when the bears are killed. Bear hunting is a favorite Ainu sport.

Akan National Park extends over Kushiro, Abashiri and Tokachi districts and contains approximately 218,000 acres of lofty mountains, primeval forests and crater lakes. The lakes—Akan, Mashu and the large Kutcharo—are noted for fresh-water trout and the *Marimo* (in Akan), a strange spherical weed found only in two other places —Switzerland and the Russian island of Sakhalien. Boats are available for scenic runs on the lakes. Alpinists can make arrangements to climb some of the peaks in the area.

For other dramatic scenery, Hokkaido has three more national parks, Daisetsuzan, Shikotsu-Toya and Shiretoko, all primeval wonderlands—each of which should be seen with special guide service.

Daisetsuzan, called the "roof of Hokkaido," is the largest of Japan's national parks (905 square miles). Site of the island's highest mountains and a part of the Kurile volcano chain, it has lofty forested peaks and many beautiful gorges and ravines. Hot springs abound, and on numerous routes into the park, well-equipped spas are tucked away in secluded gorges.

One of the most beautiful Daisetsuzan touring routes is from Ashikawa eastward along the northern edge of the park to Sounkyo Spa. This is a 2½ to 3-hour trip by bus. The spa, tourist center for the district, is in the middle of Sounkyo Gorge, a defile flanked by unusual rock walls rising to 450 feet with several waterfalls cascading over them. A national highway opened a few years ago runs from the Gorge for another 40 miles through beautiful virgin forests and natural scenery typical of Hokkaido. At Onneyu Spa, the route turns south toward Akan.

Shikotsu-Toya National Park, covering 375 square miles in the southwestern part of Hokkaido, is connected by roads to neighboring major cities: Sapporo, Muroran, Tomakomai, Chitose and Otaru. The park has various types of volcanoes and caldera lakes, as well as diverse scenic attributes in its forests, valleys and hot springs. Of the volcanic mountains, 6,209-foot Mt. Yotei is celebrated for its graceful contour and 3,359-foot Mt. Tarumae is renowned as a triple volcano. Another of the principal features of this national park is Lake Toya, a caldera lake 27 miles in circumference. On its shores are gushing hot springs, and the Toyako Spa (a thriving base for tourists) is located on its southern shore. The Forest Museum is situated on a wooded island, Nakanoshima, in the middle of the lake. Lake cruises are available throughout the year.

The hot spring bath house at the Daiichi Takimoto Hotel in Noboribetsu, on the edge of Shikotsu-Toya

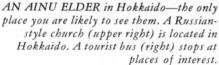

AN AINU ELDER in Hokkaido—the only place you are likely to see them. A Russian-style church (upper right) is located in Hokkaido. A tourist bus (right) stops at places of interest.

National Park, is famous for its score of hot spring pools, a swimming pool and volcanic steam baths. The latter are unusual: you lie on wooden gratings and the steam percolates up from the earth through the gratings. Colored lights shine dimly through the steam-filled bathroom, giving a nether-world atmosphere.

Shiretoko National Park, located on the Cape Shiretoko peninsula on the eastern shores of Hokkaido, is less easily accessible by road, rail or air than are Hokkaido's other national parks. Access is by a service route going north from Nemuro, but in terms of mileage and time, it's an impractical side trip for those with limited time for touring. Shiretoko's topography is volcanic in origin, but some of its most dramatic features—rocks eroded by the sea and over-hanging precipices as much as 600 feet above the water—are best seen by sightseeing boat. Such boats are available in summer at Utoro and Rausu. The round trip from Utoro to the cape and back takes about five hours; from Rausu, it takes six.

Hokkaido may be reached by jet from Tokyo in 1 hour and 10 minutes, or by train in about 18 hours. Plane passengers land at Chitose, aerial gateway to Hokkaido, and are taken by car or bus on a 50-minute speedway ride to Sapporo, the capital city. There are about 36 flights daily from Tokyo during mid-May to October and fewer in other seasons. Japan Air Lines, All Nippon Airways, and Toa Domestic Airlines serve the area and the Japanese National Railway operates frequent services between Tokyo and Hokkaido with ferry service operating from island to island.

Tours should be arranged through your travel agent before departing for Japan if possible. However, if you decide to visit Hokkaido after you arrive in Japan, the Japan National Tourist Organization offices in Tokyo and Kyoto or the Trade and Tourist Service Centers of Hokkaido Prefectural Government can assist you.

A number of package tours from Tokyo to Hokkaido are available—ranging from three to eleven days.

ANCIENT RITUALS mark Japan's festival calendar. Wild Horse Chase (above) in July in Soma dates from the 17th century. Children (right) prepare decorations for the New Year Festival. Armored men (far right) parade at Toshogu Shrine in May and October festivals in Nikko.

"Fortune In---Devils Out!"
... a Calendar of Events

Festivals are meat and drink to the Japanese. They fill a need at once social and religious, bringing vast numbers of people together in both gay and solemn observances.

The ritual of the festival usually dates back hundreds of years, commemorating some incident in history, or fable, and generally paying deep homage to one or another enshrined deity. In tune with the philosophy of ancestor worship, a Japanese festival must be enacted in the same way that it was first observed. Costumes, colors, decorations faithfully follow centuries-old traditions. So when you see a procession of palanquins carried down a long avenue to a cherished shrine, you can imagine what it was like 800 or 900 years ago.

Since the same events are held at the same time each year, and since every month sees some sort of celebration all over Japan, you can check this annual calendar of festivals and match up your visit to Japan with at least some of them. You should feel no embarassment about taking pictures—there'll be more Japanese than tourists using cameras.

Here is a list of the main yearly celebrations, but it is far from complete. Before taking off for other parts of Japan, check your itinerary with the Tourist Information Center in Tokyo (see page 9). They can tell you what events are scheduled in the areas you will be visiting.

January

January 1-3. The New Year is celebrated for the first three days of the year. The little arrangements of pine twigs and bamboo stalks you see at every door mean good luck. Within the homes a wooden stand is traditionally set with two round rice-cakes, one on top of the other. These are also good luck symbols. For the first seven days of the year, it is customary to make early-morning visits to shrines. You will see women wearing their most colorful kimonos at this time.

January 2. The members of the Royal Family each

GRAND FESTIVALS of Toshogu Shrine in Nikko (above left) feature processions of 1,000 costumed men. Port Festival of Shiogama (above) is held on Matsushima Bay. Tug-of-war (left) is holiday sports event for young boys.

year greet the Japanese people from the Imperial Palace in Tokyo, and crowds throng across the Nijubashi, the double bridge, which is the main entrance to the palace grounds, from early in the morning.

January 6. The day of the *Dezome Shiki,* when the fire brigades, in colorful regalia, perform. They race up high bamboo ladders, from the top of which they do exciting acrobatics. This is particularly celebrated in Tokyo, but it takes place in other cities too.

January 15. The first of Japan's 11 national holidays, *Seijin-no-hi* (Adult's Day). All boys and girls who have turned 20 are considered to have become adults and now have the right to vote. This is their special day.

Mid-January. The first of six *sumo* (Japanese wrestling) tournaments, each lasting 15 days, begins, this one held in Tokyo.

February

February 3 or 4. The *Setsubun* is the annual last-day-of-winter celebration observed all through Japan. It is the custom to throw beans about, with the shout, "Fortune in —Devils out!" Sometimes popular heroes like sumo champions or *kabuki* actors throw beans to the crowd.

Setsubun literally means "change of season." Thus the Japanese rush the season a bit, but since they have adopted the Western calendar, all their holidays have been advanced nearly a month. In Japanese homes on this day of alleged seasonal change, every father is supposed to throw handfuls of beans into every corner, for the good luck it will bring, and each child eats as many beans as he is years old. The fete has big celebrations at the Ikegami Hommonji Temple in Tokyo and at the Narita Fudo Temple in Chiba Prefecture.

February 3 or 4. The *Mandoro* Festival celebrated in Nara, for here on the day after the general observance of the *Setsubun*, Kasuga Shrine, on the hillside above Nara, lights all its 3,000 lanterns. Thousands of Japanese travel there to see them.

March

March 3. The Doll Festival is also known as Girls' Day. Although it is primarily observed at home where little girls display their finest dolls, the festival is played up in stores where elaborately dressed dolls, representative of classic early-day costumes are displayed. These are ceremonial dolls—not dolls that children play with—and many of them have been handed down in a family from generation to generation.

March 12. The date of the Water-Drawing Festival in Nara, as exotic a ceremony as you're likely to see in all Japan. It takes place at the Todaiji Temple (the temple which houses the Great Buddha) at 2 A.M. on a stage before the main hall. Here Buddhist priests brandish huge burning torches (a foot around and 24 feet long) in rites of exorcism. Watchers rush toward the bits of fire that are shaken off the high torches, for the fire flake is said to have a magic power against evil.

Mid-March. Osaka is the setting for Japan's second *sumo* tournament.

April

About April 1. The famed cherry blossom dances, magnificently staged, are performed in the all-girl theaters of Tokyo, Osaka and Kyoto in honor of the season. (Ask the JNTO's Tourist Information Center or your travel agent for the exact dates when these dances will be performed and where.) They may start in late March and go into early May.

April 10, 15, 28 and 29. Numerous kite-flying contests take place in Nagasaki. This is more fun than it may sound, for great crowds of contestants take part, flying kites of the most elaborate design. The contest is to try to cut off the strings of others' kites through skilled maneuvering. It is an exciting spectacle to watch.

April 8. Buddha's Birthday Festival, is also called the Flower Festival. Often children in festival costume parade at Buddhist temples throughout the country.

Early April. For three weeks, beginning in early April, the International Trade Fair is held alternately in Osaka and in Tokyo.

April 12 to May 5. Osaka's big International Festival, featuring ballet, opera and music from both Japan and Western countries.

April 29. The Emperor's Birthday (a national holiday). All day long the Imperial Palace is opened to the public, and enormous crowds attend.

May

May 5. This is Children's Day, but primarily it is a day for boys, and families who have sons hoist paper or cloth carp (signifying courage) above their homes.

May 11. This is the beginning of the cormorant fishing on the Nagara River in Gifu, a nighttime spectacle that rates with any festival for exotic glamor. The season continues through October 15. (See page 91.)

May 15. The Hollyhock Festival in Kyoto. This is a fine one for picture-takers, for it has a tremendous parade, and the marchers are in all manner of costume. The festival reenacts an ancient imperial procession including an ox-drawn carriage decorated with flowers. The processional winds through the streets to the shrines of Shimogamo and Kamigamo.

Mid-May. The third *sumo* tournament of the year begins in Tokyo.

May 17-18. The Sanja Festival of Asakusa Shrine in Tokyo is observed with a parade of colorful palanquins.

May 17-18. The Grand Festival of Toshogu Shrine at Nikko is another one to record on film. More than 1,000 people, clad in the costumes of Japan's feudal days, take part in a gala procession. Marchers are armed with swords and spears.

Third Sunday. The Boat Festival of Arashiyama, Kyoto, takes place on the Oi River where a fleet of gaily decorated boats rides down the river as in ancient days.

June

All month. During June the Peiron boat race held in Nagasaki features boats modeled after ancient whaling craft. They race to the beating of gongs and drums.

June 14. A dozen pretty girls transplant rice seedlings in the paddy field of the Sumiyoshi Shrine in Osaka. Folk songs accompany their planting rites.

June 15. Shrine palanquins into the streets again in Tokyo, this time in a procession to the Hie Shrine in observance of the Sanno Festival.

July

July 7. The date of the Tanabata (Star) Festival. Colored streamers brighten houses and streets all through Japan in celebration of a romantic legend. The two stars, Vega and Altair, are legendary lovers, allowed by the King of Heaven to meet just once a year. The celebration at Hiratsuka is well known, the one in Sendai more traditional.

July 16-19. The Festival of the Wild Horse Chase (*Nomaoi*) in Soma, near Sendai in northern Japan, is just what it says, a wild horse chase, though the horses aren't wild any more. It starts with a procession of three shrine palanquins escorted by thousands of parishioners who, clad in traditional armor, follow on horseback. Then comes the *keiba*, or race, and exciting demonstrations of horsemanship.

On the second day of the festival, the horsemen vie for a flag which is launched into the middle of a broad field amid a shower of brilliant light made by bursting fireworks. The final day features another chase which is carried out in faithful obedience to ancient patterns.

July 13-15. The Bon Festival, or the Feast of Lanterns, is celebrated by Buddhists throughout Japan. It is all said to have begun in 657 A.D. when a Buddhist disciple in Japan performed dances of joy because his deceased mother had been admitted to paradise. Twentieth century celebrations continue the same theme, that of honoring the souls of ancestors returned for earthly visits to their former homes. Special dances called *Bon Odori* are held in many cities, particularly at Nikko and at Sado Islands in the Japan Sea. The dances, done to music of drum and flute, are given before the Buddhist temples.

Perhaps the most charming custom as seen by visitors, however, is the floating of thousands of tiny boats carrying lighted paper lanterns. They are launched on rivers and lakes to carry back to heaven the spirits who had returned to earth for the Bon Festival.

Mid-July. Another 15-day *sumo* tournament begins— this one in Nagoya.

Mid-July. The date of the Music Festival at the lovely island shrine of Itsukushima, Miyajima, on the edge of the Inland Sea. Brightly decorated boats parade to the accompaniment of classic *gagaku* music.

July 16-24. The Gion Festival of Yasaka Shrine, Kyoto, is one of Japan's biggest and most spectacular festivals, one well worth trying to fit into your travel schedule. The special dates to remember are the 17th and 24th, because on these days the beautifully decorated and tremendously tall floats (often higher than nearby rooftops) highlight the processions that make their way through the streets of Kyoto. The festival dates back to the 9th century when a priest organized a procession to intercede with the gods, asking their protection against a pestilence.

Lending additional color is a group of knights on horseback, clad in ancient armor; bearers of divine spears, swords, bows and arrows; a band of musicians; a number of priests, and a sacred page who is a young boy especially chosen and honored during the festival.

This youngster, who receives the rank of *chigo*, or sacred page, is received with the greatest respect wherever he goes during the time of the festival, and one of his duties is to dance on a *hoko* (a float atop four huge wooden wheels) during the two main processions.

The parades start from the Yasaka Shrine near Gion, and they are easy for tourists to see, for they march down many streets. On Oike Street, there are covered bleachers.

Another thing that is especially intriguing for visitors is the custom on the evening of the 16th of leaving the anterooms of all private homes open to public view. The rooms are decorated with folding screens, and every house displays a lantern.

July 25. The Tenjin Festival of Temmangu Shrine, in Osaka, is a colorful water carnival. Some hundred boats are gaily decorated with flags and dolls, and there are lots of fireworks.

July 31. The Feast of the Lanterns is held at Lake Hakone. Thousands of tiny lanterns are set afloat on the lake in the evening, and there are colorful fireworks.

July 31-August 1. The Sumiyoshi Matsuri (*Palanquin Festival*) ends Osaka's series of gay summer festivals. Youngsters carry decorated shrine palanquins across the Yamato River en route to the resting place in Sakai.

August

August 3-7. The Nebuta Festival, held in Aomori, is one of the most colorful events of the year in this prefecture. *Nebuta* (dummies or huge papier-mâché dolls representing animals, birds and men) are placed on carriages and pulled through the streets. The *nebuta* are said to have originated from a legend in which they were used to misguide the enemy in a skirmish to subjugate the rebels. At Hirosaki, a large city in Aomari Prefecture, the festival is observed from August 1 to 7.

August 6. The Kanto Festival, held in Akita, is dominated by paper lanterns hung from *kantos* (long bamboo poles with horizontal ribs from which as many as 40 or 50 lanterns are hung.) During the festival, young men try their skill at balancing *kanto* with their hands or on their foreheads, shoulders or hips. The festival is celebrated to invoke help for a good harvest.

August 6-8. The picturesque Tanabata (Star) Festival (see July 7) is observed in Sendai on an especially large scale. Bamboo trees set in front of every house carry romantic poems written on strips of colored paper, streamers, and glittering ornaments of fanciful design. Main streets vie with each other in decorations. Young people make offerings of melons, peaches, pears and cakes to the two stars in honor of their happy annual union.

August 13-15. The Bon Festival, held in July in other parts of Japan, is observed in Nagasaki at this time. The ceremony is marked by more solemnity here.

August 15. The *Mandoro* Festival of Kasuga Shrine at Nara is repeated (see February). All the lanterns which line the avenue to this lovely Nara shrine, and which hang beneath the eaves of its gracefully curving roof, are lighted at once.

August 16. Kyoto marks this date with a great bon-

*TANABATA FESTIVAL (below) is held in Sendai
in August. Men display balancing skills at Kanto
Festival (right) in Akita in August. On Children's
Day in May (lower left), boys study swords, banners,
dolls that represent feudal generals. Huge floats
(lower right) at Kyoto's Gion Festival in July.*

fire which has been built on Mt. Nyoigadake in the shape of the idiograph which means "large." Once a Buddhist deity, says the legend of the fete, appeared on a hillside in a blaze of light.

August 15-18. The Awa Odori Festival in Tokushima. A four-day event at which practically the whole population dances in costume, accompanied by *samisen*, flutes and drums in a long parade through the city. A colorful (and somewhat abandoned) four-day-and-night dance.

August 26. The Fire Festival of the Sengen Shrine at Fuji-Yoshida marks the end of the Mt. Fuji climbing season. Huge bonfires crackle throughout the city and on the mountain along the Yoshida Trail.

August 26-27. The Festival of the Suwa Shrine is held annually on the shores of Lake Suwa in Nagano Prefecture. A tradition since ancient times, the festival features huge lanterns created to frighten away the sea devil.

September

September 15-16. The Festival of Tsurugaoka Hachimangu Shrine, at Kamakura, offers a most unusual sight in its exhibition of archery on horseback, or *yabusame*. As in most festivals, the participants wear costumes representative of ancient times. Cantering around a track within the shrine compound, the horsemen, without reining in their horses, shoot their arrows as they pass the target which is set up on one side of the field. It is a rare display of an unusual skill.

Mid-September. A 15-day *sumo* tournament in Tokyo.

KITE FLYING FESTIVALS (upper left) are held in Nagasaki in April; in Shirone, Sanjo and Kamo in June. Huge lanterns (left) are displayed at Festival of Suwa Shrine in August. Winter Festival in Sapporo (above) features parade plus huge ice carvings.

September 23 or 24. The day of the autumnal equinox, is a national holiday.

October

October 7-9. Nagasaki celebrates the Okunchi Festival of Suwa Shrine. The Dragon dance of Chinese origin is a part of the picturesque dancing and processionals.

October 14-15. This is a strange one, the Quarrel Festival, held at Matsubara Shrine, Himeji, in Hyogo Prefecture. Marching uphill to the shrine, the men carrying enormous palanquins battle by jostling each other to see who will gain the leading position.

October 17. The Autumn Festival of Toshogu Shrine in Nikko. A thousand townsmen, armed as in the days of feudal warlords, parade.

October 22. Kyoto's *Jidai Matsuri*, or the Festival of Eras, is held at Heian Shrine. The parading celebrants, wearing costumes that represent the chief periods of Kyoto's history, commemorate the founding of the city in the eighth century.

November

During November. Tokyo's *Tori-no-Ichi*, or the Cock Fairs, are observed around the Otori Shrine in Asakusa. Good luck bamboo rakes are sold.

November 3. The *Daimyo Gyoretsu* at Hakone brings out more processions like those of feudal times. It is a good time to visit in Hakone, for the marchers wind in stately fashion around the various hot springs resorts.

November 3. Known as Culture Day, this is a national holiday. Officially it is a day on which "to love freedom and peace and to advance culture."

Mid-November. The year's final *sumo* tournament is held in a different city each year. Ask JNTO's Tourist Information Center where it will be held this year.

November 15. The Shichi-go-san Festival, held throughout the country. *Shichi-go-san* means seven-five-three. On this day, parents with girls of seven, boys of five and either boys or girls of three take their children to their guardian shrines to express their thanks to the deity for allowing their children to reach their respective ages safely and to invoke future blessings. It's a perfectly delightful and easy to see festival. The Meiji Shrine and Asakusa in Tokyo are both places where especially large numbers of children are taken. Before the festival, you will find special displays of *kimonos* and accessories (some costing several hundred dollars) in the main department stores.

November 23. A national holiday, known as Labor Thanksgiving Day. A holiday established since the war, it is not much observed as such (a day on which to "respect labor and felicitate production"), but it fits more naturally into age-old celebrating of a bountiful harvest with parading, dancing and shrine fetes.

December

December 1-26. During these dates a famous troupe of *kabuki* actors appears at the Minami-za Theater in Kyoto. The series of plays is known as the Kaomise Kabuki Plays.

All month. December is one of the busiest months in the year for the Japanese, who are expected to pay up their debts and meet their obligations before the start of the next year. It is called *Shiwasu*, the end of all things. Decorations to be used to welcome the New Year appear for sale at shrines and temples, stores and shops everywhere. Tokyo's Ginza Street, its stores and its cabarets and bars, are all decorated for the coming season.

December 24. The time for many Christmas Eve balls. The most important one is the ball held at the Imperial Hotel, a truly gala affair. (Reservations must be made well in advance for this.)

December 29. Greeting cards and gifts are exchanged at New Year's. This is Japan's real holiday, and it continues for an entire week. The government gets the holiday started by closing all offices December 29.

December 31. Everything is a buildup to *Omisoka*, the Last Grand Day, and Japanese families sit up until midnight to hear the thunderous pealing of the bells. For as the old year dies away, the temple bells all peal 108 strokes, the *Joya-no-kane*. And Japan is ready to start all over again on another year of fete and ritual, carrying on traditions begun a thousand years or so ago.

SETSUBUN on the last day of winter, it is the custom to throw beans and shout "Fortune in—Devils out!"

Supplementary Reading

The Book of Sumo, by Doug Kenrik. The sport, the spectacle, and the ritual of this activity (Walker/Weatherhill Company, New York and Tokyo).

A Dictionary of Japanese History, by Joseph M. Geodertier. Arranged from A to Z, all concentrated on history (Walker/Weatherhill, New York and Tokyo).

Enjoy Japan, by Walt Sheldon. A personal "guide," emphasizing the author's experiences (Charles E. Tuttle Company, Rutland, Vermont, and Tokyo).

Imperial Villas of Kyoto, by Tadashi Ishikawa. A small paperback text with excellent color plates (Kodansha International, New York and Tokyo).

Japan, by Edward Seidensticker and the editors of *Life.* A sensitive interpretation, with an emphasis on modern Japan (Time Incorporated, New York).

The Japan I Love, by Pierre Landy and François Meilleau. A handsome book, enhanced by photographs in color and black-and-white (Tudor Publishing Company, New York).

Japan, An Intimate View, by Colin Simpson. A perceptive account of the author's travels in Japan (A. S. Barnes & Company, Cranbury, New Jersey).

Japan: Patterns in Continuity, by Fosco Maraini. An impressive color pictorial (Kodansha International, New York and Tokyo).

Japanese Arts—What and Where, compiled by Sadao Kikuchi. A compendium which also includes photographs (Japan Travel Bureau, Tokyo).

Japanese Festivals, by Helen Bauer and Sherwin Carlquist. An excellent source book, with an expanded calendar of events (Doubleday and Company, Garden City, New York).

Japanese Homes and Their Surroundings, by Edward S. Morse. A paperbound book with a multiplicity of drawings that give a rich profile of the Japanese home (Charles E. Tuttle Company, Rutland, Vermont, and Tokyo).

A Japanese Inn, by Oliver Statler. Gives you some understanding of the traditions of a *ryokan* within a historical framework (Pyramid Publications, New York).

Japanese Interiors, by the editorial board of Gakuyo Shobo. Concentrates on interiors which are unique to Japan (Gakuyo Shobo Ltd., Tokyo).

Japanese Pottery, by Soame Jenyns. The definitive book on the subject (Praeger Publications, New York).

Japanese Sense of Beauty, by Seiroku Noma. A book of full-page, close-up color plates which enlarge one's sense of beauty in Japan (Ashahi Shimbun Publishing Company, Tokyo).

Kyoto, A Contemplative Guide, by Gouverneur Mosher. In-depth reporting about Japan's second largest city (Charles E. Tuttle Company, Rutland, Vermont, and Tokyo).

The Land and the People of Japan, by Josephine Budd Vaughan. A book in which all the basics are spelled out (J. B. Lippincott Company, New York).

Legends of Japan, retold by Hiroshi Naito. Includes chapters on "No melons to spare" and "The flying water jars" and 20 other legends in similar vein (Charles E. Tuttle Company, Rutland, Vermont, and Tokyo).

Meet Japan/A Modern Nation with a Memory, by Tsuneji Hibino. A book-length look at modern Japan (Charles E. Tuttle Company, Rutland, Vermont, and Tokyo).

Meeting with Japan, by Fosco Maraini. A 467-page book by a very knowledgeable writer-photographer (The Viking Press, New York).

New Japanese Architecture, by Egon Tempel. An architecturally exciting book (Praeger Publishers, New York and Washington).

New Official Guide to Japan, compiled by the Japan Travel Bureau. A compendium of Baedeker-type information (Japan Travel Bureau, Inc., Tokyo).

Palaces of Kyoto, by Tadashi Ishikawa. A small paperbound book with excellent color plates (Kodansha International, New York and Tokyo).

The People of Japan, by Pearl S. Buck. An interesting book by the author of *Oil for the Lamps of China* and other popular books about the Orient (Simon & Schuster, New York).

Performing Arts of Japan: Buyo, The Classical Dance by Masakatsu Gunji; *Kabuki, the Popular Theater,* and *Noh, The Classical Theater,* both by Yasuo Nakamura. Three separate volumes dealing with these performing arts (Walker and Company, New York).

The Puppet Theatre of Japan, by A. C. Scott. All about puppetry, including a chapter on the anatomy of a puppet (Charles E. Tuttle Company, Rutland, Vermont and Tokyo).

These Splendored Isles/The Scenic Beauty of Japan, by Magoichi Kushida. A splendid color pictorial with interpretive text (Walker/Weatherhill, New York and Tokyo).

Tokaido Hiroshige, by Tomikichino Toburiki. A book written in the context of the Tokaido Road and Hiroshige's famous block prints (Hoikusha Publishing Company, Ltd., Osaka, Japan).

Tokyo: Tradition and Megapolis, by Atsushi Azumi and Hiroshi Kaneko. A small paper-bound book with up-to-date text and good color plates (Kodansha International, New York and Tokyo).

The World of Japanese Business, T. F. M. Adams and N. Kobayayashi. An analysis of Japanese businessmen and methods of doing business in Japan (Kodansha International, New York and Tokyo).

INDEX

PHOTOGRAPHERS

David Bartruff: 83. **Bob Butterfield:** 104 (lower right). **Shirley Fockler:** 28 (lower right), 29, 42 (bottom), 58 (top left, lower left), 70 (top), 97, 146 (upper right). **Norman S. Gordon:** 42 (top), 44 (top), 48 (top), 57 (lower right), 78 (top left), 79, 90 (lower left), 93 (left), 116 (lower right), 118 (lower left), 122 (right), 125, 126 (top right), 128 (lower right), 131, 136 (bottom). **Martha Guthrie:** 7 (top left, top right, lower left), 8 (top right), 19 (top right, lower left), 21 (left), 24 (bottom), 25, 28 (top right), 31 (top right), 35, 36, 37, 39 (top right, center right, lower left, lower right), 40, 41, 59, 63 (lower left, lower right), 73 (bottom), 74 (top right), 81 (bottom), 90 (top right), 93 (lower right), 103, 109 (lower left), 110 (lower left), 152 (lower left). **William L. Hewes, Jr.:** 78 (lower left), 128 (top right, lower left). **Walter Houk:** 4 (bottom), 114 (top), 126 (left), 132 (bottom), 137 (right), 139 (top right, lower right), 140, 141, 142 (bottom), 143, 145 (lower right). **Kiyoko Ishimoto:** 24 (top), 44 (lower right), 45, 47, 104 (top left, lower left), 109 (lower right). **Japan Air Lines:** 4 (top), 5, 7 (top center, lower right), 8 (lower right), 10 (lower left), 13 (top left, top right, lower right), 19 (top left), 22 (top left, lower right), 26, 31 (lower right), 32 (lower right), 48 (bottom), 49, 51 (top right), 54 (lower left, lower right), 57 (left, top right), 58 (right), 61 (left), 63 (top left), 64, 66 (bottom), 69 (right), 71, 73 (top left, top right), 93 (left), 113 (top right, lower left), 115, 119 (top), 121 (bottom), 122 (left), 133, 149 (left), 150 (top), 152 (top left), 155 (lower left), 156 (top left). **Japan National Tourist Organization:** 7 (lower center), 8 (top left, lower left), 10 (right), 13 (lower left), 15 (lower right), 16, 19 (lower right), 22 (top right), 27 (top), 31 (left), 32 (top right, lower left), 39 (top left), 54 (top left), 56, 61 (right), 65, 66 (top), 70 (bottom), 72, 74 (top left, lower left, lower right), 77 (right), 81 (top left), 82, 84, 85 (top), 86, 87, 88 (bottom), 90 (top left, lower right), 95 (top), 96 (bottom), 101, 110 (upper left), 111 (bottom), 113 (top left, lower right), 114 (bottom), 116 (top left, lower left), 118 (top left, right), 119 (bottom), 124 (bottom), 127 (right), 128, (top left), 132 (top), 134 (top left, top right), 135, 136 (top), 137 (left), 139 (top left), 146 (upper left, lower left, lower right), 148, 149 (top right, lower right), 150 (bottom), 151, 152 (right), 155 (top left, top right, lower right), 156 (lower left, right), 157. **Kyoto Municipal Government:** 100 (right). **Martin Litton:** 21 (top right), 28 (left), 102 (right), 121 (top), 126 (lower right), 127 (left). **Janeth Nix:** 107. **Pacific Area Travel Association:** 10 (top left), 43, 44 (lower left), 69 (top left), 78 (right), 85 (bottom), 95 (bottom), 96 (top), 109 (top left), 123. **Pacific Travel News:** 15 (top left), 88 (top), 106, 110 (right), 111 (top), 116 (top right), 145 (top right, lower left). **Qantas:** 21 (bottom right). **Lawrence L. Smith:** 100 (left), 134 (lower right). **Chuck Wilfong:** 77 (left).